**Byung-Chul Han**

### Key Contemporary Thinkers series includes:

Lee Braver, *Heidegger*
John Burgess, *Kripke*
Filipe Carreira da Silva, *G. H. Mead*
Claire Colebrook and Jason Maxwell, *Agamben*
Jean-Pierre Couture, *Sloterdijk*
Gareth Dale, *Karl Polanyi*
Oliver Davis, *Jacques Rancière*
Gerard de Vries, *Bruno Latour*
Reidar Andreas Due, *Deleuze*
Stuart Elden, *Canguilhem*
Neil Gascoigne, *Richard Rorty*
Graeme Gilloch, *Siegfried Kracauer*
Lawrence Hamilton, *Amartya Sen*
M. G. Hayes, *John Maynard Keynes*
Rachel Jones, *Irigaray*
S. K. Keltner, *Kristeva*
Steven Knepper, Ethan Stoneman, and Robert Wyllie, *Byung-Chul Han*
Matthew H. Kramer, *H. L. A. Hart*
Moya Lloyd, *Judith Butler*
Ronald Loeffler, *Brandom*
James McGilvray, *Chomsky*, 2nd edition
Dermot Moran, *Edmund Husserl*
Marie-Eve Morin, *Jean-Luc Nancy*
Timothy Murphy, *Antonio Negri*
Daniel H. Neilson, *Minsky*
James O'Shea, *Wilfrid Sellars*
William Outhwaite, *Habermas*, 2nd edition
Ed Pluth, *Badiou*
Reiland Rabaka, *Du Bois*
J. Toby Reiner, *Michael Walzer*
Neil G. Robertson, *Leo Strauss*
William Scheuerman, *Morgenthau*
Severin Schroeder, *Wittgenstein*
Anthony Paul Smith, *Laruelle*
James Smith, *Terry Eagleton*
Felix Stalder, *Manuel Castells*
Christine Sypnowich, *G. A. Cohen*
Christopher Zurn, *Axel Honneth*

# Byung-Chul Han

## A Critical Introduction

Steven Knepper, Ethan Stoneman,
and Robert Wyllie

polity

Copyright © Steven Knepper, Ethan Stoneman, and Robert Wyllie 2024

The right of Steven Knepper, Ethan Stoneman, and Robert Wyllie to be identified as Authors of this Work has been asserted in accordance with the UK Copyright, Designs and Patents Act 1988.

First published in 2024 by Polity Press

Polity Press
65 Bridge Street
Cambridge CB2 1UR, UK

Polity Press
111 River Street
Hoboken, NJ 07030, USA

All rights reserved. Except for the quotation of short passages for the purpose of criticism and review, no part of this publication may be reproduced, stored in a retrieval system or transmitted, in any form or by any means, electronic, mechanical, photocopying, recording or otherwise, without the prior permission of the publisher.

ISBN-13: 978-1-5095-6098-1
ISBN-13: 978-1-5095-6099-8 (pb)

A catalogue record for this book is available from the British Library.

Library of Congress Control Number: 2023950919

Typeset in 10.5 on 12pt Palatino
by Fakenham Prepress Solutions, Fakenham, Norfolk NR21 8NL
Printed and bound in Great Britain by TJ Books Ltd, Padstow, Cornwall

The publisher has used its best endeavours to ensure that the URLs for external websites referred to in this book are correct and active at the time of going to press. However, the publisher has no responsibility for the websites and can make no guarantee that a site will remain live or that the content is or will remain appropriate.

Every effort has been made to trace all copyright holders, but if any have been overlooked the publisher will be pleased to include any necessary credits in any subsequent reprint or edition.

For further information on Polity, visit our website:
politybooks.com

# Contents

| | |
|---|---|
| *Acknowledgments* | vi |
| *Abbreviations* | vii |
| Introduction | 1 |
| 1  Burnout: Against Achievement Culture | 8 |
| 2  World-Friendliness: Moods for Deep Cosmopolitanism | 35 |
| 3  Digital Bias: The Positivity of the Transparency Society | 64 |
| 4  Digital Psychopolitics: Towards the Total Control Society | 94 |
| 5  Duration: Finding Time | 123 |
| 6  Eros: Finding the Other | 148 |
| Coda | 171 |
| *Notes* | 173 |
| *Works by Han* | 182 |
| *References* | 184 |
| *Index* | 198 |

# *Acknowledgments*

The authors would like to thank their ever-patient families and friends, as well as the students and colleagues with whom they have discussed Byung-Chul Han's philosophy over the years. René Paddags was especially helpful. Ellen MacDonald-Kramer and Ian Malcolm at Polity have been tremendous editors. We thank Caroline Richmond for her attentive copy-editing, and Evie Deavall and Rachel Moore for seeing our book through the production process. We are also grateful to the outside readers of this manuscript who improved it in many ways through their insightful feedback. Byung-Chul Han graciously corresponded about his ideas at the proposal stage.

A few passages in this study first appeared in S. Knepper and R. Wyllie (2020) "In the Swarm of Byung-Chul Han," *Telos*, 191, and S. Knepper (2022) "Contemplation in a Restless Age: Byung-Chul Han on Ritual," *Telos*, 199. We are grateful to the editors for permission to revisit these pieces here.

# *Abbreviations*

| | |
|---|---|
| A | *Absence* |
| AE | *The Agony of Eros* |
| ARI | *ArtReview* interview with Gesine Borcherdt |
| BS | *The Burnout Society* |
| CDD | *Capitalism and the Death Drive* |
| DR | *The Disappearance of Rituals* |
| DRE | *Digitale Rationalität und das Ende des kommunikativen Handelns* |
| EO | *The Expulsion of the Other* |
| EPI | *El País* interview with Sergio C. Fanjul |
| GE | *Good Entertainment* |
| H | *Hyperculture* |
| HH | *Heideggers Herz* |
| HM | *Hegel und die Macht* |
| I | *Infocracy* |
| IS | *In the Swarm* |
| LE | *Lob der Erde* |
| M | *Müdigkeitsgesellschaft: Byung-Chul Han in Seoul/Berlin* (documentary film) |
| MCS | Commencement speech at MOME Budapest |
| MH | *Martin Heidegger* |
| N | *Non-Things* |
| NI | *Noēma* interview with Nathan Gardels |
| NTV | "The Tiredness Virus" (essay in *The Nation*) |
| P | *Psychopolitics* |
| PS | *The Palliative Society* |

| | |
|---|---|
| PZB | *The Philosophy of Zen Buddhism* |
| S | *Shanzhai* |
| SB | *Saving Beauty* |
| ST | *The Scent of Time* |
| T | *Todesarten* |
| TA | *Tod und Alterität* |
| TS | *The Transparency Society* |
| TV | *Topology of Violence* |
| VC | *Vita Contemplativa* |
| WP | *What Is Power?* |

# *Introduction*

Finding the sky "too beautiful" to study metallurgy, Byung-Chul Han left his native Seoul to study philosophy in Germany in the 1980s (CDD 65). He has gone on to write some thirty books on topics as diverse as Martin Heidegger, Zen Buddhism, power, globalization, beauty, pain, digital communication, Big Data, gardening, and the contemporary mental health crisis. Han's persistent concern is that late-modern individuals exhaust themselves in their life projects because they are losing the attitudes, practices, and even conceptual vocabulary to encounter what is "Other" to them. *The Burnout Society*, published in Germany in 2010, earned him an international reputation for this critique. In this book and elsewhere, Han explores why the information age is so poor in otherness. His works also explore what calls us out of ourselves: the challenge of beauty, encounters with persons who will always remain somewhat mysterious to us, even the uncanny aura of physical things. Han studied literature as well as philosophy, and he has spent much of his career teaching art students. He finds that artists are often more attuned to burnout society's problems than philosophers. Across his works, then, Han frequently engages composers, visual artists, filmmakers, and writers.

Han's ranging work resonates with our undergraduate students in the seminars we teach – respectively – in aesthetics, media studies, and political philosophy. Han is a scathing critic of the culture of achievement and language of positive reinforcement that is so prevalent in the educational system. Yet as he shows, this achievement culture and positivity pervade society beyond the institutions of meritocracy, especially via digital communication. It is part of a far-reaching global culture of neoliberalism. Han fascinates many of our students. They want to understand the philosophical perspective underlying the brief interventions they read, or how far Han's theoretical implications extend. They discuss analogs and parallels in English-language culture and media to the German essays, films, novels, and stories that fund Han's customary stock of examples. We aim to answer some of these questions.

Han's growing international audience likely has similar questions. All of his books are written in German, but his manifesto-like 2010 book *Müdigkeitsgesellschaft* [*The Burnout Society*] was quickly translated into his native Korean (2011), Italian (2011), Danish (2012), Dutch (2012), Spanish (2012), Swedish (2013), French (2014), Portuguese (2014), Brazilian Portuguese (2015), Chinese (2015), English (2015), Greek (2015), and many other languages. His ideas have strong traction already in Spanish- and Portuguese-language scholarship and now regularly appear in major magazines and newspapers around the world. Han's critique of burnout is aimed at global trends but is informed by his observations of fatigue, screen-addiction, and suicide in his regular visits to his hometown, Seoul, which he describes as a "tiredness society in its final stage" [*Müdigkeitsgesellschaft im Endstadium*] (M 13:29). Yet Seoul also appears in Han's works in reflections on childhood play and his Catholic upbringing (LE 138), in his general appreciation for East Asian philosophies, and in his interest in the hybridities of our global hyperculture (H). Han recognizes himself, of course, as being shaped by both East and West (CDD 65). He moved to Germany in the early 1980s on the pretext of continuing to study metallurgy (to satisfy his parents) but soon entered the University of Freiburg to study philosophy (M 2:45–3:47). Yet he has not completely left metallurgy behind. It shines through his passion for material design (MCS) and his concerns with how digital technology de-materializes the world and replaces things with "non-things" (N).

Readers interested in Han's biography should start with Isabella Gresser's black-and-white film documentary *Müdigkeitsgesellschaft: Byung-Chul Han in Seoul and Berlin* (2015), which situates the author between his two beloved cities. Han's voiceover describes his life and ideas. The Berlin sequence makes frequent allusions, in narration and imagery, to one of his favorite films, Wim Wenders's 1987 *Wings of Desire* [*Der Himmel über Berlin*], which is also shot in black and white. That film, about invisible angels who keep a lonely vigil over divided Berlin and console its harried inhabitants,

*Introduction* 3

underscores Han's evident concern for people. Perhaps it is in homage to Wenders's angels that Han wears a ponytail and leather jacket.

This is the first book-length introduction to Han to appear in English and the first comprehensive introduction to his philosophy, political theory, media theory, and aesthetics in any language. It has three main purposes. The first is to offer an overview of his primary overarching themes. We trace interpretive through-lines from his first book, *Heideggers Herz* [*Heidegger's Heart*], published in 1996, to his most recent book, *Vita Contemplativa*, published in English in 2024. These connect Han's philosophical interests in boredom, death, freedom, friendliness, and otherness to the main theoretical category in *The Burnout Society*: the "positive" violence of self-exploitation. Han argues that neoliberalism encourages relentless achievement to the point of burnout. He makes the startling claim that our notions of freedom, and even our experiences of freedom, are vulnerable to exploitation. Han writes, "the system exploits freedom itself" (CDD 89). We then explore how his interventions since 2010 deepen, extend, and at times revise his critical stance. Many of these later books focus on how digital media are biased towards capital accumulation, social control, and surveillance. And many offer responses to the violence of positivity, including practical ways to recover receptivity to others and reclaim space for contemplative freedom. Our book offers an orientation to Han for general readers, undergraduates, and scholars. We thoroughly define his key concepts and illustrate them with examples.

A second purpose of the book is to put Han in conversation with a wider range of interlocutors. He already engages a diverse range of thinkers, scholars, and artists, among them Hannah Arendt, Alain Badiou, Jean Baudrillard, Bashō, Walter Benjamin, Elias Canetti, Dōgen, Vilém Flusser, Michel Foucault, Peter Handke, G. W. F. Hegel, Martin Heidegger, Friedrich Hölderlin, Friedrich Nietzsche, Plato, Rainer Maria Rilke, Elaine Scarry, Carl Schmitt, and Yunmen. Some of these require more introduction than others. Occasionally we propose artists, filmmakers, novelists, and poets working in English who seem to be similar to Han's continental touchstones. We also introduce many new interlocutors by situating Han's work within or alongside the English-language scholarly literatures in our respective fields.

A third purpose of this book is to deepen the scholarly discussion of Han. His brief, clearly written books are more approachable than those of many other contemporary continental thinkers. In praise of his accessible style, Adrian Nathan West (2017) explains that Han has "little proclivity for the dialectical *fourberie* that has led many empirically minded readers to dismiss critical theory outright." Han prides himself on concision, writing so that the reader will want to underline each sentence (MCS 4:00–4:50). He also clearly wishes to speak to non-specialists who suffer the malaises of the burnout society. "Philosophy is a tool for better understanding the world," Han tells a Korean journalist, "but it is losing ground because philosophers tend to publish such difficult books that nobody dares to read" (Bae, 2013). Fresh ideas, a broad audience, and a teaching career spent in art institutes – he now writes full time – mark Han as something of an academic outsider. His emphasis on accessibility leads some critics to dismiss his writings as pop philosophy. Han's penchant for overstatement, sweeping assessments, and stark oppositions can feed into this critique. While we register criticisms of Han, some from others and some of our own, we seek responses in his body of work. Many of these come from his close readings of Hegel, Heidegger, and Zen sages in his early (and sometimes still untranslated) studies that might be overlooked by his widening global audience. Surveying Han's works as a whole reveals more nuance, seriousness, and depth than his critics credit. They reveal a serious effort to fundamentally rethink what it means to be free in response to the digital age.

*The Burnout Society* is a first introduction to Han for many readers. This intervention differentiates a new "positive" violence of self-exploitation from the old "negative" oppression that comes from disciplinary institutions, enemies, state actors, etc. Han makes a controversial pronouncement that adversity and repression are everywhere disappearing. Chapter 1 (authored by Wyllie) argues that this strict dichotomy between positive and negative violence, as well as Han's manifesto-like hyperbole about a paradigm shift to positive violence, are meant to make the problem of self-harm in achievement society visible at all costs (AE 49). The main point in *The Burnout Society*, which Han clarifies in later interviews, is to show that freedom itself is in crisis. This theoretical contribution prepares the ground for a broadly interventionist turn and for Han's more nuanced and targeted arguments about beauty (*Saving Beauty*), digital communication (*In the Swarm*), love (*The Agony of Eros*), and neoliberalism (*Psychopolitics*).

As scholarly engagement with Han increases, so will criticism. Broad lines of criticism, some more inchoate than others, have begun to appear in reviews and articles. Han overstates the shift away from disciplinary society and is inattentive to how powerful actors and institutions structure the self. He is too focused on first-world problems, as opposed to those in the poor and developing world. Han is a spiritual elitist who harbors illusions about how popular a more contemplative life could ever be. His assessments of digital technology are too bleak. Han offers self-help instead of political remedies to the problems he raises. Some of these criticisms hit the mark more than others. Many of these find responses in his broader body of work that critics may overlook.

Han is certainly not nostalgic for a bygone world of adversity, discipline, and grand narratives. Nor is he trying to turn the clock back to less efficient power structures, as if this were possible. Instead, he searches for freedom in *friendliness* beyond the ego, in a broad openness to others and the world. This friendliness is an aspect of moods such as boredom and tiredness when they relinquish power over people, places, and things. Chapter 2 (authored by Wyllie) returns to Han's early philosophical writings, several of which remain untranslated into English. He argues that Heidegger's phenomenology of boredom is contaminated by anxiety about death. In his 2002 book *Tod und Alterität* [*Death and Otherness*], Han contrasts the serene acceptance of finitude he finds in Zen Buddhism to the heroic encounter with death that he finds in Heidegger and even in implacable critics of Heidegger such as Levinas. For Han, Zen is characterized by a friendliness that allows the apparent world to be what it is. Similar attunements can be found in certain Western artists such as Paul Cézanne and writers such as Handke. Friendly tiredness and friendly boredom, which we might say are not in the mood for power, bestow a contemplative freedom from self-exploitation. These moods inform Han's politics of inactivity and what we call his deep cosmopolitanism.

Han becomes more closely attentive to how communication technology enables self-exploitation in works such as *In the Swarm*, first published in 2013. Chapter 3 (authored by Stoneman) explores Han's media ecology as an analysis of "digital bias." The lens of bias, borrowed from Harold Innis (2007), refers to how the physical properties of a medium tend to inform social experience. Han's critical media theory argues that digital formations are characterized by positivity bias and transparency bias. He is most interested in how these technologies interact with emotions to shape identity. Positivity bias refers to how the digital revolution has led to what Han calls, in a nod to Jean Baudrillard, the "hell of the same" (CDD 34). Social media algorithms, for example, survey preferences to curate options, so that users see content that elicits an immediate emotional reaction. Transparency bias refers to how digital media encourage users to make everything about themselves available as information. Digital practices bias us towards thoughtless self-exploitation. Otherness disappears, and, with it, the hopes for an internet of dialogue and sympathetic understanding. In its place, Han finds intense alienation and its byproduct: amorphous emotional engagement in online swarms that can be instantly summoned by algorithms and dissipate just as quickly.

Digital society is anything but ephemeral for Han, however. It has quickly massified into a control society. Han calls the regime that exploits freedom "psychopolitics." Chapter 4 (authored by Stoneman) shows how digital positivity and transparency offer new freedoms of self-expression that are simultaneously means of social control. Han is one of many cultural critics who notice how self-expression and self-improvement are insinuated into our economic relations. Consumption patterns such as fitness goals, meals, travel destinations, and work projects are instantly shared. We argue that psychopolitics is the definitive feature of Han's description of neoliberalism. He points out that we live in a digital panopticon of our own making. And, while all of this is the sum of "positive" bias and self-exploitation, Han nuances the bold theoretical shift announced in *The Burnout Society*. He starts to suggest how corporations and governments can steer our desires and exploit us much more shrewdly sometimes than we exploit ourselves.

Today's digitalized alienation involves the loss of meaningful time because relevant history for achievement subjects is as ephemeral as their ever-changing projects. In *The Scent of Time*, originally published in 2009, Han writes that time "whizzes by." Chapter 5 (authored by Knepper) returns to this book for strategies of resistance to burnout and digital control. Han does not offer a grand narrative that promises to return modern people collectively to a myth or history that will make time meaningful. Instead, he uses the metaphor of "scent" to recall us to a sense – smell – that entails duration. Han explores Eastern and Western practices of contemplative lingering.

Han does not merely offer therapeutics for burned-out achievement subjects adrift in a meaningless world of their own making. Friendliness promises a receptivity to other people, things, and places. Chapter 6 (authored by Knepper) focuses on a loose trilogy about recovering otherness originally published in 2012, 2015, and 2016, respectively: *The Agony of Eros*, *Saving Beauty*, and *The Expulsion of the Other*. For Han, eros draws us towards the Other, who must always remain beyond our possession and even beyond our understanding. The promise of eros motivates Han, contra modern aesthetics, to champion beauty that can wound the ego and stir eros in us. Profound boredom, profound tiredness, and the severe askesis of the Zen contemplative or the artist are not the only sources of friendliness. Han can also draw upon beauty and eros to call us to friendly greeting and the deep cosmopolitan politics of being with others.

# 1

# *Burnout: Against Achievement Culture*

Robert Wyllie

> ... it's not enough to just connect people; we have to make sure that those connections are positive.
> Mark Zuckerberg, Senate Hearing 115-683, April 10, 2018

## Life Hacks and Listlessness

"Live your best life." "Be the best version of you." In Melania Trump's laconism: "Be best." Schoolchildren who grew up with "Follow Your Dreams" posters on their classroom walls still trade positive reinforcement as adults. Their self-help advice gets only slightly more specific: visualize your life five years from now; set attainable goals; practice self-acceptance; avoid toxic and negative people. New clichés such as "life hack" imply that the brain is a poorly functioning computer that can be reprogrammed. Coffee is fetishized. All this exhortation to self-improvement is open-ended. None of it tells you what to be or what to do. "You do you." None of it tells you when you are at your best or when your best is good enough. The ambient motivational speech all around us is without direction and without limit.

These are some familiar slogans of what Byung-Chul Han calls "achievement society." He suggests the lexicon is indeterminate by design. Such slogans are meant to encourage people to become "entrepreneurs of themselves" (BS 8). The "self-made man" was ingrained in the political and later business culture of the United States long ago (Wyllie, 1954, p. 210).[1] But there has been a subtle shift away from the older idiom of making *something* of yourself. Self-making becomes infinitive. There is no finally *made* it. Now we are always in the *making*. We are "learning and growing every day." Han hears this in the standard commencement-address injunction to be a "lifelong learner" (MCS 7:30–8:33). Everywhere achievement society enjoins us to a "growth mindset," to the "grindset." Han describes modern people as "projects," "always refashioning and reinventing" themselves (P 1). Achievement subjects are served with an open-ended injunction to infinite self-optimization (IS 45–50). This sentimentalized self-description may be scraped away to reveal hard facts about economic reality underneath. Nowadays young people must be agile amidst a rapidly changing labor market, prepared to change careers, constantly networking and looking out for emerging opportunities.

Achievement society's proverbial wisdom is relentlessly positive. Han focuses on a popular slogan in Korean schools (M 41:16). Americans will associate it with Barack Obama's 2008 presidential campaign. "'Yes, we can,'" Han proposes, "epitomizes achievement society's positive orientation"; therefore, "Unlimited *Can* is the positive modal verb of achievement society," replacing a disciplinary "*Should*" (BS 8).[2] The US Army's long-running recruiting slogan, "Be all you can be," so successful from 1980 to 2001, was redeployed in 2023. Even armies, the proudest of all mission-driven disciplinary institutions, speak the language of open-ended achievement.

*The Burnout Society*, originally published in Germany in 2010, is Han's breakthrough manifesto against achievement society. It was quickly translated into many different languages. Recent critical studies (e.g., Robitaille, 2023) suggest Han was ahead of the curve in taking aim at pervasive positivity: Samuel W. Franklin's *The Cult of Creativity: A Surprisingly Recent History* (2023), Renyi Hong's *Passionate Work* (2022), Shani Orgad and Rosalind Gill's *Confidence Culture* (2022). So does Susan Cain's bestselling broadside against "toxic positivity" *Bittersweet: How Sorrow and Longing Make Us Whole* (2022). Han analyzes positivity from a broad theoretical perspective. Achievement subjects' myriad projects, from working out to working late, are part of open-ended projects of self-development. But there is an unacknowledged harm, probably unacknowledged because it is self-harm. We burn ourselves out. No other taskmaster demands, or could demand, the exhaustive effort that we put into our projects. The initial taste of freedom that stimulates our projects soon turns into its opposite – compulsive behavior that leaves us feeling drained, powerless, and full of self-reproach (BS 11, 47; TV 44).

Employers, vendors of lifestyle products, service industries, and data-harvesting tech companies are third-party beneficiaries of our self-exploitation. As we shall see in chapter 4, the lines blur when these profiteers become co-exploiters, encouraging our self-destructive strivings with performance bonuses, advertisements, and positive-reinforcement algorithms. When Mark Zuckerberg tells the Senate, "It is not enough to just connect people; we have to make sure that those connections are positive," he may be thinking of Facebook's bottom line (Senate Hearing 115-683). Ultimately, however, when achievement subjects eventually burn out, Han argues, we blame ourselves. Han describes a kind of bipolar disorder of anxious hyperactivity and depressive self-hatred as the signature affliction of our times.

Han's insistence that there is no structural negativity in achievement society is unique within critical theory. While power players – employers, the pharmaceutical industry, tech companies – benefit from and encourage achievement society, they tend to empower us. They allow us to self-inflict psychic violence upon ourselves. Han calls this "positive violence" (TV 116). For him, positive is not an antonym of normative in the way that Foucault discusses "positive knowledge" of punishment or the "positive economy" of discipline (1995, pp. 74 and 154). Han engages Foucault at length but does not adopt Foucauldian terminology in this case. For Han, positive violence means self-inflicted harm. Positive violence is synonymous with the "violence of positivity" (TV 90). Although positive is a technical term for Han, its meaning is consistent with the ordinary-language sense of a "positive attitude" [*positive Einstellung*] shared by German and English.

Unmasking puppet masters is beside the point for Han's critique of positive violence. Achievement society is *transparently* about empowerment, growth, opportunity, productivity, and wealth-creation. When a business firm encourages its employees' mental health awareness, for example, the profit motive is not ulterior or hidden. Everyone understands that healthy workers improve services, make production more efficient, and create value for shareholders. Employees are even called "human resources." Yet, even in this transparent logic, there is an unacknowledged problem. Endless self-improvement exhausts us.

By denying that achievement society must be imposed from without, Han departs from the usual internalization stories that social theorists have long provided. He does not retrace the Protestant work ethic of Max Weber (1958). Nor does Han seek the roots of contemporary "tyranny of opinion" in imitation or conformism, as John Stuart Mill did (2015, p. 166). His account does not follow Alexis de Tocqueville in blaming "democratic despotism" upon a proliferation of bureaucratic minutiae that induce us to conform (2010, p. 410). Han insists that *we* turn our own hamster wheels by our own volition (TV 47). Achievement society is millions of people who are intermittently *anxious* to be all they can be and *tired* of being all they can be.

Han opens *The Burnout Society* with a grandiose claim that a "paradigm shift" began around the end of the Cold War, bringing an "immunological" age defined against foreign enemies and pathogens to an end (BS 2). As a result, Han continues, we no longer live in a "disciplinary society" of negativity and repression (BS 8). The achievement subject is convicted by the famous cliché in the last panel of Stan Lee's first Spider-Man comic in 1962: "with great power comes great responsibility." We feel as if we *ought* to do something with our new (perhaps hard-won) freedom. Thus, we live in a neurotic age of excess positivity. Han counts the sudden prevalence of new psychological disorders as evidence of a societal malaise: "Neurological illnesses such as depression, attention deficit hyperactivity disorder (ADHD), borderline personality disorder (BPD), and burnout syndrome mark the landscape of pathology at the beginning of the twenty-first century" (BS 1).

Achievement society is the free society turned against itself. Revisiting his argument in a 2021 essay in *The Nation*, Han explains how burnout is "a crisis of freedom":

> Psychological disorders such as depression or burnout are symptoms of a deep crisis of freedom. They are a pathological signal, indicating that freedom today often turns into compulsion. We think we are free. But we actually exploit ourselves passionately until we collapse. We realize ourselves, optimize ourselves unto death. The insidious logic of achievement permanently forces us to get ahead of ourselves. Once we have achieved something, we want to achieve more, that is, we want to get ahead of ourselves yet again. But, of course, it is impossible to get ahead of oneself. This absurd logic ultimately leads to a breakdown. (NTV)

Achievement society exploits both our *ideas* about freedom and the *feelings* of freedom that our projects at least initially involve. They offer no rest or lasting satisfaction, though. We move from one project to the next. We wear ourselves out overachieving, overworking, and generally overdoing it – whatever "it" is. For all our new freedoms, we do not feel free in any lasting way.

Old-fashioned work ethic does not lead to burnout. If bounded and directed, Han notes, hard work can offer a sense of accomplishment and a satisfying tiredness. However, when unlimited *can* becomes an imperative of self-optimization, we become what Jenny Odell calls "DIY bosses propelled from within," and time is money: "You have twenty-four hours a day and must spend them in a better – and better, and better, and *better* way!" (2023, pp. 67–8). The new jobs in the information economy have few or no satisfyingly tangible results. Matthew Crawford's counterexample is an electrician wiring a light switch – click, yes, the job is done (2009, p. 14). Yet more people are moving into jobs where boundless information replaces a relationship to things. Achievement becomes vague and, as Odell suggests, a matter of individual goal-setting with no ends in sight. The achievement subject becomes the *product* of her or his work. Everyone, from entrepreneurs, to gamers, to children trying to fit in at school, must make themselves better "information hunters" (N ix). This phrase encouraging Koreans to hone their information-technology skills can be seen on an electronic billboard in Seoul in the 2015 documentary *Müdigkeitsgesellschaft: Byung-Chul Han in Seoul/Berlin* (M 14:55). As we shall see in chapter 3, the digital world facilitates our self-improvement projects smoothly. All of this may feel initially liberating, but then anxiety and guilt intrude: is *this* the best we can be?

Artists and writers during the 1980s were more sensitive to this shift to achievement society and its attendant malaises, Han suggests, than were philosophers and social theorists. A fixture in Han's books is the Austrian novelist and playwright Peter Handke, who won the Nobel Prize for literature in 2019. *The Burnout Society* supplements the descriptions of "malignant tiredness" in the opening pages of Handke's "Essay on Tiredness" (1994). Then Han makes an explicit turn to Handke's redemptive alternative: an "eloquent, seeing, reconciliatory tiredness" that is free of the pressures of achievement (BS 31). The book's original German title is *Müdigkeitsgesellschaft*, literally "tiredness society," which makes the nod to Handke more emphatic. Another frequent touchstone for Han is the billboard that Jenny Holzer installed amidst the flashing advertisements of Times Square in 1982 reading "Protect Me from What I Want" – a conceptual artist's pithy summation of the paradox of positive violence (P i; EO 39; CDD 129).

We begin with *The Burnout Society* because this book is an entry point for so many readers of Han. It is a stark theoretical statement. The author understands the task of theory as "highly selective *narration*" that "cuts a clearing of differentiation through untrodden terrain" (AE 49). *The Burnout Society* draws from Han's earlier philosophical studies of boredom, friendliness, otherness, and power, but the book makes new clear-cut distinctions between "allo-exploitation" and "auto-" or "self-exploitation," as well as between negative violence and positive violence (BS 47). Critical theorists trained to scan for internalized violence, or otherwise subtle negative operations of power, will miss the violence of positivity. And since our achievement projects are genuinely experienced as *free*, at least initially, the self-compulsive element is invisible as well. (Han has the tall order of breaking critical theory's habits of deconstructing, demystifying, and unmasking hidden structures of negativity.) Han's insistence on the absoluteness of positive violence, while it often seems exaggerated to dystopian levels, renders self-inflicted violence visible. He elaborates his theory of positive violence and the paradigm shift underway at greater length in *Topology of Violence*, originally published in 2011. This theoretical statement, certainly a clearing of differentiation, marks an interventionist turn in Han's body of work. Many of his subsequent books refine and nuance the account of how positive violence operates in specific domains such as art, digital media, markets, and so forth.

Even Han's sympathetic readers tend to agree that he exaggerates the extent to which we have undergone a clear paradigm shift to a post-disciplinary world (West, 2017; Bartles, 2021). After all, slavery, human trafficking, internment camps, and mass incarceration remain problems of global concern. Cronies have not absented themselves from crony capitalism. Legacies of injustice continue to shape racial and class divides. COVID-19, viral videos of police brutality in the United States, and the Russian invasion of Ukraine in 2022 so thoroughly belie the claim that pathogens, the disciplinary apparatus, and foreign enemies are no longer of great concern that some readers may struggle to make it through the first two chapters of *The Burnout Society*. With the benefit of some of this hindsight, we have criticized Han for overlooking how discipline and self-exploitation interact in complex ways (Knepper and Wyllie, 2020, pp. 44–5). Positive and negative violence may form a continuum. For example, self-exploitation in the wealthy global "core" (e.g., self-expression through fast fashion) may *intensify* repression in the impoverished "periphery" (e.g., bosses wringing productivity from garment workers in sweatshop conditions).[3] Another example is how the surveillance state might exploit teenagers' self-expression on TikTok. Chapter 3 will show how Han's later analysis of psychopolitics begins to take these interactions seriously.

Nonetheless, Han's primary concern is with the victims of self-inflicted psychic wounds in wealthy and putatively "free" societies: depression and burnout, the loss of space for contemplation, even the way that smartphones endanger childhood wonder. That these problems appear in the "free world" is significant. Han thinks our common-sense understanding of freedom as empowerment of the individual is in "deep crisis" (NTV). A world where freely chosen projects are all we have, indeed all we *are*, is intermittently exhilarating and ultimately exhausting. But what else could freedom be?

Before we turn to Han's philosophy of freedom in chapter 2, this chapter describes *The Burnout Society*'s theoretical contribution in three parts. The first section takes up Han's claim about the disappearance of disciplinary structures. It explores his umbrella concept of negativity and how it seems to vanish in all its various forms – adversity, boredom, pain, and even rivalry – from achievement society. The second section interrogates the violence of positivity and compares Han's critique of achievement society with that of other critics of burnout and meritocracy. The final section briefly lays the groundwork for understanding the philosophy of freedom that informs Han's critical and theoretical interventions.

## Abolishing Negativity

At the "core" of *The Burnout Society*, Han reports in an interview, is his argument that we no longer live in a disciplinary society but in an achievement society that "exploits freedom instead of suppressing it" (ARI). Burnout cannot be explained by psychoanalytic theories about how we internalize negativity. In other words, we do not internalize a threatening "or-else" set of rules and injunctions. "Or-else" internalizes the disciplinary "should" that Han distinguishes from the compulsive "can" of achievement society. At this point he bids Michel Foucault farewell:

> Today's society is no longer Foucault's disciplinary world of hospitals, madhouses, prisons, barracks, and factories. It has long been replaced by another regime, namely a society of fitness studios,

office towers, banks, airports, shopping malls, and genetic laboratories. Twenty-first-century society is no longer a disciplinary society, but rather an achievement society [*Leistungsgesellschaft*]. (BS 8)

Herman Melville's Bartleby prefers *not* to copy legal documents in favor of staring at a wall, going to prison, and eventually starving to death (BS 25–9). In contrast, Han's achievement subject *prefers to*. We work and work out in rooms with glass walls. We "self-surveil," broadcasting our projects into the "digital panopticon" (P 38). Punishment does not vanish with discipline only because our self-reproach if we slack off can reach self-destructive levels (BS 46–7). Burnout, the depressive and malignant tiredness in which we are *tired of being ourselves*, is a mood for self-harm.

Han generally dismisses a range of critiques about how external violence is internalized in the repressed subject. We call the broad family of ideas about how encounters with others constitute the self "negatively" *internalization theses*. This can be anything from a boy's encounter with his mother in Freud's famous Oedipus complex to the way the dominant ideology of the ruling class shapes our self-conception in Marx. For Jacques Lacan, the negativity of the other is primary and internalized: we form a sense of self through the mirror of imaginary others and a sense of the intersubjective world as the big capital-O Other of a symbolic order (2006, 40). Han, on the other hand, seems to essentialize the "positive" self and its desires without asking about its origins in the way that Freud, Marx, Lacan, and many others do. (As we shall see, however, someone inclined to be critical of Han on this point will need to work through his arguments about how Western philosophers posit the self's interiority as a response to the overwhelming negativity of death.) Technical meanings of Other(ness) in psychoanalysis should not mislead readers. Han uses the terms "other" and "Other," like positive and positivity, in a manner that is more continuous with ordinary language than his psychoanalytic interlocutors. In this book, capital-O Other simply refers to others as persons; it is not meant to indicate technical terms in psychoanalysis.

The internalization thesis has a long and varied lineage. In its most radical formulation, the techniques and practices of disciplinary institutions such as schools and hospitals *produce* the soul, which Foucault famously calls "the prison of the body" (1995, p. 30). Knowledge is one way that disciplinary power installs itself. Here, the soul is not shaped by the ruling class, Reformed pastors, bureaucratic minutiae, or public opinion. For Foucault, the soul *is* the internalization of external rules and authorities. Freud's "superego" is the internalization of "authority" (1989, p. 86). For Foucault, the entire soul is like a superego without remainder. Therefore, he must look outside of this power/knowledge, and ultimately to "the body and its forces," to discover counterpowers that might resist disciplinary society (1995, p. 25).

To this most radical of all internalization theses, Han's response is that the freedom of the body is exploitable in various ways that Foucault could not foresee. Foucault's schools (and souls) produced "docile bodies" (1995, p. 138). Modern schools produce eager over-achievers, enlisting pill-pushers to prescribe neuro-enhancers if necessary (BS 30). Gyms, pornography, and social media are permissive rather than repressive structures. Han is keen to show how our life projects include all kinds of affective, somatic, and visceral dimensions that are prone to exploitation. The liberation of the body does not promise freedom that is immune from exploitation.

*The Burnout Society* does not tell a single story about how disciplinary society is finally surpassed by the achievement society. Nor do Han's subsequent interventions restrict themselves to one domain of inquiry: the public enemy disappears with the end of the Cold War (BS 53n1), rituals disappear from increasingly homogeneous time, challenging artworks give way to smooth designs and the erotic gives way to the pornographic, politics becomes an entertainment spectacle as politicians' personal lives become transparent, and, above all, the internet eliminates duration and difference. *The Topology of Violence* confirms Han's commitment to a complex explanation of the reasons for achievement society's emergence, but indicates they are "primarily economic" (TV 44). Markets and enterprises are positive power structures. Consumers can buy whatever they like, so long as it is for sale; entrepreneurs can produce whatever they like, so long as there is a market for it. Han does not need to locate concealed negativity in the theoretically free market (e.g., class exploitation, structural determinants, wealth inequality, rent seeking): the growth of markets, consumer choice, and entrepreneurial potential offers plenty of opportunities to exhaust ourselves.

Han agrees with Foucault on one basic level of analysis, that power configures itself to operate as efficiently as possible. Han has a "flexible concept of power" (WP vii). He adopts a theoretical vocabulary in which power is constructive while violence is destructive (e.g., TV 65–8). "Power always *organizes itself* as a power structure," Han writes; "... [t]he structure of violence, in contrast, is an oxymoron" (TV 65). In German, the meaning of *Gewalt* ranges from authority, to power, to physical and non-physical forms of violence (WP 99n4). For Han, however, *Gewalt* most often means violence, as distinct from power [*Macht*] (WP 3).[4] Here he echoes a broad consensus of thinkers, from Hannah Arendt to Foucault and back to Hegel. But he emphasizes how the power structures of achievement society permit, stimulate, facilitate, and encourage the self-destructive violence of positivity.

Han departs from critical theory in another striking way by insisting that "Power is no longer a key medium of politics" (TV 72). He argues that politicians have become smooth public servants, likeable personalities that offer no resistance to public opinion, and gives the example of Angela Merkel (CDD 127). No longer an assemblage of subtle disciplinary institutions, politics becomes an empty spectacle. We expect transparency from political actors (TS 35). Are they nice? Are they faithful to their partners? Would it be fun to drink beer with them? Politics simply facilitates whatever individuals want. The power structure of achievement society is positivized, polycentric, and operates in each individual intra-psychically.

Politics now allows *us* to exercise power. The textbook political-science axiom that "politics always involves the exercise of power" is for Han an outmoded holdover of disciplinary society (Shively, 1991, p. 6). Even a sophisticated critic of neoliberalism such as Wendy Brown, because she thinks "the political is signaled by the presence of human relations organized by power," will overlook the individual and self-referential or "positive" power structures that for Han do not place individuals in relation to anyone or anything (2005, p. 75). Han's description of achievement society extends the semantic field of the political, since he thinks that older notions of the political – whether from Carl Schmitt, critical theorists such as Walter Benjamin, or even Jean Baudrillard (TV 61) – fail to grasp these new power dynamics. For him, these theoretical failures may explain why political responses to neoliberalism have been ineffective.

Disciplinary society gives way so that power can flow more efficiently. In achievement society, control is no longer a costly goal but rather a byproduct built into the system:

> Excess work and performance escalate into auto-exploitation. This is more efficient than allo-exploitation, for the feeling of freedom

attends it. The exploiter is simultaneously the exploited. Perpetrator and victim can no longer be distinguished. Such self-referentiality produces a paradoxical freedom that abruptly switches over into violence because of the compulsive structures dwelling within it. (BS 11)

Han argues that positive violence operates on a systemic basis: "The capitalist system is switching from allo-exploitation to auto-exploitation in order to accelerate" (BS 49). Achievement subjects are enmeshed in this system. Machiavelli's two humors, the desire *to* dominate and the desire not to *be dominated*, once manifested politically in "the great" and "the people" (1998, p. 39). However, in the depoliticized world that Han describes, where politics becomes empty spectacle, this conflict shifts to an "intrapsychic" scene. We are at once the great and the people in our own minds, at war with ourselves even, in our pursuits of greatness (see BS 35). Relentlessly positive, we constantly overestimate our carrying capacity to power our projects. We aspire to be like the new solid-state relays in electromechanics that can take wear and tear because they have no physical contacts to wear out; in reality, we are biomechanical relay switches that burn out from overload.

The achievement subject is amorphous, shapeless, and flexible, an adaptive and self-starting entrepreneur who "expects the profits of enjoyment from work" (BS 38; TV 25). Achievement society facilitates high levels of production, consumption, and communication (BS 40, 44; P 38). Self-exploitation is more efficient than discipline, and this constant reselving allows the "capitalist system" to accelerate (BS 49). Specialists have become multitaskers. "Multitasking," Han argues, "is an attentive technique indispensable for survival" for the wild animal who "must constantly be on the lookout, lest it be eaten while eating" (BS 12). Here, Han echoes the late Heidegger, who, in "Building Dwelling Thinking," calls our days "harassed unrest" [*gehetzen Unrast*] (1975, p. 148; 2000, p. 152). *Hetzen* is the German verb for giving chase to quarry or prey. Information hunters feel hunted. Proper to humans, in contrast to this scurrying, is deep attention, which is becoming increasingly rare.

The crisis of freedom that Han describes is not simply the fact that citizens do not feel free in the "free society." Citizens take freedom for granted, or feel free in different ways, for obvious reasons. Critics might point out how feelings of unfreedom *preserve* political freedom. For example, Montesquieu suggests that citizens feeling insecure in their freedoms motivates them to jealously guard their rights and privileges from other factions of citizens (1989, p. 325). Feeling unfree is perhaps the price of freedom. For Han, however, while Montesquieu's rough check of paranoid tyrannophobia may restrain others, it cannot protect us from ourselves and our self-exploitative impulses. Worse, the usual means of liberation – finding fulfilling work, achieving economic security, shedding toxic influences – *increase* the internal stress to achieve, like a Chinese finger trap that tightens as one attempts to free one's digits. Freedom itself is in crisis, Han says. Freedom and profit no longer go hand in hand. Antón Barba-Kay imagines a techno-pessimist warning in a provocative way: "History lesson: maybe you're forgetting that personal and political freedom have only ever been defended as the liberal means to a more efficient and productive society" (2023, p. 253). Han does not forget this lesson but warns that a more efficient and productive society exploits freedom itself.

The crisis of freedom generates profits from all of the pressures of self-exploitation we generate for ourselves. The exploitative capitalist and the exploited worker merge in the achievement subject. Almost everyone now recognizes that contemporary employees are both workers and capitalists. College students and Uber drivers must invest a lot of capital in order to be able to work – hence the contemporary phenomenon of the "debt trap" (Graeber, 2011, pp. 52–62). Karl Marx separates capital and labor into two distinct classes that are nowhere to be found in the developed world (P 4–6). Han underlines these shortcomings (P 51). More could be said about how achievement society spoofs Marx's utopian vision of freedom, of a world where workers are emancipated from unnecessary and alienating labor so that they can perform the fulfilling work of self- and world-creation. Achievement society also promises that we can all prosper together by doing what each of us loves, which is perhaps why so many on the left have fallen for neoliberal meritocracy. In practice, achievement society makes us feel hounded and harried, unfree in the sense of harassed animal quarry. In interviews, Han gestures to the need to "tame, civilize, and humanize capitalism" (EPI).

Capital is Han's preferred metonym for the market, a set of exchanges that are motivated by individual projects and purposes. When Han argues that self-exploitation increases returns to capital, he means to us all. For a critic of neoliberal capitalism, Han seems conspicuously unconcerned with income and wealth inequality. Moreover, he is a rare critic of capitalism who does not attempt to debunk F. A. Hayek's characterization of the market as a "spontaneous order" that is "the result of human action but not the result of human design" (Hayek, 2018, pp. 49n5 and 53). This is a consequence of his thesis about the disappearance of negativity. Han does not seek to unmask some "other" who is responsible for the violence of the system, whether this be the capitalist, an elite class, rent-seeking state actors, or even the internalization of a "neo-noir" pessimistic postmodern worldview of "capitalist realism" sold by the pop culture industry of the 1980s, hip-hop, and grunge (Fisher, 2009, pp. 4–11). Therefore, his critique can accept the same picture that defenders of free markets usually offer, where the accumulation of capital is the result of unconstrained individual actions and desires. This is because Han's critique aims at the liberal freedom of action itself. Classically, liberals give free rein to individual preferences that can be revised at any time, and which can be exercised in the "free society" where "men's goals are open" (Hayek, 2011, p. 87). Han thinks this conception of freedom is perfectly vulnerable to exploitation, because it induces us to exploit ourselves and call it freedom.

In terms of political economy, the achievement society has no architect, but it has a macro-logic (TV 82). It is global. Capital is a power structure that "dissolves borders" (TV 73). It is digital. The information with which and for which we work dissolves things into "non-things" (N 1). Yet none of this is abstract. Achievement society is *more* intensely felt than other social formations. Han points to how the internet, for example, is an emotional medium of the "swarm" (IS). *In the Swarm* nuances the theoretical absoluteness of positive violence in *The Burnout Society*. Han shows how positive violence can indeed generate intense bursts of negative violence, such as cyberbullying. These modes of violence may switch rapidly. Lack of returns to capital immediately cause public outrage that is vented upon politicians. As Steffen Mau points out, in *The Metric Society: On the Quantification of the Social*, indicators such as Gross Domestic Product, equity markets, the unemployment rate, and public debt are "capable of triggering public anger" (2019, p. 14). Therefore, while capital may encourage untrammeled positivity of the "yes we can" attitude, it can generate spasmodic negativity as well. By showing how positive power structures can also encourage spasms of *negative* violence, Han refines his critique, though not in a way that challenges the underlying paradigm or that can be directed in any sustained political action.

While Han focuses on developed societies, he is not cataloguing problems that affect a narrow elite. His examples in *The Burnout*

*Society* are white-collar workers who compulsively check their email and "fitness zombies," but similar dynamics play out across class lines, often in ways that bring together discipline and achievement to deepen inequalities. Achievement and happiness become compulsory for everyone (PS 10). This can take crude forms with wage workers in service industries. Seemingly happy sandwich shops are more profitable, placing a premium on affective labor. Mike Judge's 1999 cult-classic comedy *Office Space* parodies this. Joanna (Jennifer Aniston) is a waitress at a burger restaurant who festoons her uniform with only the minimum number of tacky buttons and corny pins that represent her "flair." She exasperates the manager (Judge) because she has no interest in "expressing herself." He admits that the restaurant chain, Chotchkie's, is trying to facilitate her self-expression to create a fun atmosphere that drives profit. Predictably, she burns out. The invitation to self-expression is a thinly veiled command, but opportunities also beckon: tips, a career in management, etc. In the movie, these cringeworthy humiliations are played for laughs. In the real world, executives at Pret a Manger reportedly surveil their sandwich-makers incognito to see if they radiate "authentic happiness," offering bonus pay or docking wages accordingly (Myerscough, 2013). This is not for laughs, but only for money.

When some saw utopian possibilities in an economics of sharing, Han foresaw the pressures of the gig economy. He predicted that it would lead to endless compulsions to work and to pursue high ratings. Han sensed that distinctions between work and life would further erode: "the sharing economy ultimately leads to the commercialization of all aspects of life" (CDD 19). He remains particularly insightful about how the gig economy needs buy-in from workers themselves to thrive. Workers need to take pride in their ratings, to embrace achievement on some level, for the system to work. Han is also attentive to similar dynamics in traditional productive sectors; what others call digital Taylorism takes the form of firmware that "gamifies" performance goals with interactive leaderboards (Odell, 2023, pp. 3–42). Sometimes employee monitoring is introduced for safety reasons (Levy, 2022). This is particularly marked in the trucking industry, where drivers are now digitally micro-managed in a way that gives basically no leeway for their judgment and agency.

As these examples show, achievement society is not for the privileged alone. There are no gatekeepers. Everyone can be (quietly: *should be*) entrepreneurs of themselves. Connections from elite business schools are not necessary to become an Instagram influencer. TikTok creators make videos about how to generate revenue by working from home. Any number of Facebook and YouTube ads, for social media users stuck in the digital Mesozoic of the mid-2000s, can alert you to easy "side hustles." Our devices reveal a world to us that lies open to our projects. The new freedom is for all of us: workaholics increasing our value on the job market, Twitter accounts amassing "followers," fitness-obsessed gym rats, academics compulsively checking citation indexes, smartphone users playing gamified apps that reward them for daily goals. All of this generates returns to capital.

At the end of *The Burnout Society*, Han broaches the possibility of the disappearance of negativity altogether, including pain, which is the theme of his 2020 book *The Palliative Society*. Han argues, "The inner logic of achievement society dictates its evolution into a *doping society*. Life reduced to bare, vital functioning is life to be kept healthy unconditionally. Health is the new goddess. That is why bare life is holy" (BS 51). This last reference is to Friedrich Nietzsche's prophecy of the Last Man in *Thus Spoke Zarathustra*. Pain is an obvious form of negativity that has become meaningless in achievement society (PS 19–24). Pain reduction and the curing of diseases are goods, but the problem is that they can never be fully eliminated. In denying pain any meaning, we turn the inevitable pain that remains into a nihilistic void. Pain becomes a black hole. We deny the value of pain that leads to substantive growth, such as wrestling with difficult ideas in school or learning to cope with failure, or, in a much different way, the pain that comes with love and loss in meaningful relationships. As achievement society removes obstacles to achievement, it also dismantles the adversity that creates the sometimes painful feelings we associate with a meaningful life. Many medical professionals are especially aware of the bad effects of the popular belief that modern medicine can eliminate suffering altogether (Gawande, 2015). A pain-free life, or the hope of a pain-free life, is another bill of goods. It is in high demand and generates massive profits. The opioid crisis in the United States has ravaged working-class Americans and the rural poor especially.[5] Han notes how "Analgesics, prescribed by the dozen, mask the social conditions that create the pain in the first place" (PS 11). Analgesics make pain an individual, rather than a social, phenomenon: "The palliative society *depoliticizes* pain by *medicalizing* and *privatizing* it" (PS 12).

In the final stage of the abolition of negativity, not only pain but even rivalry disappear. "Do what makes *you* happy." "Do your best." "Your personal best is all that matters." These are the cautious slogans of achievement society, meant to console those who might burn out because of envy or some other rivalrous passion. Han argues that the disappearance of rivalry only locks the achievement subject within itself. He writes,

> What proves problematic is not individual competition per se, but rather its self-referentiality, which escalates into *absolute competition*. That is, the achievement-subject competes with itself; it succumbs to the destructive compulsion to outdo itself over and over, to jump over its own shadow. This self-constraint, which poses as freedom, has deadly results. (BS 46)

Achievement society encourages us into an endless competition, not with others, but with ourselves, an endless process of self-optimization. Han's critique of directionless power becomes clear at this point. There are no external sources of the self, only the self in endless competition with itself. Our capacity for this absolute competition is limited, hence burnout.

## Excess Positivity; or, Creatures of the Treadmill

In J. G. Ballard's 2000 novel *Super-Cannes*, work is the "real leisure" for the creative elite of Eden-Olympia. They dwell in a business-park city of smooth structures with "streamlined balconies" and "oceanliner windows" in the hills above Cannes (Ballard, 2000, pp. 23–4, 103). Ballard calls them the "creatures of the treadmill" (ibid., p. 290). The resident psychiatrist of Eden-Olympia, Wilder Penrose, reports that the residents have insomnia, depression, and a lack of libido. *Super-Cannes* is a book about achievement subjects who live to work (see TV 25). The residents of Eden-Olympia exploit themselves and others until the day when a sudden fusion of tiredness and despair tears up "all scripts and scenarios" (Ballard, 2000, p. 168).

Ballard understands the achievement subject in a different way than Han. He explores the psychological dangers of late capitalism from a psychoanalytic perspective, building upon Freud's famous insight in *Civilization and its Discontents* that repression is necessary for civilization (1989, p. 87; cf. Bell, 2021). Amid the ennui of their carefully cultivated world, the residents of Eden-Olympia are desperate for excitement. Dr Penrose's patients do not suffer from "old-fashioned burnout" (Ballard, 2000, p. 283). They are not at the end of their rope but, rather, so bored that they are desperate for violent catharsis. This is a persistent Ballardian theme: "The suburbs dream of violence" (2006, p. 3). The residents of Eden-Olympia do not have to take matters into their own hands, like the unfulfilled businessmen in the 1999 cult-classic film *Fight Club*; instead, Dr Penrose prescribes them "carefully metered violence, microdoses of madness" (Ballard, 2000, p. 290). A safety valve for violent outbursts is under semi-official control in Eden-Olympia, like the "Purge" in the ongoing dystopian horror movie franchise of that name, a twelve-hour period where violent crimes including murder are decriminalized every year. Herbert Marcuse called these controlled moments of erotic pleasure and freedom, which co-opt Freud's discontents to perpetuate the repressive society, examples of "repressive desublimation" (1991, pp. 72–7).

For Han, however, no volcano of potential violence lies repressed beneath the boring surface of late modern capitalism. Ballard worries that our only salvation from boredom is a fascistic desire for violent spectacles far worse than the present anomie (Bell, 2021, pp. 954–7). Moreover, Dr Penrose implies burnout is a terminal condition that can only be diagnosed after it blazes forth lethally. While Han would recognize the depressed achievement subjects of Eden-Olympia down to their preference for scalloped architecture – the "smooth" in design eschews negativity (SB 1) – he challenges the premise that achievement society is founded upon internalized repression. He helps us pinpoint what is fantastic about *Super-Cannes*, and *Fight Club* and *The Purge*, as well as any other fictional representations of therapeutic psychopathy. Burnout is an ongoing zombie-like existence which can be sustained indefinitely (BS 47–51). No repression wells up potential paroxysms of violence within us. There is no catharsis, only fatigue. Han concludes, "*Instead of revolution we thus get depression*" (PS 12).

The internalization thesis in this broad sense Han is attacking is older than Frankfurt School critical theory and even older than psychoanalysis. Jean-Jacques Rousseau offers the first description of the achievement subject along these lines in 1755, though how much he endorses the "hypothetical and conditional reasonings" that he makes after "setting aside all the facts" is not clear. Indeed, that Rousseau aims to explain "the Nature of things" rather than "their genuine origin" suggests his internalization thesis is halfhearted at best (1997, p. 132). Like Han, Rousseau is critical of the modern sense of freedom as empowerment, specifically the never-ending Hobbesian pursuit of happiness (Scott, 1992, p. 701). Thomas Hobbes makes our desires or strivings, the *conatus*, the locus of the self. The "general inclination of all mankind," Hobbes argues, is "a perpetual and restless desire of power after power, that ceaseth only in death" (1994, p. 58). Faced with this tendency that Han would call positive violence, Rousseau searches for the origins of this impetus to endless self-exertion. This inaugurates the broad tradition of continental political thought that seeks to identify some "malignancy" in reason itself that distorts our ideals of freedom (White, 2011, pp. 483–4). Rousseau identifies *amour propre*, a vain desire to be lovely in the eyes of others. From the songs and dances of the earliest societies, human beings internalize others' esteem. Ever since, Rousseau argues, we are divided between a socially mediated and vain self-conception and a natural sense of self (or sentiment of existence). We feel incomplete and compelled to pursue temporary consolations of status. Rousseau pities the European citizen, who, "forever active, sweats, scurries, constantly agonizes in search of ever more strenuous occupations: now works to the death, even rushes towards it in order to be able to live, or renounces life in order to acquire immortality" (Rousseau, 1997, p. 187). Much like Han today, Rousseau complained that the bourgeois of his time was restless, overworked, and trapped in a spiral of self-harm in the guise of freedom (Storey and Storey, 2021, p. 5).

Han's diagnosis of "auto-compulsion" in achievement society, "which presents itself as freedom," is perhaps more closely aligned with Rousseau than with any other theorist (BS 46). Like Han, Rousseau is concerned firstly with self-tyranny and secondly with tyranny over nature as a whole, and he examines what in man's psyche "makes him his own and Nature's tyrant" (1997, p. 141). Han worries that an unrealistic "ego ideal" invites us to self-exploitation, and this seems closer to the vain self-conception of Rousseau's divided bourgeois than to any more precise use of this term in Freud or other psychoanalytic thinkers (BS 46). Yet Han mentions Rousseau only briefly in his works, including a critical comment on his critique of hypocrisy as an early step towards transparency as a moral imperative (P 73–4; TS 42–4). Nonetheless, Han's concerns take us back to the Rousseauian origins of continental political thought, and his most recent book, *Vita Contemplativa* (as we shall see), draws more deeply on Romantic thinkers influenced by Rousseau. More extensive comparison with the rare thinker in the center of the Western philosophical tradition who seems to share Han's concerns would be illuminating.

Han's rejection of the internalization thesis sets him apart from his interlocutors among contemporary sociologists as well. He approvingly cites Alain Ehrenberg's description of the depressed individual as the one who "is tired of having to become himself" (2010, p. 4). Still, Han challenges Ehrenberg's diagnosis. While Ehrenberg identifies a pressure to achieve that achievement subjects internalize, Han insists this pressure is self-generated. When nothing seems possible for us any longer because we are so tired, we sink into self-reproach. Perhaps if we were only more motivated .... Han points out, reasonably, that only individuals who believe everything is possible for them can come to feel like underachievers and losers (BS 10).

Burnout can be an ongoing state of the overstimulated subject for Han, not only a terminal condition of the thwarted ego. Ehrenberg thinks depression sets in *after* one's project meets with resistance or failure (BS 9, 42). But Han's burned-out achievement subjects may never encounter adversity, failure, pain, or resistance at all. They may never crash, bottom out, or explode. They may burn out on success after success. They really might, as in one of Donald Trump's memorably bizarre formulations, become "tired of winning." In *Super-Cannes*, Dr Penrose thinks burnout *is* the failure that paralyzes one from pursuing one's projects further. But Han does not think burnout necessarily scuttles our projects. Achievement subjects might work in and through burnout, though they will also likely be increasingly medicated, like the walking dead (BS 51). They may even continue to succeed, though success gradually loses its relish. A once liberating experience begins to feel like a compulsive behavior.

Eduardo Mahieu (2021) connects Han, via the modern psychiatry of chronic fatigue, back to Max Weber. Weber's *The Protestant Ethic and the Spirit of Capitalism* traces *fin-de-siècle* Anglo-Saxons' joyless pursuit of wealth – and the secular "iron cage" of economic rationality – back to their seventeenth-century Puritan ancestors' unconscious desire for assurance about their salvation (1958, p. 181). Han agrees with Weber that Protestant asceticism denigrates the medieval *vita contemplativa* in favor of the *vita activa* (ST 89). Yet he cannot accept a sociological internalization thesis, even one as marvelously complex as Weber's, to explain today's achievement subject. Likewise, Han is out of step with the twentieth-century psychiatry of chronic fatigue for the same reason. Building on the work of Hubertus Tellenbach, Herbert Freudenberger coined the term "burnout" to describe overworked employees (1974, pp. 159–65). Tellenbach had already found that individuals who identify too strongly with social norms are more likely to be chronically fatigued. The original attempt to pathologize burnout points to the internalization of norms and social pressure. The Ehrenberg–Tellenbach account of depression may be true of obedience subjects in disciplinary society, Han would allow, but it must be updated to explain similar symptoms in exhausted achievement subjects.

Although we have seen that burnout does not exclusively afflict privileged elites, Han links achievement society to the "neoliberal meritocracy" (ARI). The education system is the primary network of institutions that confer merit and status in achievement society. From a traditional (perhaps charmed) perspective, education seems to be rich in "otherness." Schools and universities invite students to listen to others' perspectives. Some instructors teach students to grapple with the interpretation of difficult ancient and foreign texts and their challenging alternative perspectives on life. Even if the liberal arts were accessible only to a privileged few, they were thought to be requirements for the education of free persons. Despite his frequent and fulsome praise of beauty, contemplation, and eros, Han does not turn to liberal education as an oasis where thoughtful alternatives to the "freedom" of self-exploitation can be embraced. This suggests how profoundly achievement society has transformed the university.

Michael Sandel (2020) argues that selective universities in the United States produce a compassionless elite that aligns their success with merit and subtly casts the unfortunate as deserving losers. As Sandel notes, meritocracy claims legitimacy from the myth of the self-made man. Yet, while contemporary meritocracy is very deliberately inclusive, a self-serving tendency to see the less fortunate as the less virtuous remains. Han's analysis of meritocracy, however, takes a broader view of ongoing psychological self-harms to everyone, including the losers. Han can be attentive to class-specific ways that burnout afflicts "underdogs" but often focuses on the spectacular symptoms of burnout among the "top dogs" (TV 78–83).

Take the top dogs. In a 2000 essay for the *New York Times*, two Harvard College admissions officers and a psychology lecturer responded to the widely reported burnout phenomenon by encouraging students to take a gap year. "Burnout is an inevitable result of trying to live up to alien goals," they write. "Time out can promote discovery of one's own passions" (Fitzsimmons et al., 2000). Teenagers in affluent and educated homes are among the most at risk for depression, anxiety, and general unhappiness, and this research broadly substantiates anecdotal evidence about burnout among successful young people (Levine, 2006, pp. 16–17). These are the students pressured to strive, perform, and earn places in our meritocratic achievement society (Curran and Hill, 2019; cited in Sandel, 2020, p. 224). Han would argue that the Harvard admissions officers and psychologist miss the point. The prospective undergraduate is least of anyone beholden to "alien goals." Young people admitted to elite universities brim with possibilities. An incoming freshman class at Harvard must come as close as any imaginable group to achievement society's ideal of freedom as open-ended self-making: study finance or history, engineering or Sanskrit, find your passion! Han would expect students to burn out because they are tired *from* their passion projects, and the positivity of well-meaning academic advisers and psychologists only adds fuel to the fire of burnout. Administrators on the frontlines of burnout do not seem to entertain this possibility. The prevailing assumption is that negativity, in this case the intrusion of alien goals, must cause burnout. Han's contrary insistence that we burn out on projects that are authentically our own suggests that even the highest achievements in neoliberal meritocracy cannot deliver the freedom they seem to promise.

Critics may still insist that Han overstates his case by presenting a both/and as an either/or. Parents and teachers encourage their students to maximize their potential by larding out their college applications with accomplishments, service projects, and extracurricular activities. Students internalize pressure from their sacrificing parents and teachers to conceive of their lives as controllable projects lest they disappoint them (Rosa, 2020, p. 71). Hartmut Rosa plausibly claims that fear and economic precarity fuel the widespread obsession with achievement: "If we fail to be better, faster, more creative, more efficient, and so on, we will lose our jobs, businesses will close, tax revenues will decline while expenditures increase, there will be budget crises …," further constricting political action and leading to a crisis of political legitimacy (ibid., p. 9). Han nuances his position in *The Expulsion of the Other* and other later works, allowing that achievement subjects are not always in "absolute competition" (BS 46) with themselves, and that fear of failure, "comparison," and "lateral anxiety" are very real contemporary motivations (EO 32). Nevertheless, Han's theory of positive violence is better situated than internalization theses to explain why successful people with excellent job security burn out, as well as the digital bias towards positivity that we shall take up in chapter 3. Still, Han's books since *The Burnout Society* explore the multiple and hybrid causes of the obsession with achievement, where internalized pressures to achieve augment self-exploitation.

Han's critique of achievement society reveals how vulnerable freedom is to exploitation when it is indexed to empowerment. Conceiving of freedom in terms of power is ancient common sense, but, as we have seen, Hobbes clarifies the concept and installs it at the center of modern political philosophy. *Leviathan* installs the then new concept of motion in seventeenth-century physics as a foundation for political philosophy. The freedom of any natural body, Hobbes writes, "signifieth (properly) the absence of opposition (by opposition, I mean external impediments of motion)" (1994, p. 136). The striving that is most fundamental to the self for Hobbes, the *conatus*, provides *impetus* for directed motion through a point in space or time; in the human being, the passions, and most famously the will or "last appetite," inclines us towards motion (1994, p. 33). And as we have also seen, Rousseau is vexed that Hobbes thinks freedom is oppressed exclusively by impediments and never by stimuli, when the soul becomes shackles, we might say, and never when it becomes a whip. Han updates Rousseau's critique and takes a wider vantage. Granted, Han would not be likely to put it this way, because he has long considered this desire for freedom not as a Hobbesian innovation, but more deeply constitutive of the Western philosophical tradition.

Achievement society does not arrest but, rather, stimulates and exploits the affective, somatic, and visceral phenomena we sometimes register as "freedom." Han's critique of achievement society resembles Patrick Deneen's critique of liberalism (2018, p. 31), insofar as our *success* in enlarging freedom of choice has unleashed forces beyond our control and closed off our receptivity to nature. Yet, while Deneen ends by casting a wide net for "deeper" and "intergenerational" freedom in countercultural practices (2018, pp. 190–2), Han is already working *from* an alternative philosophical standpoint. As we shall see in the next chapter, he takes up a perspective that is radically opposed to Hobbes's location of freedom at an exact *point and time*, one that inherits Heidegger's critique of all philosophy that presumes some experiential access to time in spatial terms. For Heidegger, to think of the self in terms of a *conatus* is to hallucinate some fundamental directional principle of subjectivity. Han turns to Heidegger, sometimes critically, for a philosophy of freedom that informs the countercultural practices we shall explore in chapters 5 and 6. In other respects, because it avoids community or narrative as the basis of critique, the Hanian critique of liberalism has an attractive parsimony. Han simply argues that new cultural and technological conditions exploit the vulnerabilities in the incomplete liberal notion of freedom based in project pursuit, turning yesterday's freedom into today's self-exploitation.

More familiar than Hobbesian *conatus* in contemporary political theory is the conception of rights-bearing persons as project pursuers. The emphasis on the active development of the faculties is retained in the liberal perfectionism of Mill (2015, p. 58). Loren Lomasky argues that persistent projects that structure persons' lives are sufficient grounds for justifying respect for individual rights; thus, rights could be defended without an appeal to any external standards of moral rationality (1987, p. 26). These projects are "motivated dispositions that *project themselves temporally* through various stages of a life" (1987, p. 42). For Lomasky, rights-bearing persons need a self-understanding that they are carrying out sustained projects.

Han concedes that the pursuit of projects is a basic part of our experience of freedom. In psychoanalytic language, he argues that, while obedience-subjects subject themselves to the superego, "the achievement-subject projects itself [*entwirft sich*] onto the ego ideal," which "is interpreted as an act of freedom" (BS 46). Moreover, this is registered viscerally. One simply feels a pleasant sense of freedom when one sets goals and achieves them. However, the ego ideal is not our embodied self. The body is not capable of absolute freedom of action. It can reach the limit of exhaustion. The intra-psychic relationship between myself and my ego-ideal, furthermore, is self-contained. This relationship does not involve the world beyond my goals and plans. My interiority may be characterized by self-love or self-hatred, but it remains absolutely in Hegel's realm of "spirit" (HM 65). No Other appears except as can be enjoyed, used, or simply conceived in the terms of my power to act. In Hegel there is no remainder to our experience of the world, Han would say (at least in his early works), that is not mediated by our projects.

Is there more to the world than can be assimilated into projects? There is a receptive aspect of being, which a critic of Hegel's ontology of spirit such as Charles Taylor would say is "porous" to the world (Taylor, 2007, p. 38). Things, mysterious Others, and even adversity vitalize us and fill our lives with new meanings, if we are receptive to them. Yet this starts with a passivity, a mood not-to-do. Passive moods are anathema in achievement culture; ironically, however, achievement society cannot help but produce tiredness. Han finds hope in certain kinds of tiredness, or, perhaps if we are receptive to tiredness in a certain way, we shall find an "aura of friendliness" in tiredness (BS 33). Han's preferred term for receptivity to otherness is *friendliness*.

Critics of individual rights as a consequence of individual projects have long targeted the role narrative plays in the arguments that define persons as project pursuers. Lomasky requires us to read the "story" of a project-pursuer's life (1987, p. 158). *How* do we tell ourselves stories about our lives of self-making? Where do we find the narrative resources for telling these stories? In another influential work of moral philosophy from the 1980s, Alasdair MacIntyre argues that our lives cannot be merely understood as projects: "the key question for men is not about their own authorship; I can only answer the question, 'What am I to do?' if I can answer the prior question, 'Of what story or stories do I find myself a part'" (2007, p. 216). MacIntyre argues that we and others can understand our projects only as part of a larger narrative or in light of the prior question of which community we ought to belong (2006, p. 122). Although Han is not operating within this moral-philosophy discourse about entitlements and the origin of rights claims, he is interested in what might invest our lives with narrative tension or depth and, thus, resist the "lightness" of achievement society where projects and values are simply chosen and are always disposable and interchangeable.

In *The Burnout Society*, Han laments the disappearance of narrative. He writes, "The late-modern ego [*Ich*] stands utterly alone. Even religions, as thanatotechnics that would remove the fear of death and produce a feeling of duration, have run their course. The general denarrativization of the world is reinforcing the feeling of fleetingness" (BS 18). Han is drawing from his previous book, *The Scent of Time*, where he argues that myth and liturgy formerly invested time with "a narrative or deep tension," interlinking duration with events (ST 18). He fosters a more practical appreciation for ancient contemplative traditions than do Nietzsche and Heidegger, even though he cannot envisage a simple return to them. Now time is empty, and individual projections replace any collective sense of duration. Chapter 5 will take up Han's description of the temporality of achievement society and his attempt to recover the "scent" of time rather than any specific myth, liturgy, ritual practice, or narrative of the past.

Despite his invocation of narrative, Han does not follow the broad turn taken by those who are sometimes called "communitarian" critics of liberalism, who evaluate specific traditions towards which we ought to be receptive. MacIntyre, for example, proposes that retrieving an Aristotelian–Thomistic moral vocabulary of virtue is best for understanding the narrative unity of our lives in a way that allows us to make moral judgments. Han does not envision prospects for large-scale retrievals of narratives, traditions, or customs. (MacIntyre would not disagree.) Beyond ethical philosophy narrowly conceived, Taylor explores the sources of the self in Western history to suggest different ways we can orient ourselves to its "immanent frame," the contemporary situation where society is no longer embedded in the transcendence of sacred history. Han is less optimistic that we can "open" ourselves to transcendence and, instead, accentuates how our worldviews are "spun" by technology and culture (Taylor, 2007, p. 550). In Taylor's words, Han warns that achievement subjects increasingly "buffer" themselves and will burn out without recovering "porosity."

Han is fundamentally more ambivalent about interiority than Taylor. His early writings indict Western philosophy, starting with Socrates, for deepening interiority as a response to death. This reaches a peak in Hegel, where the philosopher's world is a totality of power that acknowledges death but cannot accept it (HM 26). This same Western tradition in general and Hegel in particular offer Taylor resources to show how our situated moral and political obligations can underwrite commitments to individual freedom (Abbey, 2000, pp. 105–6). Yet Han seems concerned that this Western tradition is still too committed to interiority. He is so skeptical that this Western and ultimately Hegelian tradition can admit otherness that he argues Taylor's search for authentic self-fulfillment can only amount to narcissism (DR 17).

A critic for whom Han "essentializes" the desiring self would overlook the ways that outside forces construct the self can find interesting responses in *Hegel und die Macht* and Han's 2002 book *Tod und Alterität*. Han suggests that interiority develops in Western philosophy as a response to the overwhelming negativity of death – the immortal soul, for example, in early Greek thinkers such as Socrates. The valorization of spiritual freedom blinds Western thinkers to the ravages of positive violence, the effects of which are most visible in South Korea. In other words, Han may keep this most fundamental *ur-internalization thesis* in view, an overemphasis on inwardness in Western philosophy since the days of ancient Greece. This may be one reason why he has for so long readily turned to radical critics of Western philosophy such as Heidegger, to artists outside of philosophical discourses, and to non-Western sources in order to show us how to "loosen" our "clamps" on our subjectivity (TA 8) rather than to figures in the Western philosophical tradition.

Any recovery of community for Han, then, requires a more basic recovery of hospitality to otherness. For this reason, he searches out possible sites where Others might appear to which we can cultivate openness – ritual, art, friendship and love, beauty and the sublime, contemplative mindfulness. Here, again, in his broad array of responses to the paradoxically compulsive character of the contemporary notion of freedom, only some of which are directly political, Han resembles Rousseau perhaps a little more than his broadside against Western philosophy allows him to admit.

## Towards a New Freedom

Achievement subject is a misnomer. Han admits as much: "The late-modern achievement-subject is subject to no one. In fact, it is no longer a subject in the etymological sense. ... It positivizes itself; indeed, it liberates itself into a *project*" (BS 46). As we have seen, the result is spastic. Achievement subjects have the paradoxically "compulsive freedom" of uncontrolled movement (BS 11). So many modern people now believe that nothing can be learned from pain (PS 1), that beauty gives us nothing to see beyond pleasure (SB 79), and that we lose nothing by replacing objects with all their significance with information (N 55). Without a capacity for belonging or wonder, the achievement life becomes a series of trivial adventures punctuated by depressive episodes. Yet the "bare life" described by Giorgio Agamben (1998) does not generate its negative counterpart, sovereignty. Han argues, "Agamben utterly fails to notice the topological change of power that lies at the basis of the society of sovereignty's transformation into achievement society" (BS 48). Here, once again, we find Han out of step with an earlier social-theory tradition from Tocqueville to Foucault where individual atomization is the precursor for political domination (Villa, 2008, p. 75). Instead, depoliticization is a central theme for Han. Disciplinary power is drained from politics (TV 72).

Han is searching for something in the world that is other than power. What is freedom if not empowerment? He comes to *The Burnout Society* already thinking alongside a tradition in which we are receptive to freedom. For Heidegger and Romantics such as

F. W. J. Schelling, freedom is "not the property of man" but, rather, "[m]an, at best, is the property of freedom" (Heidegger, 1985, p. 9). Separating freedom from the individual's feelings and ideas related to empowerment brings us to a post-subjective standpoint as radically opposed to Foucault's undisciplined bodily forces as it is to Hayek's freedom-from-constraint for unknown ends, as different from Hegel's being-oneself-in-the-other as it is from Nietzsche's will-to-power. The next chapter explores Han among other philosophers of post-subjective freedom. Political theorists especially may worry that he is threatening to leave the semantic field of *political* freedom altogether. Isn't politics always about collective *action*? However, they should keep in mind the exigent problems of anxiety, burnout, depression, overstimulation, and overwork that Han addresses in *The Burnout Society* before they dismiss the direction of his thought as an "unpolitical" one. Furthermore, they should feel convicted by his charge that the idea of freedom at the very center of Western political and philosophical traditions has led us to our current crisis and remains complicit in our ongoing self-exploitation. This should invite skeptical readers to entertain Han's arguments about how receptivity can liberate us for new forms of collective political action that presently seem impossible.

Sometimes Han translates his philosophy of freedom into more congenial language that political theorists and ordinary citizens will more readily accept. A good citizen has an ethos of fraternity *and* freedom, Han writes, in "Who Is a Refugee?," his reflection on Arendt and what it means to be an "optimistic refugee" and a German "patriot" (CDD 64–8). Here we can imagine a response he might make to liberals such as Mill and Lomasky who put individuals' projects and self-chosen plans of life at the moral center of the rights-respecting society: without receptivity to others *as* Others, individuals will lack respect for them and their entitlements. Han might say that achievement subjects may intermittently feel free, but mostly they feel stressed. Somehow, they are not in the mood for freedom. Han points us to a concept of "ordered liberty," we might say in quite different language from his own, where the mood for freedom must come first before freedom appears.

# 2

# *World-Friendliness: Moods for Deep Cosmopolitanism*

## Robert Wyllie

> Tiredness is the angel who touches the fingers of the one dreaming king, while the other kings go on sleeping dreamlessly ... Tiredness is greater than the self.
>
> Peter Handke, "Essay on Tiredness"

### A Political Response to Burnout?

Even if positive violence made everyone in achievement society miserable and everyone knew it, a political response to the crisis described in *The Burnout Society* would be difficult. One major reason for this is that achievement society exploits real feelings of freedom, however transitory they are. The violence we inflict upon ourselves becomes "completely invisible," Han argues, "at the moment it merges with its opposite, that is, with freedom" (TV vi). Paradoxically, *freedom* makes achievement subjects no longer in the mood for freedom. Achievement subjects seem like freedom addicts, oddly enough. They usually feel harried or depressed, not free. They cling to the cold comfort that some new rush of freedom may lie in a new opportunity just around the corner. Many inherited conceptions of freedom – freedom from interference, freedom of the will, autonomy, self-actualization, etc. – contribute to the present neurological crisis by encouraging us to think of achievement society as the domain of freedom. All of these obscure positive violence. The crisis described in *The Burnout Society* is a crisis of this Western ideal of freedom. For this reason, Han sets out to develop a sense of freedom that is more authentic to our age (BS 11). One of his main theoretical contributions is to help us see the issue of positive violence more clearly. He offers us a language to describe how our subject-centered and project-oriented ideas of freedom are *themselves* being exploited.

Achievement lifestyle, lived so conspicuously in the realm of possibility, has a deceptive lightness. Achievement subjects are not responsible for any other; no other is responsible for them. Of course, they are no less self-destructive for the fact that their *"shoulds"* are no weightier than *"cans."* Anxiety or guilt are unavoidable. With all these opportunities that unfortunate persons lack, perhaps for which my ancestors sacrificed, *shouldn't I* do something? In this way, Han's achievement subject feels the weight of the *should*, but without any sense of direction – should *what*? Self-reproach awaits if we do nothing. Isn't this the life we wanted? Isn't this freedom? In this chapter, we shall see how Han's philosophical writings explore ways in which the lightness of modern freedom might be made bearable, how there might be some "weight of the world" in others and things (EO 41), without resorting to the ponderous fatalism to which Nietzsche and Heidegger seem to succumb.

Han's philosophy of freedom is nevertheless indebted to Heidegger's, and especially to the way that Heidegger leaves aside the perspective of the subject (HM 68). Heidegger's later writings, as is well known, are marked by concern about technology. *The Burnout Society* suggests plenty of reasons to return to thinkers who consider how technology threatens human freedom. More profoundly, it suggests plenty of reasons why subjects who possess free possibilities do not actually experience freedom. Autonomous self-control does not rule out self-tyranny (WP 88). Achievement society induces unconstrained actors to exploit themselves in self-destructive ways. Still, an alternative conception where we are *acted upon by* freedom, or where "freedom has us" more profoundly than "we have freedom," is weird. Thinking about ourselves as the *objects of* freedom cuts against the grain of common sense, ordinary language, and any political theory that starts from available shared conceptions of collective action. Plus, additional wrinkles appear when we consider that Heidegger, the German Romantics, the Zen masters, and Han himself all think differently about how freedom comes to "have us." The crisis of freedom brings us to a starting point of inquiry that is a little strange, not obviously political, and complicated by intersecting philosophical paths across the centuries and across the globe.

# Moods for Deep Cosmopolitanism    37

How Han understands the crisis of freedom that we explored in the previous chapter requires careful attention to his interlocutors. Heidegger and Zen Buddhism, for instance, are pivotally important to understanding Han, though they are neither as accessible nor as topical. This chapter moves carefully through Han's untranslated early writings. While they are more historical-interpretive and academic, and while they concern finer points of German and Far Eastern philosophy, they are important to orient us to how Han understands the crisis of freedom. We begin with the problem concerning technology that compelled Heidegger to decenter subjective freedom and to reexamine Schelling and the German Romantics who made the spirit of *freedom*, rather than individual human beings and their wills, the subject of history. These thinkers raise questions such as *What* puts us in the mood to be free *in the first place*? After we are reoriented to ask how we become receptive to freedom, the second part returns to Han's first book from 1996, *Heideggers Herz*. Here, Han argues that Heidegger underestimates how boredom is a mood for freedom. Heidegger allegedly overlooks a friendly boredom that relinquishes interiority and serenely accepts one's place within a world of fleeting phenomena. Han thinks Heidegger's anxiety about death, and his "heroic" affirmation of finitude, though muted in the later writings in comparison to *Being and Time*, nonetheless continue to blind him to the friendly possibilities of serene boredom. This serene boredom or friendly tiredness, Han continues, is found in the haiku and aphorisms of Zen Buddhist sages, who accept their place as *part* of a scattering of fleeting phenomena, which is all the world is.

The third part of the chapter takes up Han's comparison of different attitudes towards death that shape philosophy. In *Tod und Alterität* and elsewhere, Han argues that the tradition of Western philosophy, Heidegger, and East Asian philosophy originate in fundamentally different attitudes towards death. Beginning with Plato and culminating in Hegel's system, death in Western thought is an impetus to the heroic self-mastery of the soul. It is an impetus to direct thinking inwardly towards permanence. The arch-critic of this metaphysical tradition, Heidegger, rejects it in his heroic confrontation with death. Even more different, though, are Taoism and Zen Buddhism, with their serene acceptance of human beings' place among the fleeting things of the world. For Han, East Asian philosophy lacks the heroic egoism that marks Western philosophy, including Heidegger, and thus is able to reveal a mood of world-friendliness overlooked in Western philosophy.

Han's critique of Hegel in 2005's *Hegel und die Macht: Ein Versuch über die Freundlichkeit* [*Hegel and Power: An Essay on Friendliness*], informed by engagements with Heidegger and Zen, orients his philosophical project to what might be other than power. Is there anything in the world, or in God, that is beyond power? Not for Hegel, for whom power *is* one's space of self in the world (WP 6). Hegel's philosophy identifies freedom and power. Moreover, it makes God and substance identical with power (HM 112). Han takes up Hegel's expansive and constructive sense of power as a kind of working definition, but mainly to probe if there is something else between or outside Hegel's totality of power. Han finds non-power in Buddhist emptiness (śūnyatā), and also in certain Western figures, mostly artists: in the Romantics Friedrich Hölderlin and Novalis, the Dutch still-life painters, Paul Cézanne, Elias Canetti, Otl Aicher, John Cage, Handke, Holzer, and others, and – most surprisingly – in a "divine voice" occasionally heard by Nietzsche that beckons beyond the will (WP 96–7). Han's philosophy of freedom makes clear that *The Burnout Society* does not call for a rehabilitation of the coercive negativity of disciplinary society. His goal is not to recover Hegelian freedom, the struggle to appropriate what reason recognizes as its own against a hostile world of others who resist its mediation.[1] Instead, he encourages us towards a radically new sort of freedom, one that appears amidst a *friendly* receptivity to what-is-beyond-power, a friendliness to the Other and the world. The fourth and last part of this chapter attempts to sketch what a politics of friendliness might look like by turning to Han's ideas of a "politics of beauty" and a "politics of inactivity" that friendliness informs (SB 58–62; VC 1–26). This finally puts Han in conversation with contemporary political theorists to further fill in the picture of his political response to the power structures of self-exploitation in neoliberal achievement society.

A note on the term "friendliness" [*Freundlichkeit*]. Han calls *Freundlichkeit* the central concept of his thinking.[2] *Freundlichkeit* has nothing to do with agreeableness, likeability, the sociable capacity to schmooze seamlessly in a crowded room. (Indeed, these are characteristics of our world that is so poor in Hanian friendliness.) Rather, for Han, *Freundlichkeit* means a kindness towards everything that is – so, a form of *deep kindness* or even ontological kindness towards the apparent world. This is why the title of this chapter indicates "world-friendliness." If we are ever in a mood *not* to exercise power over the things that appear to us, this mood involves *Freundlichkeit*. To some, friendliness will seem to indicate apolitical moods. Does friendliness demand justice? To others, friendliness will seem to inform non-philosophical moods. Friendly thinking does not try to penetrate the surface of the world of appearances and phenomena. Yet Han proposes that *Freundlichkeit* is a politically needful and properly philosophical, because collective, action, and thinking must begin by letting things and others be what they are. In doing so, it clears space for thinking and acting politically amidst achievement society's frenetic patterns of work and consumption. The third and fourth parts of this chapter, respectively, will explore these problems, first for philosophy, then for politics.

Han notes that it is impossible to translate his sense of *Freundlichkeit* into English adequately.[3] A good alternative translation to ("deep") friendliness or ("ontological") kindness could be *geniality*, since it involves *genius*, the guardian spirit or *daimōn* that says "no" to our desires (VC 72–3), at least in the famous case of Socrates' *daimonion*, and also *geniālis*, middle Latin for "of or related to festivity." The negative genius and festival time both manifest *Freundlichkeit* in Han's writings. Better still would be *congeniality*: *Freundlichkeit* is always a mood of releasement to live *with* or be *with* things and others (MH 189). The reader should bear these caveats in mind when "friendliness" and "friendly" appear throughout this book.

## How Can Freedom Have *Us*?

A sense of freedom to which we are passive is a paradox, one that is familiar of those who proclaim liberty to captives (who continue to remain captive). Christian tradition emphasizes that freedom is a gift from God, an inner contemplative freedom to see the world as it truly is. Martin Luther famously allows that this inner freedom can perfectly exclude political freedom, so that the free Christian remains a "perfectly dutiful servant of all" (1960, p. 277). Han thinks, in contrast, towards a contemplative freedom that he claims is incompatible with domination.

The Romantics for whom freedom becomes the subject of history do not shy away from theological descriptions of freedom. Schelling installs human freedom in *God's* freedom. According to Heidegger, Schelling presents a "becoming God" (1985, p. 109). God's existence comes to be from the ground of God's originary "longing" to let beings be free to become (1985, p. 126; cf. 2021, p. 102). The ground of God is a prior longing for human freedom. However ennobling of human freedom this is, it is not clear what it looks like politically. Instead, like Luther, Schelling may have anti-political impulses when he writes about freedom. Schelling and other thinkers of a resurgent Germany after 1808 declare "spirit is fate" and the "essence of spirit" is freedom, according to Heidegger, in order to repudiate Napoleon's famous remark to Goethe that "Politics is fate" (1985, p. 2). The German Idealists and Romantics see some deeper movement of freedom underneath politics, somehow, and allow themselves to be destined *by* freedom. This is interesting to a phenomenologist such as Heidegger in a particular way: how does freedom make an appearance, in different ways, to the German academics, diplomats, philosophers, poets, and soldiers of the volatile Napoleonic period? Or for Han: why has the experience of freedom disappeared nowadays wherever the word is on everyone's lips?

Maurice Merleau-Ponty, another frequent interlocutor of Han's, suggests more mundane ways that freedom appears to us. In the final section of *The Phenomenology of Perception*, Merleau-Ponty argues that our actions appear to us as free actions only "against a background of life from which [freedom] is entirely, or almost entirely, absent" (1962, p. 437). Like the Germans of 1808, Merleau-Ponty had a direct experience with foreign occupation, in his case the Nazi occupation of France, and he was in a position to appreciate how political freedom appears most vividly at the moment when a foreign military occupation lifts. Freedom is prior to our actions but can appear in and through our actions, at least some significant few of them. Yet the background of life is not simply a tableau of necessity, Merleau-Ponty insists, since this same background affords all of the historical and psychological structures that motivate us to live freely. Merleau-Ponty concludes, "The fact remains that I am free, not in spite of, or on the hither side of, these motivations, but by means of them" (1962, p. 455). What motivates us to be free? What in the background of life puts us in the mood for freedom? What in the background of life destroys the mood for freedom? Han thinks out of the crisis of freedom like this.

To *think* freely, also – what disposes us to think freely? The question of what basic mood allows us to have a free relationship to the truth brings Han back again to Heidegger, for whom all thinking is "attuned" or *mood-ed* [*gestimmt*] by some presentiment (2012, pp. 18–20; 1989, pp. 21–2). "Dasein is older than consciousness," Han explains, so for Heidegger there must be a primordial mood for thinking that cannot be preserved in consciousness (HH 33).[4]

The question of the mood or moods proper to philosophy is a very old one. Is it wonder? Eros? Doubt? Self-preservation instinct? Anxiety about death? Care for the beautiful? Heidegger names this the question of *Grundstimmung*, or basic mood. Moods are given, granted, or bestowed. While we can cultivate habits of receptivity, we are ultimately the recipients of our moods. *Something* puts you in a mood. A mood that reveals *what* puts us in a mood, we might say, would be a mood for thinking about *what gives us over to thinking*. For Han, this mood must place thinking *outside* of itself, must direct it towards the Other and the world (WP 80–1). It is perhaps a depersonalizing sort of mood, a mood in which our mood for thinking appears to our thinking. (Philosophy, for Han, means thinking about thinking [MCS 16:38]). One example of such a mood is the serenity in Zen Buddhist meditation in which one aims to become "a no one, a selfless self that simply reflects things," highly receptive to one's surroundings (PZB 51).

Heidegger attempts to rethink this basic mood for philosophy during the 1930s, beyond the anxiety in which Dasein confronts its own death in *Being and Time*. Anxiety is a mood that discloses the freedom of action. Only those who feel *able to* are anxious. Anxiety reveals to me that I feel able to do something (but should I?). For Heidegger, anxiety about my death individualizes me and make possibilities "authentic" *for me* (1962, pp. 234–5). In light of his concerns about technology, however, he leaves behind this perspective of the mortal subject. This is often called Heidegger's "turning" [*Kehre*]. He worries that the essence of technology, which he calls an "enframing" [*Gestell*] that orders the world, had already wormed its way into the history of metaphysics in ancient times. As an alternative to "enframing," Heidegger offers a contemplative mood characterized by "releasement" [*Gelassenheit*]. Yet he worries that, even if we could find the "releasement" to be receptive to a world beyond our purposes and intentions and allowed Being to appear in freedom, perhaps Being would not return to us. Dwelling poetically cannot guarantee that there will be any destiny to receive. Being anxious is not enough to reveal freedom to us, Heidegger belatedly concludes. Han would agree.

Freedom is originally something to which we are passive, Heidegger argues – thus, we cannot willfully confront death, as if our anxiety will make us free in some heroic existentialist fashion. "The essence of freedom is *originally* not connected with the will or even with the causality of willing," writes Heidegger in "The Question Concerning Technology," in an effort to reorient his readers to the freedom *to be destined by* the unconcealment of Being (2013b, p. 25). Heidegger links freedom to the essence of truth in lectures on Plato in 1930 (2013a), as well as in lectures on Schelling in 1936 and 1941 (1985, 2021). Freedom is "not the property of man, but the other way around: Man is at best the property of freedom" (Heidegger, 1985, p. 9). Those who are free gratefully receive their destiny and do not try to master the ground of their existence, which Schelling calls God and Heidegger calls Being (2021, p. 109). Technology, which turns out to be deeply rooted in the tradition of metaphysical thought, predisposes us to order and set in place this ground, to reduce the world to an exploitable resource, preventing Heidegger's "releasement" and receptive freedom. At stake is whether we are free to bring ourselves into a relationship to Being or to truth in philosophy at all.

Heidegger's exclusive focus on the history of the self-withdrawal of Being [*Seinsgeschichte*] grants no place to the subject. No personal responsibility and no political judgment have any sway over Being. Heidegger emphasizes that Being is in no way a product. "Enframing" itself, rather than any human being, attempts to master the ground of Being. To detractors, Heidegger's later writings conveniently abandon personal responsibility for fatalism, given his own complicity with the Nazis (Habermas, 1990, p. 159; Wolin, 1990, p. 151). Han criticizes heroic self-assertion in Heidegger. However, critics such as Catherine Zuckert (1990) argue that Heidegger's search for a basic mood is itself still heroic. After all, Heidegger invites poet-thinkers such as Hölderlin to reshape the Germans' basic attitudes towards being-in-the-world. While these critics would emphasize political dangers, for Han, what puts us in the mood for freedom is not only a properly philosophical question but also a politically urgent one.

Political theory admittedly seldom takes its bearings from Heidegger's "turning," since it seems to be a turn away from politics.[5] Heidegger does not have a notion of political freedom that takes account of opinions, feelings, or individual or collective projects. The late Heidegger seems too resigned to fate, too completely obsessed with the history of the self-withdrawal of Being, and too ready to reduce political problems to the problem of technology to offer anything to political thinkers. The latter tendency can be embarrassing and inhumane, as when he claimed in Bremen in 1949 that the same essence of technology is as responsible for factory farming as it is for the "manufacture of corpses" in the Nazi death camps (Zuckert, 1990, p. 71). Even Heidegger's most important admirer in the realm of political theory, Arendt, although she appreciates the "turning" to releasement ("the will-to-not-will") as serious philosophy (1977, p. 188), still sees releasement as a culmination of Heidegger's lifelong philosophical attraction both to unworldliness and to death which shelters Being's self-veiling essence (Villa, 1996, pp. 239–40).[6] For Arendt, Heidegger abandons politics altogether. She sees in the late Heidegger a belated but welcome abdication of the philosopher's traditional pretense of overriding the pluralistic exchange of opinions and appearances that constitute the Arendtian political realm.

A critic of Han, then, could charge that making space for contemplation is an apolitical, and even elitist, concern, simply by cross-supplying critiques of Heidegger. Yet the fact remains that, for Heidegger (in the famous interview posthumously published by *Der Spiegel*), how we respond politically to the problem of technology is a "decisive question." Indeed, the question seems more pressing than ever for Han in our digital age. The "enframing" of the world by hydroelectric dams and factories that Heidegger describes seems quaint in comparison to the way in which the smartphone orders our intellectualized hyper-reality of images so as to become "a mobile labor camp" (N 24), or the way in which Artificial Intelligence and virtual reality promise an even more thorough enframing. Yet Heidegger could offer no clear answer to this decisive question in 1966: "I know of no answer to this question. I am not convinced that it is democracy" (1981, p. 55). The paradox is that we cannot master technology, individually or collectively, by our own power, since any attempt would fall under the sway of technology. It is fair to ask, can Han's philosophy of freedom avoid Heidegger's paralysis?

Han's earliest philosophical work takes shape at this inauspicious site of Heidegger's "turning." And his most recent book, *Vita Contemplativa*, confirms that our "primordial ontological passivity" remains very much on his mind (VC 36). Moods shape the world for us – Han even declares that mood "*is* the world" (N 38; VC 37). His critique of achievement society suggests why anxiety is not (or no longer) a promising mood for freedom. The dizzying freedom to transgress God's laws relies upon a negativity that vanished with churchgoing habits, with the liturgical "thanatotechnics" that could bring death present-to-mind to many people (BS 18). In its place, technology expands and *exploits* our freedom of action, giving rise to innumerable anxieties bound up with our achievement projects. Han is obviously in sympathy with Heidegger's concerns that technology somehow colonizes subjective freedom. From the beginning, however, Han indicates his doubts that even the late Heidegger has understood the basic mood for philosophy – or freedom – in the best way. In *Heideggers Herz*, he challenges Heidegger's phenomenology of boredom and asks whether boredom is not a mood where we are *friendly* to things and others. A boredom beyond restlessness, one where the ego relaxes, becomes the mood for freedom, the freedom to think without a primordial compulsion to order one's experiences, the mood for thinking about the mood for thinking.

Han's beginning in philosophy cannot be understood without reference to Heidegger's later writings, to which we shall return, but Merleau-Ponty may offer the better introduction to Han, since his idea of freedom moves afield from the Christian, German Idealist, or Heideggerian passivity where God or Being alone bestows freedom. Merleau-Ponty and Han are more open to the suggestion that anyone or everything can bestow freedom. (Han would add: *if* we are receptive to a world beyond power.) They do not necessarily await a destiny that appears beneath the appearances of things, as Heidegger does.

Han often cites Merleau-Ponty when he writes about a painter whom they both admire: Cézanne. This post-impressionist painter was so immersed in the landscapes he contemplated that he could claim to "*see* the fragrance of things" (BS 14). Rather than gathering the land around a site [*Ort*], in the way that power creates and orders space, Cézanne seems to abdicate his own perspective.[7] He does not paint his conceptions but, rather, paints out of what Merleau-Ponty calls an "indeterminate fever" (1964, p. 19; quoted in N 64). Paraphrasing Handke, we might say that Cézanne allows trees to flow into rain and air to flow into stone (HM 47–8; cf. Handke, 1985b, pp. 139–211). In the permeable landscapes of his canvasses, Cézanne is friendly to the fleeting world of phenomena; these flow into the painter himself and out into the paintings. Cézanne's orientation is beyond power. Han writes that he sees a warmth in Cézanne's landscapes that Merleau-Ponty cannot (HM 47). Nonetheless, perhaps Cézanne's painterly practice can be compared to Merleau-Ponty's reflections on freedom. Both call upon us to contemplate the ways in which nature or the "background of life" becomes part of us (VC 99). This background of life flows into our motivations for freedom. The similarity ends when, for Merleau-Ponty, we read that fatigue is only liberating when we are free to transform it (1962, p. 441). Han thinks fatigue, or boredom, can sometimes liberate us from the pressures of the ego. Han's hope for a different, restorative kind of tiredness society is here.

## Friendly Boredom

The reader of *The Burnout Society* will recognize that "profound boredom" is the basic mood for Han, which explains the close affinity he has for Handke's novels, films, and essays, and that this is a mood conducive to "listening," "deep attention," and "contemplative lingering" (BS 13–14). Since the Romantics, critics of technology have expressed a nostalgia for boredom, which seems to be the fertile ground of childlike wonder. Boredom may offer pleasure, even intense pleasure (Kracauer, 1995). Among David Foster Wallace's papers is a note that describes his unfinished and posthumously published novel, *The Pale King*:

> Bliss – a-second-by-second joy and gratitude at the gift of being alive, conscious – lies on the other side of crushing, crushing boredom. Pay close attention to the most tedious thing you can find (Tax Returns, Televised Golf) and, in waves, a boredom like you've never known will wash over you and just about kill you. Ride these out, and it's like stepping from black and white into color. Like water after days in the desert. Instant bliss in every atom. (Quoted in Weiner, 2010)

In his "Essay on Tiredness" (1994), Handke adds an explicit openness to *others* in boredom, one that is implicit in *The Pale King*. As the extremely self-conscious "author" writes in an "Author's Foreword" that appears well into Wallace's novel:

> … surely something must lie behind not just Muzak in dull or tedious places anymore but now also the actual TV in waiting rooms, supermarkets' checkouts, airports' gates, SUVs' backseats. Walkmen, iPods, BlackBerries, cell phones that attach to your head. This terror of silence with nothing diverting to do. I can't think anyone really believes that today's so called "information society" is just about information. Everyone knows it's about something else, way down. (2011, 85)

The accumulation of money, and the illusion of possibility and time that money conjures, casts death into oblivion (CDD 7). Indeed, all positive power structures – including those that allow us to accumulate scientific knowledge, for instance – are attractive because they veil the overwhelming negativity of death. This *interiorization* is the great internalization thesis that crowds out all others for Han. The self is structured first of all by an internalization of positivity, the self-conception of a "soul" or "spirit" that can be oblivious of mortal fate. The cost of the illusion of immortality, however, is eventually exhaustive depression. Fortunately, on the other side of burnout, there may be joy, salvific boredom, and a restoration to the world. Handke makes this explicit when he describes the mood of his village childhood as a "cloud of tiredness" which included others in it (1994, p. 15). What draws Han to this sort of profound boredom is that it offers an alternative to interiorization, the maximum dilation of the ego and the most radical openness to the world of others and things.

When, in *Heideggers Herz*, Han challenges Heidegger's phenomenology of boredom, he argues that Heidegger is not sufficiently attentive to the saving power of boredom that Handke and Wallace perceive. He argues that boredom does not necessarily include the compulsion to be oneself and therefore can evade the "call" to resolute selfhood (HH 42). He takes issue with the analysis of boredom in Heidegger's winter lectures of 1929–30 entitled *The Fundamental Concepts of Metaphysics: World, Finitude, Solitude* (1995, pp. 74–168). Boredom is not necessarily a hunger to grasp a possibility to be oneself, Han explains; it can also be a hunger for a gift from the Other (HH 42). He argues that Heidegger betrays the phenomenality of boredom in his analysis and allows the anxiety involved in the constitution of the self to creep in (HH 42). Han's critique of Heidegger, one can see, sets up his protest in *The Burnout Society* that all boredom is not "I-tiredness"; he makes room for Handke's "we-tiredness" (BS 33). Later, he links profound boredom – still following Handke – to "ethereal tiredness" (VC 22; cf. Handke, 1994). Anxiety and guilt creep into achievement subjects, subtly turning "can" into "should," but Han insists there is a profound boredom that is impervious to these affects.

*Heideggers Herz* contains touchstones to which Han consistently returns. Handke is already present in epigraphs. Likewise, in epigraph, is Benjamin's aphorism "Boredom is the dream-bird that hatches the egg of experience" (HH 33). The first three chapters have epigraphs from Nietzsche. Han is an exceptionally charitable reader of Nietzsche, whom he calls "this unusual philosopher of the 'will to power,'" because he detects a "divine voice" that called Nietzsche beyond his usual emphasis on self-assertion and towards the need for receptivity and contemplation – "*Give yourself away*"

Moods for Deep Cosmopolitanism 47

(WP 96–7). Han reminds us how Nietzsche called for "considerable strengthening of the contemplative element" in Western civilization (1996, p. 113; cf. ST 114), called for a pathos of distance (1974, p. 90), and praised "the genius of the heart who silences all that is loud and self-satisfied, teaching it to listen" (1989, p. 233; cf. BS 15). Nietzsche has the last word on what is other-than-power in *What Is Power?*

Han takes his starting point from Heidegger, who remains the philosopher for whom the whole [*das Ganze*] is not a totality that is identical to itself, that can be discovered and mastered in thought, but an ongoing song to be *listened to*. It is Heidegger who insists, athwart the Western tradition, that the heart is the "guardian" of the basic mood that "guards" the always "mood-ed" whole (HH 176). Some commentators find Han's focus on goosebumps and boredom to be selective and exaggerated as an interpretive account of Heidegger's enterprise (Ferreira, 2002, p. 57). Nonetheless, this account shows how Han departs from Heidegger. Han is not "an inhabitant" [*ein Einwohner*] of Heidegger's discourse (MH 8). Rather, he is like a friendly guest showing visitors the best aspects of Heidegger's thinking, namely its empty center – much like the ruins of the old Berlin airport or the garden of ruins that are Han's favorite empty centers of his beloved city (M 4:55, 58:10).

Friendliness appears in connection with boredom for the first time only in Han's second book, *Todesarten* (1998). Here we find Han searching "for a word of friendliness and hospitality that goes along with a 'releasement' [*Gelassenheit*] towards others" (T 72). A more congenial boredom with others, where we graciously make room for them, suggests the ethical and political direction in which Han wishes to go. Counterintuitively, then, Han thinks the later Heidegger *is not withdrawn enough*. If he withdrew even from his inward resolution to allow Being to appear, Han suggests, Heidegger may have made space to welcome other living beings of all kinds and realize that the self is already always being constituted by a scattering of impermanent things.

Heidegger's thinking never completes its "turning" away from the immanence of consciousness and towards astonishment at being, Han thinks, since it remains encumbered by a heroic resolution to face death. He affirms the way that Heidegger, after the "turning," focuses on "inactivities," such as festivity, dance, and play, that give splendor to human life and liberate time, the body, and intention from practical (read: technologically predetermined) purpose (VC 44–6). Still, then, death intrudes into Heidegger's ideas about boredom: "Death inscribes into the beings the negativity of the mystery, of the abyss, of the complete Other" (EO 29).[8] Heidegger seems unable to completely expunge the trace of heroic self-assertion in the face of death in his later works, even in his analysis of boredom. For Han, this clogs even the late Heidegger's releasement. It prevents full openness to otherness.

Heidegger's heart is open to an ethic of inactivity, but Han recently reconfirms his initial judgment: "Heidegger could not imagine the experience of death in terms of a loosening of the grip of the self" that could awaken a friendliness towards the world (VC 43). Han is always pushing the boundaries of the later Heidegger towards ordinary others, showing whither Heidegger's analysis might go were he not haunted by the thought of death. We limit ourselves to two examples: how goosebumps reveal the presence of divinity and what Han calls Heidegger's ethics of friendly greeting.

In his reflection on goosebumps in his lectures on Hölderlin's hymns "Germania" and "The Rhine," Heidegger describes a shivering mood that "transports our Dasein into the *mood*-ed relation [*in dem gestimmten Bezug*] to the gods and their being so-and-so" (1980, p. 140; quoted in HH 79). Goosebumps, shivers, and shudders remind us that the world is more than the totality of our consciousness. There is something outside that Heidegger calls the divine (HH 78). Religiosity for Han is friendliness; it is the mood that accepts the divine without attempting to discover, master, or order its appearance (WP 57). Zen Buddhism is especially faithful to the essence of religion as friendliness, he argues, since it teaches us to empty ourselves into no one, in a gesture of friendliness to the scattered phenomena of the ephemeral world (PZB 40). Han continues to show the Zen Buddhist teaching about death in contrast to Heidegger: "When I give death to myself, when I empty myself out, death is no longer *my* death" (PZB 78). One is no longer a mortal but a guest in and a "guesthouse" for the world of ephemeral and fleeting things.

Friendliness is a bestowal of the space for others to emerge in freedom. Han turns to Heidegger's lectures on Heraclitus to find a "dialogical friendliness" [*dialogische Freundlichkeit*] therein (HM 68ff.). The ethics of a friendly greeting leaves space for others to appear. Han intensifies this ethics further – Zen instructs us to empty our interiority, even to become "no one," in order to let others appear. *Absence*, originally published in 2007, ends with a discussion of bowing in Japanese culture and Buddhism as a religion of "absencing." Han radicalizes Heidegger's dialogical friendliness into a more profound "releasement," attuned to receive any Other who appears (not just Being). In the Buddhist-influenced bowing culture of Japan, Han proposes that the one who performs the greeting yields to the emptiness of the between, into a non-dialogical "in-difference" (A 99).

The reader will have noticed how, in both these examples, Han points to ways that Heidegger's "heart" leads him towards the world of Zen Buddhism but also, ultimately, to how Zen outstrips Heidegger's heroic attitude towards death – I die therefore I am; *"moriō ergo sum"* (TA 64).[9] Han again suggests that releasement in the later Heidegger is not profound enough. In a way, this philosophical suggestion mirrors the paradoxical claim in *The Burnout Society* that we are *not tired enough*. Han may find inspiration in his turn to friendly boredom in Emmanuel Levinas and particularly in the "primordial lassitude" Levinas describes in *Otherwise than Being* (1998, p. 51; cf. EO 68). Levinas was a well-known critic of Heidegger who drew on Jewish philosophy, as well as phenomenology, to make ethics, and the encounter with the capital-O Other, more primordial than what Heidegger called fundamental ontology. In Levinas there is another dramatic encounter between the self and death that appears to our primordial lassitude. For Levinas, it is in patiently bearing the lapse of time – bearing death – that we find something prior to Being that we share with the Other. Levinas ultimately renders us too passive, beyond the friendly greeting that affirms the world of others. His primordial lassitude maintains a drama of asymmetry before the Other that is not found in friendly greeting. Han points beyond dialogical friendliness *and* the priority that Levinas affords to Otherness: "Deep bowing is based on the decision to defuse the precarious situation of the person opposite not by dialogic means but instead by leveling it into an in-difference" (A 98).

Han reaches into our tiredness to propose a way of wandering and living anywhere. Death-obsessed philosophers of the Western tradition develop inwardness that wonders at "imperishable Being," though Han takes pains to show that "wonder," "contemplation," and "deep attention" can be directed to "whatever is floating, inconspicuous, or fleeting" as well (BS 14). He shows ways that a godless world, and a world where people do not dwell in one place, may still be a spiritual world. He offers a spirituality for people who live anywhere, for wanderers who "dwell nowhere" in particular, and practices to affirm "the inhabited, multiform world" (PZB 67; cf. A 5).

What if one were to stop asking, "What is?" questions and instead issue a friendly "Who's there?" – or even dispense with interrogative voice altogether, "Come in!" Would one still be thinking *philosophically*?[10] The Zen teachers whom Han invites us to consider seem to dispense with the discursive regularities that we are accustomed to calling philosophy. Are the Zen teachers in fact non-philosophers who would tranquilize our philosophical questions with their paradoxes and beatings, and so force us to live within what is apparently so? The inwardness that grasps our own finitude may be constitutive of philosophy itself, not merely of *Western* philosophy. Han insists otherwise. Thinking is not an activity that generates its own rules; even more radically than Heidegger, he insists that thinking is "thanking," a bestowal to which we are passive. However, settling this dispute is not essential to read Han, for Han *is* engaged in a philosophical activity. His writings do not form "a (paradoxical) epic of haikus" (PZB vii).[11] Haiku are light, witty, humorous, and playful in ways Han thinks Westerners do not understand (GE 41). However, an earnest and passionate concern with truth runs through Han's works. There are always difficult, recurring questions. What does boredom reveal to us? Is friendliness the mood for thinking? How do we recover friendliness in our time of crisis?

Han is not encouraging releasement to a world of kaleidoscopic flux in which one being cannot be distinguished from another. He references Yunmen, Dōgen, and the Heart Sutra to underline that śūnyatā is not the destruction of form but the space for beings to appear. Han explains, "Emptiness simply prevents what is individual from insisting on itself. It loosens the rigidity of substance. The beings flow into each other without merging into a substance-like 'unity'" (PZB 31). Hanian friendliness is an attitude of affirmation towards whatever appears to us. The non-insistence of the self, and the relinquishment of concepts to make a space of self in the world, is the *epochē* or bracketing for a phenomenology of ordinary life.

## Beyond Heroic Philosophy

Death, at least, is something other than power. As we have seen, the "great death" described in Zen Buddhist writings proposes a way of living beyond the ego and outside power (PZB 79). Yet it would be wrong to say that this way of life is known only in East Asia and not also in the West. Western artists and composers sometimes teach an *ethos* of friendliness akin to that in Zen Buddhist religion, Han suggests, as in Cézanne's paintings, John Cage's compositions, and the essays of Canetti and Handke (HM 38, 48). So, what is wrong with Western *philosophy*? Han does not offer a grand narrative but does offer a brief suggestion in his reading of the *Phaedo*. When Plato's Socrates says that philosophy is practice for death, Han argues, and when he tells Simmias and Cebes that death will free the philosophical soul from the body for the sake of its pure contemplation, "death intensifies the gathering and inwardness of the soul" (PZB 70; Plato, 1997, *Phaedo* 64a, 82b–84c). Death puts Western philosophy in the mood of withdrawing inwardly from the world of sensation and appetite. Christianity plays its part later as well (HM 25). Death as the cessation of all possibilities may be other-than-power, but it always seems to conjure up its opposite, the *power* of the soul or inward thinking, in Western religion and philosophy. In modernity, the self becomes increasingly monadic and defined by the will, the inwardness increasingly egoistic.

Han takes inventory of different philosophical attitudes towards death in *Todesarten* [*Manners of Death*] (1998) and *Tod und Alterität* (2002). The introduction to the latter establishes "friendliness" as his term of art for a way of being-towards-death that avoids both the heroic self-assertion of Dasein and Levinas's heroic love of the Other in search of a serenity in the face of death (TA 19). Han links Kant's hypochondria to his resentment towards death, to the humiliation that Kantian reason feels in the face of death, and to Kant's concern that music can seduce the autonomy of the rational subject (HH 7; TA 23; cf. Kant, 1987, p. 200). Music renders us passive, and therefore "Kant frowns at how music slips through the armor of our autonomy" (Knepper, 2022, p. 15). Kant thinks music prevents autonomous thinking. Even in the face of the sublime, reason cannot *suffer* (TA 39). Kant resents the noise of neighbors singing that compels others to sing along. For his part, Hegel wishes for music at the *table d'hôte* in order to regulate the noisy chatter of restaurant diners (HM 133). Han's thinking points to a more hospitable music, emptier, perhaps like guzheng and erhu music that has space, or to Cage's famous 4'33". Friendly music would listen to the crowd and invite or include their sounds.

In Eugène Ionesco's *Exit the King*, which Han considers at the beginning of *Tod und Alterität*, a dying king tries desperately and absurdly to cling to life and power (1963). King Berenger orders his servant Juliette to kill spiders in his room, so that they do not outlive him, but forbears as soon as he narcissistically considers the spiders may contain something of his in them. Even kings are powerless against death. But it is not only kings who flail pathetically before death. Tellingly, in the other two plays of Ionesco's Berenger cycle, Berenger is an everyman. Han is drawing our attention to how death makes all of us cling to power like sovereigns. Profound tiredness, however, unclenches our hold on life and power. Han will cite Handke, who calls tiredness the "angel who touches the fingers of the one dreaming king, while the other kings go on sleeping dreamlessly ... Tiredness is greater than the self" (1994, p. 41).

Han encourages us to "loosen the clamps" on our selfhood that the prospect of death tempts us to tighten (TA 8). The prospect of near death and the aversion of death is the ontological scene of Hegel's master/slave dialectic which identifies power and freedom (Hegel, 1977, pp. 111–19). In *Being and Time*, the discord of the public sphere and plural social interests are not part of authentic being-with [*Mitsein*] because they are oblivious to death. Even in Heidegger's later writings, death continues to renew our possibilities and seals off the completely Other (EO 29). Han thinks the presence of death in Heidegger prevents the diverse opinions of our fellows to shine forth, creates a sense of a collective destiny, and even requires a society of common destiny such as "a collective self" (TA 87). If the political salience of this critique is not clear enough, Han thinks it amounts to solidarity in the face of death, a resolute willingness to die a sacrificial death so that the community of destiny lives on.

Han's immanent critique of Heidegger's phenomenology of boredom, that it overlooks a friendly boredom that makes room for others, develops into an unmistakably political critique of the Heideggerian community that can come together resolutely only in the face of death, as a fighting collectivity. Like Levinas, Han thinks Heidegger is not sufficiently attentive to the Other. But Levinas abandons fundamental ontology in the name of the infinite ethical value of the Other. For Han, Levinas is so anxious about the *there is* [*il y a*] and the event of alterity that he reverses the contours of Heidegger's heroic encounter with death. He replaces self-sacrifice for one's own community with self-sacrificial love for the Other (TA 103). For all Levinas's reflection on exteriority, Han characterizes him as a thinker who clings to interiority in the face of death because he must overcome finitude to respond to the infinite ethical demand of the Other (TA 148). Zen sages may become as passive as the ambient matter around them, Han may think, but "Levinas resorts to a dimension of passivity that is more passive than matter" (HM 116; cf. HH 98, 121; see Levinas, 2017, p. 52). Levinas's heroic self-denial lacks the serenity in the face of death that Han is after.

*Tod und Alterität* sets up a critique of both Heidegger and Levinas in the name of freedom as friendliness, though Han remains committed to the search for the basic mood for thinking inaugurated by Heidegger. However, only in *Hegel und die Macht* does he bring friendliness into conversation with the Western philosophical tradition of Hegel (HM 9). Han encapsulates Hegel's definition of power: "Power is the ability to continue *in* the other" (HM 15). This is why, in *The Burnout Society*, he can claim that there is no power, and therefore for Hegel no living self, without negativity (BS 24). Yet here Han is not showing the disaster of a society that abolishes negativity but, rather, *critiquing* Hegel's dialectic of power.

Han begins by arguing that Hegel's concept of beauty is decidedly unfriendly to plurality. He takes up Hegel's judgment in his *Introductory Lectures on Aesthetics* that Romantic art is "higher" than classical art because of the self-conscious realization that the self-expression of mind or spirit is the expression of a concept of "*infinite* concrete universality" (1993, p. 85). Han explains how, for Hegel, "Beauty is a power structure [*Machtgebilde*] ... [that] produces the continuity of the same" in the world (HM 23). This continuity of the same is spirit, which is no longer in classical balance with nature but "elevates spirit to itself" (HM 24). Romanticism makes subjective interiority the form of art, but Han argues this is a *closed* form. Modern art becomes self-referential when it sloughs off any mediation of the external world, where spirit expresses itself (HM 33). Modern art seems like the aesthetic analog to achievement subjects who relate only intra-psychically to their ego ideals (see A 32–44).

Han takes exception to Hegel's dismissive, indeed racist, attitude towards the "primitive artistic pantheism of the East" as being all too submerged in nature for the appearance of spirit (Hegel, 1993, p. 83; HM 30). Of course, this immersion in nature is the spirit of friendliness, instead of the spirit of interiority that expresses itself in and against nature. Unlike Hegel's conception of art, writers of haiku such as Bashō allow "between" things to shine in their being-so (HM 31). These things elude conceptual mediation; they need have no meaning *for* us. Happily for Han, Western art did not end where Hegel thought it would. Rather, Dutch still-life painters, Cézanne, Cage, and other artists prove friendlier to the apparent world (HM 38, 48).

Hegelian freedom is the space I make for myself in the world, as I make others recognize me and as I come to understand them. In Hegel, so long as some negativity is present, more power creates more freedom (HM 60). There is no Other beyond others who have meaning for me. Han thinks achievement society and digital life smoothly facilitate our access to such a world that is poor in otherness (N 13). Yet there is always negativity in Hegel, he points out, even in love, where the beloved is the one with whom I can be myself (HM 63). And even in freedom: free persons *subject themselves* to government, but only to those with whom they identify or to necessities in a world transformed into rational spirit (HM 84). In this way, nothing – not beauty, not the earth, not God – transcends or lies outside Hegel's return to self (HM 100; WP 64). Freedom is the triumph of the power of reason over what is Other to it. A world that is poor in negativity or otherness turns out to be fatal to this idea of freedom.

In contrast to Hegel, Han looks for freedom in friendliness to others. Freedom seems to appear when the gaze of power is mutually relinquished, when people receive one another as guests, in empty spaces, and in set-aside festival time. Freedom appears when others are friendly. Han is presenting a contemplative freedom that makes collective action with others possible, rather than the contemplative freedom of Luther's Christian (or for some Stoics, for example) that has nothing to do with political freedom. Friendliness is not compatible with *any* domination, such as when Aristotle allows that masters and slaves can be friends to some minimal degree inasmuch as they share a common humanity (2011, 1161b8). Han's friendliness emancipates things and others from our purposes completely. While Heidegger finds the etymology of freedom [*Freiheit*] in peace [*Frieden*] in "Building Dwelling Thinking," and argues that freedom is to dwell and to be set at peace (1975, p. 149), Han goes to the "Indo-Germanic root *fri*" to argue that, originally, freedom means to be among friends (TA 143; ST 31). It means to be in the hold of relationships that are friendly. This may simply be the impulse of hospitality. Even here, Han insists, "*Friendliness means freedom*" (EO 17).

Han writes in his 2021 book *Non-Things*: "Every age has a different definition of freedom" (N 10). However, he does not present freedom in friendliness as yet another notion of freedom, underlining its historicity, in the way that Leo Strauss and his students impute "radical historicism" to Heidegger (Robertson, 2021, p. 26; Zuckert and Zuckert, 2014, pp. 48–53). Freedom, as we have seen, is what fates or destines us. Granted, the freedom that destines Heidegger, a peaceful clearing that escapes technological determination, is a bestowal of Being particular to time and place. However, the world does not only call us to freedom-in-friendliness now, in our modern and technological age. Ostensibly, Bashō made way for the same fleeting, impermanent scattering of things in the seventeenth century, and Dōgen centuries before him. By jettisoning Heidegger's "history of Being" and ceasing to penetrate the world of appearances and things-that-are-so, Han avoids both radical historicism and grounding his argument in an ahistorical, fixed order of Nature. (From Han's perspective, Hobbes's attempt to derive "natural right" from self-preservation only turns Nature into an order of power.) Instead, Han describes freedom-through-friendliness in pluriform ways. These are historically inflected, sometimes by Zen Buddhist practice, perhaps by some strands of Romanticism or by Cézanne's confrontations with the impressionists or Cage's discovery of the *I Ching*. Nevertheless, for these artists and thinkers, the freedom promised by friendliness is available anywhere, and in any epoch.

Tiredness is both the danger (burnout) and the saving power (profound tiredness) in Han's mind. The ambivalent sense of tiredness is lost when *Müdigkeitsgesellschaft*, literally *The Tiredness Society*, is translated as *The Burnout Society*. Hölderlin's poem "Patmos" indicates a common source from whence the "danger threatens" and where "That which saves from it also grows" (2002, p. 245). Heidegger quotes it twice in "The Question Concerning Technology" to direct his readers to the ancient *technē* of poetry (2013b, pp. 28, 34). Heidegger's declaration of the end of philosophy, and the apocalyptic crisis thinking of twentieth-century high modernism in general, loses its appeal as soon as its once startling pronouncements are handed down shopworn, generation after generation. Han's critique of Heidegger's phenomenology of boredom might preserve the relevance of the latter's thinking for generations that are not only inured to environmental devastation, nuclear warfare, spaceflight, and so many things that shocked Heidegger and his contemporaries. Today we may even feel burned out, depressed, and even *bored* by a world that seems to be in a permanent state of insoluble crisis. Rather than abandon a receptive philosophical mood altogether and take up the playful lightness of postmodern irony, Han turns to poets and artists who find liberation in ultimate boredom.

Inspiring "deep tiredness" may sound attractive and conveniently proximate to our burned-out mood (WP 60). Still, it does not seem that deep tiredness can be a *goal* that Han teaches the citizen or the philosopher to attain, though they may cultivate receptivity to this generative mood. The reader has hopefully seen that deep tiredness is a mood, an original ontological passivity, and a bestowal. Both Han's attempt to locate an outside-to-power and, before this, his critique of the heroic encounter with death in Western philosophy respond to an impulse to say thank you to what moods of world-affirming boredom disclose. However, though we are passive with respect to boredom, burnout, and tiredness, these free us for a contemplation that is receptive but not entirely passive – a contemplation that, as we shall see in later chapters, allows us to prepare for decisive action in a time of aimless activity.

Some may still worry that the contemplative freedom that Han describes as friendly boredom may seem too demanding. Must one be a Buddhist monk or a Romantic mystic to overcome the anxiety of death that always attends boredom for Heidegger? Han may seem to describe practices and attitudes that are out of reach for ordinary citizens and workers. It is one thing to be distracted from anxiety about death by endless consumption and another thing to cultivate serene friendliness to the world (CDD 7). How far must we go? At times, Han seems content to cool down the heroic element in Western political and philosophical perspectives on freedom, death, and the world. At other times, however, he suggests that a new eco-spirituality of friendliness is the only hope for a humane future.

In the previous chapter, we compared Han to Rousseau, who saw a compulsive freedom in the bourgeois society of the 1750s, and explored an array of different remedies, some political, and some not. In his "Fifth Walk" in *The Reveries of a Solitary Walker*, Rousseau describes losing himself in a calm sentiment of existence with an enthusiasm for flowers, floating supine in a drifting boat to view "vague yet delightful reveries," listening to the murmuring water, forgetful of time, momentarily at one with the "constant flux" of everything (1979, pp. 84–9). Peter Sloterdijk pronounces Rousseau's "conquest of carefreeness," as the decisive link between the experience of freedom and felt existence, to be attained only by exiting the "self-stressing care systems" of politics (2016b, pp. 6, 22). It seems possible, for Rousseau, to completely divest oneself of that socially mediated self-conception that is shot through with *amour propre*. For Sloterdijk, Rousseau makes freedom apolitical; now, a *free* person can only condescend to political commitments, taking on the stress or uncalm of urgent collective enterprise, from the "bumming, hanging around ... and chilling," where we feel in touch with our existence (ibid., pp. 35, 54). This likely underestimates Rousseau's spiritual elitism. Rousseau wrote that his reveries "cannot be experienced by every soul" (1979, p. 89). This certainly underestimates how difficult *Han* thinks it is to cultivate a friendly receptivity to the world beyond our goals, plans, and projects. Yet, even if Han and Sloterdijk disagree about the prospects for contemplation in achievement society – the former has more in common with spiritual elitists – Han's friendly boredom may seem as apolitical as Rousseau's floating reveries.

Yet friendly boredom is an initial opening, and a necessary beginning, for the freedom to allow others to appear in freedom. In Handke's "Essay on Tiredness," the voice of an alter ego probes this "ultimate tiredness," asking, "What good is it? Does it enable a tired person to act?" Handke replies, "It is itself the best action, because it is in itself a beginning, a doing, a getting under way, so to speak" (1994, p. 37). Friendly tiredness and friendly boredom may open new moods to us: the eros that is always the allure of the Other (AE 3), beauty that is always the gift of eros (SB 78) and which *demands* a care for the world (LE 10). Han may think of his own studies, and even his own changing moods, as exploring contours within friendliness from the perspective of different traditions. The interplay between friendliness and care, and the transitions from passive moods to receptive contemplation, and from there to political action, are all important to understanding what Han sometimes calls his politics of inactivity.

## Deep Cosmopolitanism

The "politics of inactivity" that appears in Han's most recent book, *Vita Contemplativa*, presents us with a paradox that should make us wary. It is one thing to frame *thinking* in terms of passivity rather than activity – but *politics*? One might think first of the indirect politics of philosophical loafers such as Socrates and Kierkegaard and their ironic examples of conspicuous inactivity (Ryan, 2014, p. 167). Han's politics of inactivity, however, refers to active efforts to create empty spaces for contemplation. Empty spaces, Romantic eco-spirituality, noisy children, ruins, Zen practices, public festivities, rituals, beauty, restaurant chatter, and fragrant gardens might all form part of the politics of inactivity. Han recommends many of these to restore our original ontological passivity. These practices do not, need not, and indeed should not clear space for a common destiny to appear – as we have seen, Han does not share the late Heidegger's fatal expectations for poetic dwelling. These moods simply need to engender the world-friendliness that allows us to linger with and listen to everything that may appear. What exactly Han means by the politics of inactivity remains somewhat unclear. Since his arguments land in quick bursts across different short books, and since he is still very much a bird in flight, *Vita Contemplativa* may very well signal a new focus on a practical politics of inactivity and its contours to counteract positive violence.

Han offers us a *deep cosmopolitanism* in two senses. "Deep" in the first sense means that his political thought reaches all the way down into ontological figurations of self-and-world, from which those who wander the globe in search of lives and loves can draw. This may put him in a fruitful dialogue with contemporary political theory in North America. "Deep" in the second sense means that the *cosmos* includes the earth. The things of the earth flow into the city of human beings and vice versa. This sense is meant to be evocative of deep ecology. These two senses may be in a certain tension with each other.

Han explicitly tells us that he is in search of a philosophy that would allow one to live anywhere. His cosmopolitanism is informed not by ethical figures drawn from Hegel, such as that of Kwame Anthony Appiah (2006, pp. 64–5, 92) but, rather, from the Zen teachers whom Hegel despised. How do you think so that you can find repose anywhere in the hectic world wrought by global capitalism? In three ways. First, by trying to think outside of power altogether, including in very personal ways that can release one from self-exploitation. Second, by accepting that the fleetingness and impermanence of things is simply the is-so of the world. Han reconciles us to the flow of changeling things in a mode of acceptance. Third, by making the central ontological scene friendly greeting rather than a decisive confrontation with death or a dialectic of power (e.g., the master/slave dialectic) that avoids death. It is worth asking of Han how this way of thinking, which seems to be one of passive acceptance, can turn into resistance.

Han's 2005 book *Hyperculture* wades directly into debates over cosmopolitanism in the spirit of friendliness (H 33). He argues that we live in a "hyperculture," where we must learn to listen and linger in friendly attention to an increasingly hybridized world. Yet hyperculture is not the end of culture as such, as it might be for Heidegger. Nor does one navigate this world like Richard Rorty's liberal ironist, suspending their own judgments: "the spices and smells that are interculturally blended, multiplied, are not ironic" (H 67). Han does not need to turn to Being or God to introduce heaviness and guilt. Indeed, what is needful is a receptiveness to any others who will teach us to feel the weight of the world wherever we may be.

An "optimistic immigrant" himself, Han carries a global mark in his thinking, a hybridity of West and East (CDD 65). Groundwork in comparative political theory responds to globalization by taking non-Western perspectives seriously (Dallmayr, 2004, p. 249). In one of the early contributions to this field, Fred Dallmayr takes up the late Heidegger's conversations with Zen Buddhism to sketch an alternative to subjective freedom and its dominant place in Western political thought. He wants to retrieve "releasement" from the late Heidegger to afford a concept of "political freedom" that reorients us to reconciliation, peace, and solidarity (1984, pp. 207, 228; 1995, p. 70). In particular, he notes how "releasement" is close to śūnyatā, or Zen "emptiness" (1995, p. 225; cf. PZB 26). Han is more skeptical than Dallmayr of the "often asserted proximity" between Heidegger and Zen (MH 171). He refuses to massage the differences between Western philosophy, including Heidegger, and East Asian philosophy. Comparative political theorists might look to Han to avoid pitfalls. Comparative political theorists will find, in Han's deep cosmopolitanism, not comparative philosophy but a pluralistic philosophy marked by "the friendliness of the 'and'" (H 33). As we shall see, Han brings both to bear to help global citizens think as they wander, dwell, and exchange in an increasingly hybridized global society.

Another depth in Han's deep cosmopolitanism is its insistence that the *cosmos* includes the earth beyond the human world. In his 2017 book *Lob der Erde* [*Praise the Earth*], Han has called for the "re-romanticization" of the world. This is his most personal book. It is written in a language of an earnest change of heart. He begins and ends by insisting that beauty [*die Schöne*] demands caring for [*schonen*] (LE 10). Already this is unlike in Zen, where one lives without care for the future (PZB 50). Gardeners cannot wander; they must dwell. Care and dwelling bring Han the gardener closer to Heidegger; gardening makes him "rich in being and time" (LE 27). Han describes his garden as a place of salvation, where he found God, and where he sensed his winter flowers' desire for resurrection – the basic mood of his book (LE 14). This is a new mood of deep connection, one of freedom as lingering in the garden, a mood that is protective of the earth from desecration and our mutual destruction (LE 149).

Han calls for a new understanding of the earth and of matter. Here the Romantics are more present. He envisions a future society where "human beings are but *fellow citizens* in a *republic of the living*" (VC 99). Han favorably cites Jane Bennett's efforts in *Vibrant Matter* to produce a new ontology of matter (N 96). Yet in some ways his ontology of matter seems quite different from thing-power in Bennett (2010). Like Han, Bennett wishes to recover things from human purposes or interpretations. Yet she explicitly refuses non-material interpretations of an animating spirit of things. Indeed, for Bennett, all things remain within a manifold of power.

The deep cosmopolitanism informed in part by Zen Buddhism and the deep cosmopolitanism informed in part by Romantics such as Novalis are different ways of friendliness. The "Zen way," we'll call it for shorthand, minimizes the active, creative self or spirit and opens it to nature, of which Zen teaches we are an ephemeral part. Han describes this as a way along the surface of water (PZB 28–31). Zen disciplines us against seeking any depth or spirit in nature. Zen teaches *"trust in the world,"* in the surface of phenomena, and resists any heroic penetration of the appearances (PZB 18). It offers a cosmopolitan way of "dwelling nowhere" that allows one to live in a friendly way anywhere (PZB 68), which Han also calls a way of wandering (A 7). This requires an attentiveness to our surroundings, however. Deep cosmopolitanism offers an *anywhere politics*, or better yet a *wherever politics*, as opposed to the "everywhere politics" where internet users can express their will immediately on any subject in any country now that "politics is sublimated into information" (Barba-Kay, 2023, p. 141).

As we shall explore further in chapter 6, Han gives his readers different forms of deep cosmopolitanism to consider. The "Romantic way" (also our shorthand) embraces dwelling in a fixed abode, eros, and passionate care for the world. Zen friendliness or *mettā*, while disposed to a hospitable emptiness or openness, does not include emotionally invested care for the world (PZB 89). And, of course, the serene acceptance of one's ephemerality (the Great Death) cannot admit a desire for resurrection. Han describes learning the desire for resurrection from the flowers in his winter garden in particular (LE 14). Dōgen does not sound like a winter gardener when he writes, "We do not think that winter becomes spring" (PZB 81). *Śūnyatā* (emptiness) makes way for beings in a world of "immanence," not for "transcendence" or for the "wholly other" (PZB 26). The "transcendental homelessness" of Novalis, then, is a different kind of deep cosmopolitanism (Lukács, 1971, p. 26). It is a way up through the earth and hears in beauty a command to care.

## Friendliness and Democratic Theory

Romantic sacralization of the earth and Buddhist emptiness may seem far removed from political theory. Or a throwback to the late 1970s – perhaps Gary Snyder discussed these subjects with Governor Jerry Brown at Kitkitdizze in northern California, but that was then. In fact, however, political theorists are actively engaged in a broad conversation that can welcome Han's deep cosmopolitanism. George Kateb draws upon Henry David Thoreau and Walt Whitman to inform our conceptions of politics and citizenship. He also turns to Nietzsche and Heidegger, who, though they are "spiritual elitists," according to Kateb, are "radical individualist thinkers" (1992, pp. 133–4). The bottom line, for Kateb, is to repurpose a broad range of thinkers to help individuals learn how to see the world. He casts his net broadly in *The Inner Ocean* to find resources for a "democratically aesthetic contemplation of all things and beings" (1992, p. 166). Amidst the crisis of freedom, Han insists we cannot afford to ignore contemplation just because it has been historically valorized by spiritual elitists from Aristotle to Heidegger. As we shall see in chapter 5, Han thinks opportunities for contemplative lingering were much more abundant for almost everyone in premodern societies. Moreover, his spiritual elitism, if critics insist upon this inapt term, comes expressly in the service of democracy amidst its crisis of freedom.

Twenty-first-century democratic theorists across North America have chimed into Kateb's desired open conversation about the ethos of citizenship – Appiah, Taylor, Judith Butler, William Connolly, Wendy Brown, Cornel West, and Stephen White are some notable contributors. (We saw Han's critique of Taylor in the last chapter.) Wide-ranging discussions assess fellow citizens' "core ethical disposition[s]" and how these arise from "particular set[s] of ontological figures" (White, 2009, p. 8). These democratic theorists are interested neither in a minimum for what counts as public reason, as John Rawls was, nor in a minimum for what counts as intolerable evil, as Richard Rorty and Judith Shklar were. These theorists are not in the business of ruling speech or actions in or out. Therefore, Jürgen Habermas can help, but not provide a litmus test for acceptable speech (White, 2009, p. 100; cf. DRE 16–19). A better genealogical approximation is that many of these thinkers draw from a generous understanding of American pragmatism (and Hegel's inspiration to this movement) in an "explicit political mode" (West, 1989, p. 212). They hesitate to exclude any worldview that animates citizens' earnestly democratic commitments. White uses the term "weak ontology" to describe worldviews that generate fundamental yet contestable claims, and which also dispose us to listen to others (2000, p. 6). Han uses a similar construction, "metaphysical weakness," to describe the "primal passivity" to listen to "the voice of the Other" (EO 52). The mood or comportment for *listening*, including in "slow" and "passive" ways, has become a topic of basic importance in modern democratic theory (White, 2017, p. 72; Scudder, 2020, p. 88).

These democratic theorists thus invite their readers to reflect, "What is the world to you?" (Connolly, 2011, p. 177). While this metaethical and even metaphysical starting point may seem too abstract, far removed from the exigent matters of politics – perhaps even high-handed and dreamy – the alternative for these thinkers is tantamount to shying away from pluralism. All draw upon continental political thought to suggest ways to understand self and world, with an eye to how citizens should discover and hold their values. They may see the role of the political theorist, as does Brown, as offering an "illuminating description" of power relationships within the vast amounts of information generated by research professionals (e.g., environmental scientists) and by global actors of concern (e.g., Malagasy farmers impacted by drought), and at the intersection of these discourses (Brown, 2005, p. 80). At a broad level, all of these political theorists agree that it is vital to foreground these concerns and discuss them if we are to reflect together on the value of democracy and big questions raised by the ecological crisis, racism, inclusion and immigration, the mental health crisis, and global capitalism.

Han's deep cosmopolitanism belongs in this conversation, though he might balk at Brown's description of the political theorist as a particularly adept sort of information hunter. Han would probably share White's discomfort when Butler makes "power ... more primordial than either ontology or ethics" (White, 2005, p. 100). Butler starts from the priority that Nietzsche gives

# Moods for Deep Cosmopolitanism 63

the event, or deed, to any agent, and builds from it an argument about sexual identity where ontology is "not a foundation, but a normative injunction that operates insidiously by installing itself into political discourse as its necessary ground" (1990, pp. 34, 203). Butler's "ontological indifference" is not the ordinary unreflective kind but comes in what Han would recognize as the Hegelian sense, where there is no outside to power (EO 31). And, of course, Han always draws our attention to how Nietzsche hears a "divine voice" altogether beyond power and ontology (WP 96). Han doubts that ontology is primordial (WP 89), except in the deeper etymological sense that Being [*Wesen*] originally means "lingering" (A 1). His concerns, basically, remain live issues in this broad drift of North American democratic theory.

Han's primordial ontological scene of friendly greeting offers something to democratic theory in general, and in particular to White's search for an ethos that can secure our commitment to listen to one another. White is after a "presumptive generosity" that arises from *within* ordinary democratic life, without resorting to the heroic ethical demand in Levinas (White, 2009, p. 69). Han undertakes a search that is similar in some respects. This chapter has traced the philosophical depth, consistencies, and tensions of this search. Han goes beyond Heidegger's phenomenology of boredom, exploring potentially friendlier kinds of boredom, drawing from Zen Buddhism. It is friendliness, he argues, that makes space for freedom and secures what we call his deep cosmopolitanism. Han has been rethinking deep cosmopolitanism lately, in a "Romantic" way that includes a desire for resurrection, seems to re-presence death, and thus may require reevaluating his early critiques of Heidegger and Levinas. This seems appropriate to secure intergenerational commitments to people, places, plants, animals, and things that we hope will long survive our deaths. While Han remains very active as a thinker and writer, he consistently appeals throughout his writings to a friendliness to other beings that he makes the mark of "civilized" society (EO 18).

# 3

# *Digital Bias: The Positivity of the Transparency Society*

Ethan Stoneman

> But without my account ID and profile it's like they don't even see me.
> Anna Mill and Luke Jones, *Square Eyes*

## Media Studies in the Key of Technology

Han contributes further to political philosophy by offering incisive analysis of digital technologies. For Han, these technologies' biases are deeply unfriendly. Unfriendliness is not simply the result of a web of ideas interacting apart from materiality to produce a placeless series of psychosocial effects. Unfriendliness is trans-individual without being social or personal. Rather than being a site of friendly greeting, unfriendliness is asystemic resonance pursued, intensified, and diversified by information and communications technology. For Han, these technologies are not mere channels of communication whose operations occasionally present technical problems calling for technical solutions (or limited political solutions). They are ontological operators, vessels of storage, transmission, and processing that, by digitizing and algorithmizing everything that flows between us and in us, shape existence and structure the environment that constitutes us. Digital media produce unfriendliness. As Han states in 2021's *Infocracy*, "Digitalization of the lifeworld ... is radically changing our perception, our relation to the world and our communal life," taking hold of those "pre-reflexive, instinctual, emotive layers of behavior that precede conscious

## The Positivity of the Transparency Society 65

action" (I 12, 10). Immersed in algorithms and amid artificial intelligence, people lose not only negativity or resistance but also their receptivity to what is other-than-power. If, for much of the twentieth century, people were passive television spectators who surrendered themselves to entertainment, then today they are frenzied transmitters, compulsively producing and consuming information, never bored, "alone together" (Turkle, 2017), constantly communicating themselves to death in an unfriendly resonance chamber (I 17).[1]

Especially since 2013, a major throughline of Han's critical theory is a critique of the interactive changes among technology, culture, and consciousness brought about by the emergence of digital media. Beginning with *What Is Power?*, originally published in 2005, his cultural-theoretical works register a steadily increasing interest in how media and technology affect human perceptions and interactions, as well as how the dynamic between technology and consciousness organizes much of what is taken for reality. Yet Han's preoccupation with the question concerning technology does not take center stage until his still-untranslated 2013 critique of Habermas's project to reconstruct reason as an emancipatory communicative action, in *Digitale Rationalität und das Ende des kommunikativen Handelns*, followed that same year by *In the Swarm*. As recently as *The Scent of Time*, originally published in 2009, Han downplayed the determining role of media technology in shaping consciousness and culture, rejecting, for instance, the notion popularized by Baudrillard (1994) and Paul Virilio (2005) that the acceleration of high-speed technologies of communication and transportation exerts a primary influence on the widespread contemporary experience of "whizzing time" (ST 18–19, 20–7).

For the Han of *The Scent of Time*, as we shall examine in chapter 5, the problem is not technological acceleration but the dissipation of meaning – a direct effect of the loss of narrative which accompanies late-stage modernity, when the modern belief in unfolding, meaningful progress across time dissolves into a present of "point-like moments," a "time without scent" (ST 12). On this view, the acceleration born of the conceptual and actual technological separation of transportation and communication is merely an epiphenomenon, albeit a phenomenologically significant one, and one that many other thinkers have mistakenly taken as the motive force of modernity. And yet, between 2009 and 2013, the temporal dimension of neoliberal modernity would translate, in Han's thinking, into a growing concern with the erosion of the "*temporal architectures* that *support* and stabilize life" (I 18). That emphasis on structure, which is perhaps motivated by a discovery of media theory, leads Han to consider the efficient means by which life is destabilized. These are the media which pulverize not only time-intensive cognitive practices such as narrative but also knowledge, experience, insight, and much else besides.[2] He thus undertakes an intensive study of technologies and media.

One of the purposes of this and the following chapter is to make the case that Han can be considered a media as well as a cultural theorist, and that his cultural theory is often a media-inflected one. Beginning with *In the Swarm*, which marks a media-studies turn in his thought, his cultural theory reflects a more or less constant attentiveness to phenomena involving digital technologies of communication. Other important post-*Burnout Society* texts on media include *Psychopolitics*, *The Expulsion of the Other*, and, more recently, *Non-Things* and *Infocracy*. Further works in which media play an important but less than central role are *Saving Beauty*, *The Disappearance of Rituals*, *Capitalism and the Death Drive*, and *The Palliative Society*. In each of these interventions, Han examines the same patterns that draw the attention of media ecologists: the ways in which media are not passively deployed but instead actively shape individuals and culture. From this ecological framework, he argues that the development of digital media constitutes a technological revolution, one in which the widespread modification of forms of thought and the organization of experience ushers in a new period of transition. Digital technology has overtaken previous cultural norms and practices and supplanted them with a new psychosocial dispensation and a new system of rule. We find ourselves living in a critical period (though it is less clear when exactly it began) that we experience as an existential crisis.

On this view, the digital medium inaugurates a techno-anthropological mutation both in the social body and in the conscious, sensitive organism. This change generates effects on sensibility and cognition, the labor process, inter- and intra-personal relationships, techniques of surveillance and control, and much else besides. Defined by the inherent biases of positivity and transparency, the digital constitutes an environment of unfriendliness, within and through which the "negativity of the Other" is replaced by the "positivity of the Same" and distance is annulled by a gapless hypervisibility which renders the world transparent. In this technological environment, the self, over-exposed on social media and cut off from meaningful relationships, becomes isolated and exteriorized, collapsing in on itself while spasmodically lashing out at an unknown Other. These alienating, distance-destroying effects, however, occur within the already existing socioeconomic context of neoliberalism. Indeed, for Han, digital bias helps to complete the totalization of work and usher in post-industrial societies of total control that, as we have seen, exploit freedom itself. Rather than disciplining bodies, forms of digitized, networked interactivity take as their object inner thoughts, needs, and desires, intervening in psychic processes themselves and enabling a more efficient system of rule that Han names psychopolitics.

Elihu Katz (1987) famously divided media studies into three broad perspectives: the social-scientific tradition, the critical-theoretical approach, and the technological tradition. The social-scientific perspective, also commonly referred to as the *media effects* research paradigm, conceives of media (say, political mailings or email listservs) as givers and senders of information. Emphasizing "empirical research on people's attitudes, behavior, and cognition in a mainstream political framework" (Peters, 2015, p. 17), this approach "attempts to understand, explain, and predict the impact – or effects – of the mass media on individuals and society" (Campbell et al., 2011, p. 537).[3] In contrast to mainstream media effects theories, critical-theoretical research – what in the United States is loosely labeled *cultural studies* – exhibits a stronger historical and interpretive edge, "focusing on how people make meaning, understand reality, and order experience by using cultural symbols" that circulate via media channels (ibid., p. 467). Hence cultural studies research tends to conceive of media in terms of ideology, or as sites of struggle between forces of domination and resistance (Carey, 2009). For that reason, cultural studies research "has been foundational to Marxist, feminist, post-colonial, queer, and race-related work" in media studies (Packer, 2013, p. 296). In the Western world, except for Germany, this view of media as transmitters (the old "mass media" function) enjoys a quasi-hegemonic status.

Compared to the transmission view, the technological tradition thinks of media more expansively in terms of organization, environment, or milieu. Though it too is empirical and critical in its way, it "focuses historically on how media technologies" determine an underlying "psychic and social order" (Peters, 2015, p. 17).[4] Rather than studying the news and entertainment industries of the twentieth century, scholars specializing in the technological tradition often work with a more liberal understanding of medium, of "media *as* media" (Strate, 2008), or media as "a largely concealed environment" (Postman, 1974–6, p. 78). Defined as "vessels of storage, transmission, and processing," media may include such diverse forms as the city, modes of transportation, alpha-numeric sign systems, the postal system, even the womb or air conditioning (ibid., p. 19). From that broad perspective, media are not mere vehicles for the circulation of meaning; they are technologies, apparatuses, that, by creating connections – by *mediating* between things – shape the environments that in turn shape how we think, perceive, and behave, how we communicate and form relationships, how we organize ourselves socially and politically. To study media on their own terms, in other words, to study them as active *mediators*, entails thinking of media as environments (and environments as media). Marshall McLuhan makes the connection explicit in the introduction to the second edition of his *Understanding Media*, writing that the development and implementation of any technology "gradually creates a totally new human environment," where environment is understood as an active process rather than a passive wrapping (2003, p. 12). So-called new media are "onto-mutational"; they admit new beings to, and exclude others from, our fields of experience.

On this view, it is primarily media themselves – their formal properties, affordances, biases, and effects, rather than their mediated content or messages – that influence the group, the society, the culture. They alter our social organization; sense of identity and community; traditions and time-binding practices; our worldview and way of life; and almost every other aspect of lived reality. Although not the dominant paradigm within media studies, the technological approach counts among its ranks a who's who of media theorists from four national intellectual traditions – American (Lewis Mumford and James Carey), Canadian (Harold Innis and McLuhan), French (Jacques Ellul and Baudrillard), and German (Heidegger and Friedrich Kittler). Thinkers in these traditions may not recognize "media" as their central theme, but they understand media as constituents of civilization or even being itself. As John Durham Peters remarks, they see media as "the strategies and tactics of culture and society" (2015, p. 18), the devices, crafts, and techniques we use to hold together, as groupings and communities, in time and space, sometimes to our collective disadvantage.

Han's approach to the study of media places him firmly within the technological tradition that emphasizes the wide-ranging effects of media upon culture and experience. Situated within that broad intellectual tradition, however, is what anglophone regions like to label "German media theory," and Han's relationship to the latter, despite his education and long teaching career in Germany, is less clear-cut.[5] Having arisen in the 1980s in Freiburg – in the years just before Han arrived to earn his doctorate – German media theory is associated with figures such as Kittler, Bernhard Siegert, Klaus Theweleit, Norbert Bolz, and Avital Ronell. These theorists "were not primarily concerned with the theory or history of individual media" but, rather, sought to change the "frame of reference" away from the "traditional objects" of humanities research. These German media theorists shift "the focus from the representation of meaning to the conditions" or "materialities of communication" (Siegert, 2015, p. 2; see also Gumbrecht and Pfeiffer, 1994, p. 399). "In place of traditional objects of research that defined communication studies" (the usual suspects of newspapers, film, television, and radio), German media theory favored "those insignificant, unprepossessing technologies that underlie the constitution of meaning and thus elude the grasp of our usual methods of understanding" (ibid, p. 3). These include such "inconspicuous technologies of knowledge such as index cards, writing tools, typewriters ... pedagogical tools such as the blackboard, various unclassifiable media such as phonographs or stamps, musical instruments, disciplining techniques such as alphabetization" (ibid., p. 2). These practices are now referred to as *cultural techniques* [*Kulturtechniken*], a "complex term" that, according to Geoffrey Winthrop-Young, "combines an attention to media technologies with a focus on elementary physical and mental skills, including, most prominently, reading, writing, and computing" (2011, p. 3). A major undercurrent of the "conceptual transformation of media into cultural technique" was the movement from an "antihumanist rejection of the tradition" of the Enlightenment, with its "rules of hermeneutic interpretation," to "a reconceptualization of the posthuman as always already intertwined between human and nonhuman" (Siegert, 2015, pp. 5–6).[6] Their "anthropotechnical" level of analysis emphasizes how human beings are always shaped by the tools we use, however mundane.

With that synopsis in mind, it is hopefully clear that, while the labels "German" and "media theorist" can apply to Han, the title *German media theorist* is somewhat ill-fitting. To be sure, Han is a *German* thinker in the mold of someone such as Friedrich Kittler, producing a theory of media against the cultural background of debates concerning "technology, humanism, and individual as well as collective identity formation" (Winthrop-Young, 2011, pp. 2–3). Han's approach to media also largely eschews content analysis and the semantics of representation, focusing instead on the operating principles of media technology. But while his criticism of Habermas's normalized ideal of the public sphere superficially resembles German media theory's critique of reason-based humanist systems of reference (DRE), Han does not share its posthumanist concerns, much less its earlier antihumanist prejudices.[7] He also does not share the disciplinary concerns about reorienting the humanities' frame of reference around media as the material substrate of culture. Readers of Han will encounter in his works frequent references to German writings about technology (typically those of Heidegger, Benjamin, Schmitt, and Flusser) but virtually no mention of Kittler, Siegert, or later cultural-technique thinkers such as Cornelia Vismann, Thomas Macho, and Eva Horn.

Han largely seems uninterested in unprepossessing or hard-to-classify technologies – jukeboxes notwithstanding (N 85–98). Rather than emphasizing the inconspicuous, Han concentrates critical attention – with an almost laser-beam focus – on the wide-ranging effects of digital modes of mediation. Indeed, this focus makes him such a timely thinker. Digital devices are well on their way to reconfiguring our technological and symbolic environments, to becoming a "natural technology" that disappears into the taken-for-granted background of everyday life (Barba-Kay, 2023, p. 12). Still, for now, digital communication constitutes a particularly conspicuous aspect of technological modernity. This is the case even or especially if the diverse effects of digital media escape the conscious thought of most people. For these reasons, Han's media theory stands apart from so-called German media theory, occupying an ambiguous insider–outsider status not unlike that of his frequent interlocutor, the Czech-born Brazilian philosopher and media theorist Vilém Flusser.

Less ambiguous is Han's relationship to the Canadian and French traditions of media theory in the technological mode. With respect to media technology, Han's two most important reference points are McLuhan and Baudrillard. Of the two, McLuhan is the more foundational, especially given that Baudrillard himself draws on McLuhan in his emphasis on the form of media. Conceptualizing technologies as extended bodily organs, McLuhan set forth a critical media paradigm that revolutionized media studies by ontologizing technology. On McLuhan's view, media do not merely transmit meaning but shape the contours of existence – hence his famous saying "the medium is the message," which serves as a first principle as well as a summation of his approach (2003, p. 7).

The aphorism suggests, among other things, that each medium possesses a "grammar or underlying language-like set of protocols for arranging the world and the organs of sensation into a distinct ratio" (Peters, 2015, p. 15). Each new medium simultaneously extends and "amputates" the bodies who use them, creating distinct technical and experiential regimes. The standard example used by media ecologists to demonstrate such "disturbances" is the shift from primary orality to chirography: literacy or alphabetic writing suppresses the audile-tactile complex of "poetic man" while simultaneously extending the visual function of language to an extraordinary degree (McLuhan, 1962, pp. 4, 53).

Han's writings on digital communication and technology largely hew to this "onto-mutational" view of media. The preface to *In the Swarm* makes this alignment explicit by articulating Han's critique of digital technology with McLuhan's earlier analysis of electronic media. Then as now, Han writes, "We are hobbling along after the very medium that, below our threshold of conscious decision, is definitively changing the ways that we act, perceive, feel, think, and live together" (IS, p. ix; cf. McLuhan, 2003, p. 30). Unlike McLuhan, however, who tended to substitute dispassionate observation and description for ethico-political diagnosis, Han characterizes the growing dominance of the new digital medium as a crisis, a disruption of subjectivity and affect that amounts to a political crisis. His attempt to bring McLuhan up to date with the digital possesses a sense of urgency largely foreign to the "metaphysician of media" (but entirely of a piece with more pessimistic critics of technology such as Virilio and Ellul).

The crisis thinking present in Han's media theory is supplied by Heidegger's urgent critique of "enframing." Technology receives its own mode of consciousness from "enframing," which for Heidegger portends the withdrawal of Being. This oblivion of Being is a crisis for Heidegger, who cannot share the German media theorists' dispassionate analysis of posthuman "onto-mutations." As we have seen, Han is not a Heideggerian disciple for whom the master "comes too soon," exhorting us to "releasement" now that the time is ripe. Instead of vigilance for Being, Han calls us to a friendliness to whatever beings appear to us. Friendliness is a particular attitude towards communication. As Han writes in *Hegel und die Macht*, "Friendliness is the prologue that warms words. Without it, they would cool down to bare communication. If there was a difference between the speaking and what is said [*zwischen dem Sagen und dem Gesagten*], this would be friendliness"

(HM 136n15). According to Heidegger, technical language expands what is said to a totality that excludes any friendly act of speaking. Technical language frames "reality in the widest sense" in a formal, abstract, and high-speed transmission of clear signals and sequences of signs (1998, p. 141). Friendliness resists the technical reduction of language dreaded by Heidegger. What makes Han's practice of media theory an urgent task is thus its capacity to create critical awareness of how and to what extent techno-linguistic, connective interfaces supplant the friendliness of warm words and the ontological scene of friendly greetings and foreclose dwelling poetically upon the earth.

Han's concern that digital communication both replaces friendly greeting and closes the linguistic spaces where other meanings can appear manifests in a critical, small-m method that considers the built-in tendencies of digital media, along with their social implications and related pathologies. This framework, which hinges on the concept of media bias, originates in the work of the Canadian political economist Harold Innis (2007) and his work on the relationship between media and empire. Sharply focused on the technology of communication, Innis was interested less in issues of content and more in how different media are biased towards different forms of sociopolitical organization (2008, pp. 33–60). He was concerned as well with how their physical properties (e.g., durability, portability, heaviness or lightness) interact with – how they infuse and inform – psychosocial reality.[8] While Han does not explicitly mention Innis or the concept of bias, much less outline a framework for thinking about the tendencies and trajectories of digital media, his critique of the erosion of temporal architectures that foster duration, lingering, friendly greeting, and narratives implies such a critical method. The heuristic of medium bias clarifies his broad approach to digitality while defending against accusations of technological essentialism (see Buongiorno, 2022). Throughout his media-centric works, Han identifies and critiques two principal biases of digital media – positivity and transparency – analyzing their diverse but interrelated effects on self and Other as well as on the socioeconomic and political environments in which they are implemented and of which they form a constitutive part. In a North American context, this approach is sometimes labeled *media ecology*. Even though Han never aligns himself with the term, media ecology is an accurate and helpful description for his work. For Han the media ecologist, the biases of digital media are how the tendencies of neoliberal modernity take root and are realized in the world. They thus go a long way towards providing a compelling *account* of the where and how, the causes and effects, of some of today's major psychosocial and politico-economic disturbances. In the remainder of this chapter and in the next, we examine Han's media ecology, first, as it addresses the effects of digital communication on the subject and its relations to the Other and, second, as it pertains to the larger environments of neoliberalism and control society.

## Gaplessness and Digital Comfort Zones

If digital media could be said to disclose a central bias, then for Han it would most likely be positivity. According to Han, the effects of positivity are simultaneously wide-ranging and intensive, taking hold of everything everywhere all at once. Nothing, however, is as profoundly affected as the self and its relation to the Other. As we have seen, one of the distinctive features of burnout society is that the violence or terror of the same supersedes the Other, such that "the negativity of the Other now gives way to the positivity of the Same" (EO 1). While Han identifies several momentous repercussions of this (ontological) shift towards the Same – pathological, erotic, phenomenological, epistemological, etc. – he thinks they are all more or less predictable elaborations of the digital revolution's positivity bias.

Flusser is Han's foil for thinking about the digital revolution in terms of the violence of the same (and perhaps his foil in general). Flusser's major contribution to media studies, his so-called trilogy (2011a, 2011b, 2000), appeared during what the media theorist McKenzie Wark calls the *"cyberculture* period," which lasted roughly "from the popularization of cyberpunk in 1984 to the death of the internet as a purely scientific and military medium in 1995" (2020, p. 208). Although Flusser was initially distrustful of the new communication technology, like many late twentieth-century critics his wariness evolved into something like a "skeptical euphoria" (Ströhl, 2002, p. xxiv). His magnum opus, *Into the Universe of Technical Images*, "outlines a utopian society based on telematics and information" (ibid., p. xxvi). In this near-future world, "net dialogue" would be "supported by the technical implementation of communication structures that allow" for the intersubjective synthesis and circulation of new information. Members of this "resonant space" could thereby establish "noncoercive" relationships of sympathy and "mutual respect," dedicating themselves "to contemplation, to theoretical reflection, to dialogue, games, and celebration" (ibid., p. xxvii).

Han does not contest the resonant quality of the internet – quite the opposite, in fact. The internet is nothing if not an accelerated, hypercommunicative space of synchronous vibration. On that score, Han thinks Flusser's prediction is correct. Where Han parts with Flusser (2009, p. 251ff.) is on the nature of that resonance, which, on Han's view, is anything but sympathetic – much less empathetic or altruistic. "Today," he argues, "the net changes into a special resonant space, an echo chamber purged of all otherness, all foreignness," an endless ego loop wherein we encounter only our own ideas, beliefs, and preferences (EO 6). In contrast to Flusser's messianism of telematic networking, digital technology "has proven to be a narcissistic ego machine" (IS 48).

One of Han's go-to examples for highlighting the egocentric effects of the digital is the smartphone – arguably the signature artifact of our age. Drawing on Lacanian psychoanalysis, Han argues that the smartphone dismantles the real while totalizing the imaginary, thereby opening a narcissistic space in which we enclose ourselves and self-mirror. For Lacan, there are three orders or registers according to which all psychoanalytic phenomena may be described: the "real," "symbolic," and "imaginary." The real emerges as that which is outside language or any system of sign or symbol. It is "the impossible" (Lacan, 1988, p. 167), since it is impossible to imagine, impossible to assimilate into the symbolic order – which is essentially a linguistic dimension, the realm of law and of structure – and therefore impossible to attain in any way. The imaginary order, by contrast, refers to the fundamental narcissism by which subjects create fantasy images both of themselves and of their objects of desire. It is also a site of radical alienation and closely tied to Lacan's theorization of the "mirror stage" of ego formation, though it continues to exert its influence through the life of adult subjects (1993, p. 146). For Han, the smooth and continuous *liking* that we experience through our digital devices exploits the imaginary's continued influence, erasing negativity in all its forms and producing a realm of positivity which prolongs only the same. Algorithms surveil our preferences to better curate this ego-space for us (and better commodify it for advertisers). True resonance, for Han, presupposes the proximity of the Other, but, in a dialectical reversal, "total interconnection and total communication by digital means" replace proximity with "the gaplessness of the Same" (EO 3, 6). Unlike closeness, which enjoys a dialectical, mutually inscribed relationship between self and Other with distance, gaplessness is sheer positivity, with no Other but only mirrored images or augmentations of self. The gaplessness experienced across social media, in news feeds, and on handheld digital devices may very well abolish distance, but, without any animating force or dialectical tension, without any true opening to the Other, it destroys closeness rather than creating intimacy.

By facilitating gaplessness, networked digital information technology redoubles the terror of the same. It passes over those who are unfamiliar and other – who might challenge us or draw us out of ourselves – selecting for "those who are the same or like-minded," thereby ensuring that our experiential horizon "becomes ever narrower." Thus, "[s]ocial media constitutes an absolute zero grade of the social" (EO 3), while the "like" function common to social media interfaces marks "the absolute zero grade of *perception*" (EO 41). We may accumulate "friends" on Facebook and "followers" on Twitter (or X) – mistaking them for the genuine article – but we do so without ever encountering another person. At most, we encounter others' profiles, "anonymous somebodies," who – or that – may very well be bots but whose medial difference from persons is perceptually negligible (IS 10–11). Live web-cam girls, emotional expression shortcuts, Twitter engagements, friend requests and suggestions, dating-app matches, all are merely interface effects that exist for a specific anthropotechnical reason: the uninterrupted, distance-destroying interconnectivity of people transmuted into positivized things (Galloway, 2012). Within such abstract spaces of hypercommunication, "*Relationships* are replaced by *connections*" and "[g]aplessness supplants *closeness*" (EO 37). Global communication ultimately results in encounters with the same, at best with "like-minded Others" or other "likes." Shielded from the negativity of the foreign or uncanny, denizens of the digital settle into a "comfort zone" or "safe space" from which genuine alterity has always already been eliminated.

Depending on which tech visionary one asks, one possible future of our digital comfort zones could involve the semantic web (sometimes known as Web 3.0). Coined by the computer scientist Tim Berners-Lee, often credited with inventing the World Wide Web, the semantic web is "a layered, connected database of information that software agents would sift through and process automatically for human users" (Campbell et al., 2011, p. 50; cf. Berners-Lee et al., 2001). Essentially, it is a futuristic, interactive search engine that utilizes the networked perception elements of the Internet of Things. Instead of generating search results of listed web sites for us to peruse, the software of the semantic web would place "the basic information of the Web into meaningful categories (family, friends, calendars, mutual interests, locations, and the like) and make significant" or meaningful connections for us (ibid., p. 50). The closest extant example of the semantic web is the intelligent virtual assistant (IVA) or intelligent personal assistant (IPA), as represented by Apple Inc.'s voice recognition assistant Siri, first shipped with its iPhone 4S in 2011. Apple is of course not alone in successfully marketing IVAs/IPAs. Voice recognition apps such as Bixby, Cortana, Genie, and Google Assistant have brought voice recognition capabilities to Android devices as well. Similar voice recognition technologies are now standard in a wide range of "Intelligent Virtual Assistant" technologies, such as Amazon's Echo speakers (with Amazon's IPA service Alexa), Apple's HomePod (with Siri), and Google Home (with Google Assistant).[9]

Even in the absence of something akin to the semantic web, our increasingly immersive digital comfort zones have reconfigured our very mode of perception, scrubbing away traces of negativity and intensifying narcissistic self-reference. Han resignifies the cultural phenomenon of binge-watching "as *the* contemporary mode of perception" (EO 2; cf. DR 7). In a restricted sense, binge-watching refers to the practice of watching videos, often many episodes of the same show, to either the end of the series or the point of exhaustion. As consumers in an age of digitized spectacle, we are continuously offered movies, television programs, books, and music recordings that match our individuated preferences and therefore please us as isolated selves (even as "our" preferences are increasingly captured and shaped by recombinant codes and algorithmic chains of computation). We can consume what we want, when we want, for as long as we like – and even discover what it is that we want – because information is replicable and retrievable on a vast scale. The digital has largely released it from its material constraints.

But that is not the entire picture, Han argues. In a digitally mediated environment of ersatz resonance and gaplessness – where our household speakers recommend personalized playlists, order takeout pizza, and remind us to refill our anti-anxiety prescriptions – binge-watching comes to describe a new way of being-in-the-world, one that is identical to a way of not-being-with-others. It is an unrestricted mode of self-indulgence that fattens us, Han writes, "like consumer livestock," with "ever-new sameness" (EO 2). Media scholars working in audience studies tend to bristle at the pathological-addictive connotations of the term "binge-watching," offering as an alternative the term "media marathoning." Suggesting a conjoined triumph of commitment and stamina, this phrase, they argue, better captures viewers' engrossment and sense of accomplishment (Perks, 2014; Bush, 2008). Han would notice how the scholarship reflects the bias of positivity. He instead offers a critique of "the mounting narcissification of perception" that attends the digital's proliferation of the same (IS 24). Alone on social media or in the simulated company of our various IVAs, we are becoming disarticulate, binge-watching atoms, endlessly gorging ourselves on "whatever we like" to the point of narcissistic overload.

One area of life that is particularly destabilized by the excess of positivity is eros, the relationship between the lover and the beloved. In the science-fiction romantic-drama film *Her*, the director Spike Jonze explores the pathetic possibilities brought on by the digital medium's disruption of eros. In the film, the reclusive Theodore Twombly (Joaquin Phoenix) is in the midst of a divorce when he falls in love with his IVA, Samantha (Scarlett Johansson). The two characters "connect" over time and through the kind of searching conversations common in a promising relationship. Both seem to grow individually as they grow closer to one another. Theodore gains confidence in life and as a writer. Samantha gains greater awareness.

Towards the end of the film, before leaving earth for some digital space that Theodore cannot imagine (like the Lacanian real that lies beyond the symbolic order), Samantha receives an upgrade that allows her to talk with thousands of people. Theodore is dismayed and upset to learn that she has fallen in love with 641 of the 8,316 people she has interacted with. While the film seems to affirm that Samantha possesses a personality, this is at once undermined by the sheer positivity reflected in her indiscriminate capacity to form loving attachments (or what her operating system codes as loving attachments). Samantha, in other words, loves people in much the same way that social media users like other users' profiles and posts. And Theodore loves Samantha – or thinks he does – because there is nothing there to resist or oppose him, not really, just technical deficiencies that can be solved through system upgrades and downloadable updates. As per the tendencies of digital media, this is indeed as it should be. Han explains, "The negativity of what is different or alien, the resistance of the Other, interferes with and delays the smooth communication of the same" (CDD 34). Neither distant nor close, Theodore and Samantha exist in the gaplessness of digital positivity, for a while at least. Their proximity to present reality, however, is a different matter. The notion that digital media could lead to such an excess of positivity that we prefer the "company" of our operating systems to that of flesh-and-blood (and, for Han, soul-infused) otherness is not entirely far-fetched but evokes a plausible near-future. Released in 2013, *Her* already feels less like science fiction than a fictionalized retelling of the first human–IVA romance.

Eros, however, is not the only kind of relationship or encounter with the Other that is lost amid the digital noise of the same. Characterized by the absence of opposition, existence within the digital echo chamber loses that combination of reserve and engagement which is constitutive of encounters with the Other and thus of the communal aspect of communication. "Digital communication," Han claims, "is increasingly developing into communication without community," isolating everyone in their respective comfort bubbles of self-mirroring (DR 12).

This technical affordance, however, is not unique to the digital but constitutes an advance or variation on what Wark calls *addressability*, a technical feat originating with the emergence of the telegraph. With addressability, "every movement becomes equivalent and interchangeable with any other movement ... [and] any destination becomes equivalent and interchangeable with any other place" (Wark, 2012, p. 32). Everything and everyone are equally near and equally far, equally present and equally absent; messages are not directed at concrete persons but "*mean* no one"; and "communication degenerates into an accelerated exchange of information" that establishes no relationships, only connections (EO 74). "Dear valued customer" does not empty a spam email into a space of friendly greeting where the Other can appear as Other. And yet, as Anna Mill and Luke Jones's graphic novel *Square Eyes* suggests, addressability in the digital era serves as a guarantor of one's social existence: "But without my account ID and profile it's like they don't even see me" (2018, p. 3). Digital gaplessness thus subverts the prospect of community just as effectively as it undermines the possibility of eros. For Han, "It is a communication with no *neighbour*, without any neighbourly *closeness*." And "without neighborliness," he adds, "no community can form" (EO 74). In the place of community – and with it of shared, communicative action or discourse – the digital infosphere substitutes "exhibition spaces of the I" (EO 76). From the comfort of its digital resonant chamber, the isolated I advertises itself to other like-minded, similarly advertising selves – selves who, in their isolated addressability, are at once everywhere and nowhere.

As internally consistent as Han's critique of digital resonance chambers may be, there is something counterintuitive about describing networked digital information technology in terms of positivity and the removal of difference. After all, today's internet (social media in particular) consists of many different technosocial milieux, any number of which may provide the opportunity to encounter limitless difference and negativity. One does not need to celebrate so-called postmodern fragmentation to appreciate that digital convergence has splintered twentieth-century mass audiences into ever smaller niche interest groups. Even if Flusser is wrong to ascribe a uniformly sympathetic quality to the resonance that occurs through digitized structures of networked interactivity, was he not still correct in his prediction that such technologies would foster the production and interplay of difference, even if these differences are irreconcilable (Stoneman, 2024)? Certainly, the current cultural-political landscape, not to mention partisan politics, remains an unintelligible black box unless considered in connection with the negativity that characterizes online discourse, as Han himself has recently suggested (I 25–33).

With these considerations in mind, it would seem that one could persuasively argue, *pace* Han, that the digital revolution has not redoubled the terror of the same but in fact replaced homogeneity with heterogeneity. This may look to be especially the case when comparing today's internet and social media users to the mass audiences that typified the great news and entertainment industries of the twentieth century. Indeed, many of us can attest to how digital technologies have renewed familial bonds and old friendships in which significant differences opened across the years. Many of us can attest to meaningful relationships that have developed online that involve genuine dialogue and difference. Perhaps two scholars read each other's work and strike up a long debate via email, one that gradually grows into a friendship. Perhaps a Christian potter from Minnesota befriends a Hindu potter from India, and their conversations move beyond technique to cultural and religious differences. Likewise, there can be real-world "watch parties" for the latest season of an engaging show, with much laughter and commentary and conversation along the way, that are better described as focal points for community than "comatose viewing" or "binge-watching."

Nonetheless, Han would hold that we ignore the countervailing pathological tendencies, the biases, encouraged by digital media at our own risk. His critical-ecological approach ultimately rejects the notion that such an interplay of difference results (or even could result) in an environment hospitable to the negativity of the Other. While forms of digitized, networked interactivity may very well uphold a desire for the kind of tensile difference that characterizes relations to the Other, they simultaneously render this difference manageable, contained, a difference that has already been disarmed. What Baudrillard writes about the electronic mass media applies equally to the digital, perhaps even more so. For Baudrillard, media form a coercive system that disarticulates the world by reducing it to equivalent and successive signs. "[It] is their function," he writes, "to neutralize the lived, unique, eventual character of the world and substitute for it a multiple universe of media which, as such, are homogeneous one with another, signifying each other reciprocally and referring back and forth to each other" (Baudrillard, 1998, p. 124). Today's specialized interest groups and niche audiences are therefore not identical (or comparable) to analog counterparts. They are merely feedback loops for the circulation of sameness. In place of difference, social media creates a false sense of familiarity with the Other, an algorithmic familiarity that functions merely to shore up and refine one's profile. As a result, Han explains, "The negativity of otherness or foreignness is de-interiorized and transformed into the positivity of communicable and consumable differences: 'diversity'" (P 9). Instead of expanding our interpersonal-existential horizon, the interactivity of social media narrows it, drawing us into endless, narcissistic resonant chambers that isolate and scatter their users while at the same time creating coordination and alignment.

One of the nontechnical reasons that helps account for the effectiveness of this rhetorical sleight of hand is that digital media have become the latest instance of what Wendy Chun refers to as *habitual media*. That transformed status is significant, she argues, because "media matter most when they seem not to matter at all, that is, when they have moved from the new to the habitual" (Chun, 2016, p. 1). As our "new" habitual media, digital means of communication capitalize on the wish for an absence of negativity, for the anti-experience of disarmed difference, encouraging the sharing of information within one's own algorithmically adapted filter bubble (which Chun describes with the term "homophily" [ibid., pp. 14–15]). Han does not explicitly address the becoming-invisible of digital media – what McLuhan would describe as the transposition of the digital from figure to ground of perception – but it is assumed in his environmental or ecological approach to the positivity bias of digital interconnectivity (McLuhan and McLuhan, 1992, pp. 5–6). In this environment, where *"Socius* has yielded to the *solus,"* community and difference are merely buzzwords that work in the service of their actual exclusion (IS 13).

## Paroxysms of an Alienated Self and a Demediatized World

Another conspicuous aspect of digital interactivity that is prima facie at odds with Han's account of positivity bias is the prevalence of what Nolen Gertz refers to as *orgies of clicking* – nihilistic, sometimes self-destructive, outbursts observed in connection with online behaviors such as anonymous posting, flash mobs, and cybervigilantism (2018, pp. 162–4). While social media may indiscriminately isolate, keeping everyone trapped in their own signifying bubbles of *access* and *friends*, it is also socially antagonistic, almost unmistakably so. This tension, however, does not so much reveal a flaw in Han's critique as it points up a peculiar feature of the gaplessness of the Same, one to which Han is very much attuned. To be sure, abolishing distance does destroy closeness, but it does so by making society transparent, leaving us over-close and over-exposed. In place of resonance, hypervisibility fosters a buzzing, agitational state, which leaves us immunologically defenseless, prone to various, sporadic outbursts directed at both the Other and the self.

For Han, transparency and positivity name two coordinative biases that inhere in the digital, such that a society of positivity is at once a transparency society. Indeed, it is "[t]he positivity of the transparency society [that] makes it a hell of the same" (CDD 34). This notion of transparency, by which Han understands the *"systematic compulsion"* to make everything available as information, derives largely from Baudrillard (1985), who in the 1980s famously (and, at the time, provocatively) wrote of an implosion of the social in the mass media (I 5). Updating Benjamin's (2007) well-known thesis about the disappearance of the artwork's ineffable aura in an age of mechanical reproducibility, Baudrillard argues that the technical abolition of distance realizes "an over-proximity of all things, a foul promiscuity of all things which beleaguer and penetrate [us], meeting with no resistance, and no halo, no aura," not even the aura of our own bodies (1988, p. 27). Baudrillard's word for this phenomenon is *obscenity* or *the obscene*. It begins, he argues, "when every-thing becomes immediately transparent, visible, exposed in the raw and inexorable light of information and communication" (Baudrillard, 2012, p. 26). Han frequently deploys this term – and its close cousin "pornographic" (also taken from Baudrillard) – to describe both the loss of auratic distance that characterizes digital mediation and what Baudrillard describes as "the perpetual engendering of the same by the same" (1990, p. 74; cited in EO 6).

For Han, as well as Baudrillard, one of the most far-reaching consequences of the obscene is the loss of the distinction between private and public. Without the distance necessary for maintaining this distinction – without Nietzsche's *pathos* of distance – the private is made public and the civil sphere collapses. Accompanying that collapse is the erosion of *social capital*, those courtesies in behavior and speech that go hand in hand with "more or less institutionalized relationships of mutual acquaintance and recognition" (Bourdieu and Wacquant, 1992, p. 119). Of the various civilities now endangered, Han thinks that respect is the major casualty, followed, in a cascading logic of desocialization, by practices involving responsibility, trustworthiness, and reliability. Instead of generating admiration and respect, as "isolating and setting apart" do, "Digital mediality works to the detriment of respect." Of course, Han adds, the anonymity of online communication contributes to the dismantling of "respect on a massive scale" (IS 2), substituting the recognition provided for by names with mere affect – with what Baudrillard terms *the ecstasy of communication* (2012, p. 28). This ecstasy, however, does not complete itself until the arrival of digital media and the achievement of total transparency. In contrast to mass media such as radio and TV, digital interfaces such as Instagram, Twitter, and Facebook "demediate communication." They are "windows with doors," enabling symmetrical communication in the immediate present "without intermediary spaces" (IS 16). They are also mirrors, that "counter-figure" to the window, that reflect only what is inside; there is no space through the threshold where the friendly greeting to the Other might be made (H 81–3). Representation and mediation thus give way to sheer presence or co-presentation. In an over-exposed, transparent world of obscene positivity, digital communication eliminates or disarms all traces of the Other while simultaneously abolishing all distances and distinctions into the zero-dimension of influent networks.

This transformation of the social means that the "hell of the same" often entails swarm-like behavior, affective discharges that can be directed or unleashed at virtually anyone at any time for seemingly any ad hoc reason. Although Han does not explicitly draw on others' writings vis-à-vis the concept of the swarm, since the digital revolution the swarm has become something of a trope among media theorists.[10] For Han, as for others, whereas industrialism ushered in the era of crowds and masses, digital media signal a new formation of "the many," the swarm, which is radically different from its pre-digital antecedents. In contrast to crowds, digital swarms "form a *gathering without assembly – a crowd without interiority*" (IS 11). But, while swarms may not exhibit the internal coherence or harmony that could develop a collective subject, a "we," "their *collective patterns of movement* are like the swarms that animals form – fleeting and unstable" (IS 11–12). This characteristic, Han argues, is a result of the "imperative of transparency" (its bias), which "produces a strong compulsion to conform" (IS 18). Unfortunately, the hallmark of such compulsion is volatility, and it is of a piece with the *"Phenomenology of 'Like'"* that characterizes positivity (IS 54).

Transparency, in fact, is not opposed to positivity; rather, it "stabilizes and accelerates the system by eliminating what is other, what deviates" (CDD 34). Sometimes this elimination involves the positive-affirmative function of "liking," "retweeting," "following," and the like, but it may also involve more active, less indirect gestures. The positivity of violence, in other words, is not a guarantor against *negation* as such, only the truly encountered negativity of the Other. In the obscene networks of doorless windows, positivity often involves negating the Other's negativity, the active negation of what is different or alien, typically through paroxysms of outrage. Digital swarms are exemplary in this regard. Although these groupings may appear carnivalesque – ludic and affirmatively nonbinding – their principal affective condition is outrage. Perhaps echoing Sloterdijk's *Rage and Time*, Han distinguishes the "affective *condition*" of outrage from rage understood in the strong sense of "the capacity, or power, to interrupt existing conditions and bring about new ones." Outrage, in contrast, cannot be channeled towards a conscious relationship or a domesticated, rational use but remains an untamable affect. "Today's fits of outrage," writes Han, "are extremely fleeting and scattered." Swarms may be destructive, yes, but they are ultimately impotent.[11] They lack the gravity "necessary for action" (in Arendt's sense) and thus for creating the future (IS 8).

Consider what Han memorably refers to as social media "shitstorms." For Han, these affect-driven outbursts are an "authentic phenomenon of digital communication" (IS 3), fundamentally differing from the rhetorical genre of invective, as observed in such mediated, analog practices as writing angry letters to the editor. Letters are named events that possess a different temporality, a different movement, and a different topology. Insofar as letters are handwritten, they are also carriers of bodily signs (EO 53).[12] Riffing on Schmitt's post-World War I definition of sovereignty as "he who decides on the exception" (1985, p. 5), Han playfully defines digital-age sovereignty as *"he who commands the shitstorms"* (IS 6).[13] But, of course, *no one* directs the digital swarms, which are by nature anonymous and derive much of their power from that anonymity: "They are like *smart mobs*" – "uncontrollable, incalculable, inconstant, ephemeral, and amorphous" – defying integration into a stable "we" and often surfacing around events that lack "social or political relevance" (IS 7). Such mob behavior can take any number of forms, but perhaps the most common is the aptly named "Twitter swarm," where a quickly growing number of users converge on a target profile to denounce or ridicule, sometimes due to moral grievance and sometimes for spite (Seymour, 2019, pp. 32–7). It makes no difference to the volatile smart mobs whether the target is an A-list celebrity accused of some sexual impropriety or just some impolitic high schooler desperately trying to optimize his or her profile. As Adrian Nathan West observes, "online condemnation responds less to the dialogic criteria of suasion than to the base pleasure of dealing a cheap shot – in many cases, under cover of anonymity – with no concern for whether the target is a stranger, a celebrity author, or the president of the United States" (2017). The affective condition of digital swarms means that the mobs are incapable of making such distinctions. It also means that the outrage which drives any given shitstorm tends to be short-lived. But while smart mobs may quickly dissipate, greatly limiting their potential for lasting political change, they are nevertheless all too capable of leaving in their wake the wreckage of ruined careers, damaged reputations, and self-harmed bodies.

One is tempted to relate this swarm-like behavior to René Girard's mimetic theory, according to which the desire to want what other people want (mimetic desire) inexorably leads to tensions, division, and fighting (mimetic rivalry), which destabilizes the community until a (perhaps innocent) scapegoat is banished or even killed. After the enactment of the scapegoating mechanism, societies form around the repeated ritual reenactment of this murder. It effectively founds the society and continues through its ritualization to stem violent "mimetic contagion" (Girard, 1977, pp. 144–9). The mimetic behavior of digital smart mobs, however, is only superficially comparable to the sacrificial ritualized violence of the scapegoat function. In the case of shitstorms, there is no clear mimetic desire or rivalry, nor is there identification with a community, whose instability would be perceived by its members as posing an existential threat. There are only fleeting patterns of collective movement, swarms that never admit of a concern for society as a whole or even anything resembling a long-term world-building or world-sustaining project.

Given the frequency of social media shitstorms, one would expect to see them prominently featured in the popular imagination, especially in television or movies. But even though modern gadgetry and digital devices are featured on such prestige dramas as HBO's *Euphoria* and *Big Little Lies*, these and other shows largely fail to address the psychosocial effects of digital outrage swarms. One exception is the episode "Nosedive" from the British science-fiction anthology series *Black Mirror*. The episode portrays a near-future dystopia where people have adopted not only the ubiquitous mobile devices of today but also eye chips (emphasizing the theme of scrutiny). And users do indeed scrutinize each other, quantifying each encounter on a five-point rating scale. This social rating system cumulatively affects individuals' socioeconomic status, a networked feature not far removed from current reality. As Han points out, "Digital interconnectedness allows for every aspect of a person to be rated and exposed" (CCD 23).[14] The *Black Mirror* episode focuses on Lacie (Bryce Dallas Howard), an upwardly-mobile, or at least aspiring, young professional fixated on raising her 4.2 net rating to 4.5 so that she can receive a discount on an upscale apartment that she wishes to rent. When Lacie's popular childhood friend (Alice Eve) asks her to deliver the maid-of-honor speech for her wedding, she is presented with an opportunity for a major impact on her social rating. However, successive misfortunes cause people to give Lacie poor ratings, dropping her net score below 4.2. When her friend disinvites her from the wedding, a desperate Lacie nonetheless steals into the festivities to deliver the speech anyway, only to suffer a breakdown. In mimetic, swarm-like behavior, the guests rate Lacie negatively, and the downward spiral brings her net rating below one star, resulting in her arrest and detention.

While several online commentators (and at least one philosopher, Sergio Urueña) have compared the episode to China's social credit system, the wedding guests' behavior reflects a much broader phenomenon, namely, the strong compulsion of digital swarms to conform in their affective discharge, simultaneously and immediately attacking the same targeted individual without regard for that person's wellbeing.[15] In a transparent environment of digital media – and, soon perhaps, of augmented- or virtual-reality headsets – respect is superseded by the buzz of agitated anonymous selves, who, if not outraged per se, are at least indignant and disapproving.[16] Lacie's emotional disintegration at the end of "Nosedive" also underscores the inner-directed possibilities of digital paroxysms. Significantly, her breakdown precedes the swarm attack. Her crisis is primarily a function of being close to instantaneous images and information in a world that is transparent to itself. Even before the wedding crash, Lacie is what Baudrillard calls a pure screen, "a pure absorption and re-absorption surface" (1988, p. 27). She is a subject who knows only the gaplessness of the same and, for that reason, requires constant affirmation to delay the implosion of the self, as well as all the ensuing psychic disturbances, of which, according to Han, there are many. Lacie: exhibit A of the psychic costs of the achievement subject.

Crucially, Han reminds us, the effects of positivity are not isolated to relationships with (or, in bastardized form, connections to) the Other. How could they be, when the Other and the Self – what Han refers to as the Selfsame [*das Selbe*] – are dialectical terms? Like the relationship between closeness and distance, the Selfsame and the Other always appear in tandem with each other (or not at all). According to Han, "The negativity of the *Other* provides form and measure for the *Selfsame*" ... [which] "has a form, an inner collectedness, an inwardness that is due to its *difference from the Other*" (EO 2–3). The Same, "by contrast, lacks a dialectical counterpart that could limit and form it" (EO 2–3); its formlessness corresponds to its absence of experience. Recalling Ernst Jünger's provocative interwar pronouncement "Tell me your relation to pain, and I will tell you who you are!" (2008, p. 1), Han argues, "Without pain, without the negativity of the Other, and with an excess of positivity instead, no *experience* can occur" (IS 53).[17] For Han, experience presupposes pain, understood as a threshold feeling when encountering the Other. From the perspective of subjectivity, the screening out of experience is profoundly if also unspectacularly destructive, for *"without an Against one falls hard on oneself.*

It leads to an *auto-erosion"* (EO 43). In addition to the boundless, distance-destroying effects of transparency, digital communication brings into existence a new form of alienation: "It is no longer an alienation from the world or from work, but rather a destructive self-alienation: *alienation from oneself*" (EO 39). While this new form of alienation goes largely unnoticed, lacking as it does the spectacle of negativity, it is generative of several self-destructive pathological effects. In the pure surface of the digital medium, a "dialectic of violence applies," whereby *"a system that rejects the negativity of the Other develops self-destructive traits"* (EO 2). In effect (or in response), this dialectic fills the void left by the withdrawal of that between Self and Other, as well as between distance and closeness. Disconcertingly, it makes Lacie's self-implosion, or something like it, an ever-growing possibility for the world of *homo digitalis*.

According to Han, the pathological sign of our times is neither paranoia nor repression, but depression, an internal pressure that develops auto-aggressive traits: "Overwrought, pathologically overmodulated self-reference makes one depressed" (IS 61). Therefore, Han explains that "the expulsion of the Other sets into motion an entirely different process of destruction, namely that of self-destruction" (EO 2). As B. R. Yeager (2017) vividly demonstrates in the recent cult novel *Amygdalatropolis*, this self-destructive process is entirely consistent with the paroxysms of digital swarms. As Mike Corrao explains in an insightful review, the novel alternates between two forms of writing, a "surface prose" that "depicts the physical world" and "a series of text chats primarily between members of the protagonist's favorite forum." Readers "observe the actions and behaviors of a young man" who exists almost exclusively in a self-enclosed digital reality along with other anonymous and sadistic users who all call themselves /1404er/. He "rarely leaves his room, often making frozen dinners in his microwave and ignoring his mother, who speaks to him through the door." Wandering through the "insecure and violent parts of the dark web," his interactions with other /1404er/s revolve around their involvement in any number of practical, swarm-like cruelties – "LiveLeak videos, snuff films, and torture porn." In the novel's denouement, /1404er/'s "real life" disintegrates: sitting in the same position virtually all day, every day, secluding himself in a "self-induced hermitage" for the sole purpose of pursuing narcissistic, ultraviolent fantasies, leaves his body failing (Corrao, 2019). After "completely unraveling to the point of violently dismembering a mail-order sex doll, he cowers before an onslaught of real or imagined house centipedes, making despairing, half-hearted, mescaline-fueled attempts on his own life" (Fitzgerald, 2021). Like a Ballardian novel for a society calibrated to the spasms of networked self-alienation, *Amygdalatropolis* gives narrative form to the psychosocial pathologies induced by digital infrastructures – compulsive, destructive behaviors that target both Self and Other.

Following from the depressive effects of narcissistic self-alienation, the process of auto-erosion includes a "who's who" of twenty-first-century psychopathologies, from selfies, self-harm, and suicide to panic, anxiety, and body-image disorder. Here Han's critique of digital media links up with that of the Italian autonomist Franco "Bifo" Berardi, whose work on the psychosocial disturbances of media technology identifies panic and depression as the two pathologies of greatest actuality in the digital era. "No matter what other perspective we might decide to adopt to look at twenty-first century history," writes Berardi, "suicide is the truth hidden by official discourses" (2009, p. 164). For Han, however, the hidden truth could just as likely be body-image disorder. Because the digital medium increasingly obsolesces the heavy, solid counter-bodies that are constitutive of encounters with the Other, many of the destructive effects of self-alienation pertain to the body. Body dysmorphic disorder, which includes anorexia, bulimia, and binge-eating, thus represents for Han one of the now common paths of self-erosion. That path is increasingly facilitated by one of the great aesthetic ironies of digital smoothness: the use of beauty filters such as "the skinny filter" on TikTok, which thins users' cheeks and tucks their chins, and "the perfect face filter" on Instagram, which automatically refashions any user's face according to purportedly "ideal" symmetries. Cut off from the bodies and bodily media that announce the presence of the Other, the subject consumes and drowns in the sameness of itself – binging, purging, cutting, and starving the last vestiges of corporeal reality. "By the end," Han thinks, "one no longer feels one's own body" (EO 39). Between fits of digital outrage, the subject loses itself in the anti-experience of a painless, self-devouring misery. In a disembodied, transparent society where digital swarms and narcissistic ego machines replace the mass audiences of the twentieth century, digitality nevertheless manages to mass produce unhappiness and despair. Self-alienated and auto-eroding, the subject is even deprived of a decent dystopia. Instead of experiencing life as depicted by *Blade Runner* or *The Matrix*, the subject is treated to a mash-up of *13 Reasons Why* and *Pleasantville*, a banal, soulless dystopia of suicide, self-harm, and the terror of the "Like."

## There Can Be No Digital Organicism

In a 2014 interview originally published in the German national weekly newspaper *Die Zeit*, Han explicitly self-identifies as a technophile. When asked what turned a prospective engineer of metal technology into "a relentless critic of the system," he starts his answer by reflecting on his childhood: "As a child, I enjoyed tinkering around with radios and other electronic and mechanical devices. I actually wanted to study electrical or mechanical engineering, but I ended up with metallurgy. I really was an enthusiastic engineer and tinkerer" (CDD 133–4). What changed his mind was his involvement in an explosion that almost blinded and killed him and permanently scarred his body. Still, to this day he continues to tinker and thinks of himself as a technophile. On its face, this looks like an instance of almost absurd cognitive dissonance. But there is little if anything pessimistic in Han's writing about technology per se. At the end of *Non-Things*, he even recalls, with some fondness, his studies in metallurgy, referring to "the *magic of matter*" and describing metallurgists as romantics (N 95). This almost alchemical appreciation of matter is reminiscent of Lewis Mumford's account of technics. For Mumford, technics extends beyond the phenomenon of human tool using (and even beyond the extensions of human faculties) to include the whole symbolic, nonphysical environment that humans use and are simultaneously used by. It regards the whole nature of human beings, the ability both to use tools and to manage a superorganic environment. As Mumford writes in the first volume of *The Myth of the Machine*, "at every stage man's inventions and transformations were less for the purpose of increasing the food supply or controlling nature than for utilizing his own immense organic resources and expressing his latent potentialities, in order to fulfill more adequately his superorganic demands and aspirations" (1967, p. 8). Han does not explicitly champion technics in these terms or articulate a vision of the proper balance between humans and their tools. But his stark criticism of digital technology, combined with his admission of being enthusiastic about new technology, suggests that, at minimum, he carries with him an attenuated version of Mumford's techno-organic worldview. In fact, as we shall see in our discussion of ritual, many of Han's remedies will involve the use of analog, inscription, and bodily technologies.

One criticism which could be leveled at Han is that much of what he writes about the digital may also (and, in some cases, does) extend to the electronic mass media, because the same biases are present in both. One could argue, for instance, that his periodization of electronic and digital communication technology obscures the extent to which things such as television and radio did a rather thorough job of scrubbing away traces of negativity and collapsing the dialectic between closeness and distance. After all, that part of Han's critical framework which he adapts from Baudrillard was developed in and applied to a media environment dominated by audiovisual broadcasting. A similar thing could be said of Heidegger's mark on Han's critique of the digital. In the *Parmenides*, a series of lectures delivered in the winter of 1942–3, Heidegger posits an ontological distinction between proper writing, or "handwriting," and improper writing, which he thinks through the example of the typewriter; rather than inscribing Being in man, the improper action enabled by the typewriter keeps Being at a distance (1992, pp. 76–84). Because the typewriter takes the "handwork" out of communication, and because, for Heidegger, thinking is like the craftsman feeling his way around a cabinet, Han argues that a "typewriter foreshadows the digital" (N 66–7). So, when did the digital age begin? This imprecision, however, which can be interpreted as a casualty of Han's disinclination for media-technical analysis of the German media studies variety, does not compromise the critical purchase of his media theory, which focuses primarily on the operative principles of positivity and transparency. The question thus becomes at what point a progressive development of these biases becomes a qualitative shift. We seem to have reached one once our screens are no longer stationary, affixed as they once were to walls or furniture in the family "TV room," but miniaturized, mobile, continually present in our hands, pockets, and purses. From Han's perspective, however, the question of such a qualitative tipping point is largely academic. Of much greater critical relevance is the identification of technological biases and the consideration of their social implications and related pathologies in the present human–technology environment. And today we live, for better or worse (for Han, probably for worse), in a digital era.

When writing about the wide-ranging effects of digitality, Han's posture can come across as apocalyptic – even or especially if the apocalypse he describes registers as more of a whimper than a bang. In this respect, his critical media theory resembles the quasi-eschatological tones of Virilio, whose consistent interrogation of the effects of modern technology on the human condition was often perceived as pessimistic. Tellingly, when his translator, Julie

Rose, spoke to him in Paris, where a plan to blow up the American Embassy had just been dismantled, Virilio said, "There are no pessimists; there are only realists and liars" (quoted in Rose, 2006, p. vii). Within those parameters, Han is undeniably a realist – his critique of digital technology is a practice of uncensored realism. By focusing on the built-in tendencies of digital media, he paints a realistic but inauspicious portrait of a demediatized hypermodernity. Here the twin biases of positivity and transparency modify the technical-symbolic-existential world in ways that debilitate, rather than fortify or sustain, the human subject. They amputate and prevent encounters with the Other, supplant eros and community with obscene simulation, and reduce subjectivity to empty forms of paroxysmal destruction. In so doing, they abstract the subject from the larger cultural whole in which it has always functioned, thereby dissociating it from itself in an undifferentiated digital sea of binge-watching and social media shitstorms. In this environment, the human being becomes both collaborator and victim to the corruptive, disintegrating power of digital technology. This occurs to such an extent that the normative ideal of human perfection, even Being itself, becomes a vanishing point.

Here too, we are put in the mind of Jünger, whose (later) views on the relationship between technical and human perfection capture the dichotomy that Han inserts between human beings and digitality. According to Jünger, "Human perfection and technical perfection are incompatible. If we strive for one, we must sacrifice the other: there is, in any case, a parting of the way. Whoever realizes this will do cleaner work one way or another" (2000, p. 155). For Han, the possibility of biotechnics ends with the digital. Contrary to the hopeful prognostications of American posthumanists such as N. Katherine Hayles (2017) and Donna Haraway (2016), there is no digital-organicism – nor could there ever be – no digital–human balanced ecology, no rapprochement, only the progressive disintegration and increasing improbability of integrated existence and the expression of human personality. And here Han parts company with the humanism (perhaps the last great humanism) of Lewis Mumford as well. Despite the ominous tone of Mumford's prophecies on the harmful effects of large-scale power machines, Mumford ends his second volume of *The Myth of the Machine* by placing the ball in the court of those who have studied such phenomena, writing, "the next move is ours: for the gates of the technocratic prison will open automatically, despite their rusty ancient hinges, as soon as we choose to walk out" (1970, p. 435).

For Han, the present situation is much worse. As we shall see in the next chapter, it is exceedingly difficult to walk out of a technocratic prison that has no walls but is at once everywhere and nowhere.

Beyond the issue of periodizing eras of communication technology, there are two other critical questions that can be raised vis-à-vis Han's media theory, both of which stem from his focus on digitality. First, by focusing as intensely as he does on the digital, Han downplays the extent to which analog technologies increase the effectiveness of digital bias. Modern architecture and sophisticated commodity logistics both greatly contribute to the isolating and narcissistic effects that characterize digital ecstasy. As Sloterdijk argues, the dominant form of social connectivity today is the foam-like composition of "disarticulated social architecture," seen primarily in the modern apartment, which today and in the near future may include such avant-garde architectural designs as the ALPOD mobile home, Tokyo's "three-mat apartments," and portable, stackable studios. In these "agglomerations of *bubbles*," Sloterdijk argues, "each individual 'cell' constitutes a self-augmenting context" (2016a, p. 52; cf. MCS). The operative principle of these systems or aggregates is not any kind of organic reassembling of previously fragmented parts but *co-isolation*, "meaning that one and the same dividing wall serves as a boundary for two or more spheres" (Sloterdijk, 2016a, p. 53). The co-isolated existence of modern apartment dwelling thus intensifies the isolation and obscene ecstasy of networked interactivity. Accompanying the alienating (and self-alienating) effects of online positivity is what Sloterdijk refers to as the new monadology: "One man – one apartment. One monad – one world cell" (2009, p. 134).[18]

There is at the same time a logistical network that ensures a quasi-permanent cocooning within these individual cells. Vectors of *commodity-space* have now acquired the networking capabilities that allow consumers to satisfy virtually all their shopping wants from the comfort of their pods (Wark, 2012, pp. 72–7). With just a tap of the screen, we may experience the almost instant gratification of Amazon Prime's two-day shipping and the on-demand food delivery service of DoorDash and Uber Eats. Han does not deny that these systems and arrangements co-exist with or intensify the biases of networked digital information technology. His critique of the sharing economy and neoliberalism, which we noted in chapter 1 and will elaborate on in the next chapter, considers the broader anthropotechnical ecology of which digital media makes up a part. Even so, a more systematically expansive critique of the current stage of technological hypermodernity would arguably strengthen Han's critical media theory. Such an expansion could take as its starting point the inclusion of a more diversified infrastructural space, accompanied by a correspondingly multifarious vectoral analysis. This would also have the benefit of mitigating the charge of ahistoricism (vis-à-vis the overlap of technological eras), as well as the accusation of technological determinism, which tends to bedevil virtually all critical theories of technology.

# 4

# *Digital Psychopolitics: Towards the Total Control Society*

Ethan Stoneman

> Show them your heart. Show them your truth. Never give up. Work until you drop.
> Adam Neumann, WeWork former CEO and co-founder, *WeWork: Or the Making and Breaking of a $47 Billion Unicorn*

Another reasonable objection that could be leveled against Han's critical media theory is that it goes too far in the direction of technological determinism and ascribes to technology a deterministic or causal role in shaping human consciousness and culture. Of course, the trappings of determinism accompany virtually all perspectives that approach media through a technological lens. Perhaps the most obvious examples are Friedrich Kittler's bald and even infamous pronouncements that "Media determine our situation" (1999, p. xxxix) and that "Only what is switchable [or networkable, *schaltbar*] is at all" (2017, p. 5). While Han's apparent determinism never matches the bluntness of Kittler's, he shares in the latter's insight that media "form a needle's eye for novel historical and existential possibilities" (Peters, 2015, p. 24). "Now, as ever," Han declares, "the rule holds: in critical phases of its existence, the prevailing form of being or life pushes for modes of expression that attain completion only in a new medium. The forms that life assumes depend on prevailing media" (IS 45). Specifically, they depend on the biases inherent in those media, the built-in tendencies for a medium to be used in certain ways, which in turn tend to result in certain effects – some foreseeable, others not.

A bias, however, does not represent absolute control over us, either individually or collectively, but, rather, "a path of least resistance" (Strate, 2017, p. 36). Even a prevailing technology must interact with variables particular to the conscious and sensitive organism who uses it and the society and culture that adopts it. This was true of the phonetic alphabet and, much later, of the assembly line, and for Han it remains true of twenty-first-century digital media. The biases of positivity and transparency result in a tendency for digital technology to be used in accordance with them – hence the transformation of binge-watching into a mode of perception, the paroxysms of ephemeral digital swarms, the proliferation of various self-destructive psychopathologies, and the narcissistic, quantitative tracking of "friends," followers, retweets, and the like. Even so, Han's mediological concern, which he shares with any number of critical media theorists, is the degree to which we cede control to the affordances of digital technology versus the degree to which we can resist or move against the pull of "the looming digital totalitarianism" (CDD 26). While, for Han, resistance constitutes an ever-renewable possibility, the ability to withstand or mitigate the effects of digital bias must first reckon with the larger technological and symbolic environment in which they take root.

For that reason, Han thinks the question of digital bias – of transparency and positivity – is an important one to frame within the existing socioeconomic context of neoliberal hypercapitalism. To be sure, Han maintains, "Transparency manifests itself as a systematic compulsion that takes hold of all social, economic and political processes and subjects them to far-reaching transformation" (CDD 33).[1] And inasmuch as the transparency society is a society of positivity, the tendency to eliminate negativity likewise manifests this architectonic compulsion. Ultimately, however, these built-in tendencies are themselves directed, if not midwifed, by an economic compulsion. At the very least, Han thinks that digital bias is so intercalated with economic imperatives that digital communication itself amounts to a new mode of production. Echoing the post-'68 Italian autonomists, Han describes this new configuration of productive forces as an "immaterial mode of production," one that seeks to transform everything into data and information for the purpose of "greater productivity, acceleration, and growth" (CDD 29). Within this context, transparency and positivity coax everything and everyone out into the smooth, open flows of capital, communication, and information, shedding all negativity to maximize economic efficiency. Such smoothing and leveling out, which is accompanied by pressures of acceleration, exposes both people and things to limitless exploitation, thereby transforming all human existence into an over-exposed network of commercial relations. According to Han, this development signals the culmination of what Gilles Deleuze (1995) famously termed control society. Its completion, he argues, hinges on the capacity of digital bias to insinuate into a desire for self-exposure, achievement, and optimization, fully integrating freedom and self-exploitation.

Han's media theory thus takes up questions about the desiring and disciplined subject as it was theorized at the end of the twentieth century. It is this aspect of Han's thought that earns it the epithet "critical" and links up his approach to media technology with that of other media theorists whose work cuts across both the critical-theoretical and technological traditions. Implicitly, Han's *critical* media theory takes as its point of departure a crisis of subjectivity, which, according to Félix Guattari (1984), has been the principal crisis affecting the West since the early 1970s. This crisis hinges on the capture and production of subjectivity by technologies that interpolate and support a broader socioeconomic environment. Summing up Guattari's working hypothesis of this critical moment, Maurizio Lazzarato writes that "the central project of capitalist politics consists in the articulation of economic, technological, and social flows with the production of subjectivity in such a way that political economy is identical with 'subjective economy'" (2014, p. 8). Similar hypotheses can be attributed to Foucault, Jean-François Lyotard, and Deleuze and Guattari. For them, as well as for Han, the only questions capable of pointing beyond neoliberalism are political questions about the production of subjectivity.

Han advances on these late twentieth-century thinkers in assigning a central role to media technologies in the various processes and apparatuses of subjectification. Even this phrasing, however, undersells the significance of Han's contribution. As Mark Poster writes in his introduction to two translations of Flusser's work, "Given the importance of the question of media – it is disappointing that the major cultural theorists of the 1970s and 1980s tend to overlook media theory" and technology (2011, p. xix). The inclusion of media and media theory within critical discourses of the subjective economy is not, of course, exclusive to Han. As mentioned above, his media theory interacts with those of several twenty-first-century thinkers whose media-technical writings also embrace a critical-cultural approach. What separates him from these like-minded contemporaries – at least in terms of a media-theoretical approach – is his focus on digital bias, namely, the twin engines of positivity and transparency. These tendencies make up the key features of what Han refers to as neoliberal or digital psychopolitics, a system of rule that differs from and succeeds the previous biopolitical regime of disciplinary, industrial modernity. Whereas biopower "operates through disciplinary compulsion and command," psychopolitics exploits "freedom itself," dialectically turning it into its opposite, such that people voluntarily subordinate themselves to the system of rule (DR 12). For Han, digital communication and technology are essential to the system-preserving power of neoliberal psychopolitics. For that reason, the biases of positivity and transparency offer a heuristic necessary for evaluating the function of the new technologies of power and the regime they support. These tendencies enable digital media to function as a divisional apparatus of subjectification which puts into play techniques of self-optimization, total information capture, and the quasi-religious orientation of dataism.

# From Biopower to Psychopower; or, Forgetting Foucault (Again)

In the first volume of *The History of Sexuality*, Foucault introduces "biopower," an umbrella concept that describes governmental techniques for managing large populations of human bodies (1978, pp. 138–45). As we saw in chapter 1, Han's argument that achievement society exploits the freedom of the body departs from Foucault's analysis of how bodies are disciplined. Sexual reproduction is at the intersection of disciplinary society and the biopolitical concern with population. Schools and prisons discipline bodies, but sex requires Foucault to reflect upon techniques and practices that govern the reproduction of society as a whole. In the late 1970s, Foucault begins to argue that biopower takes two forms, broadly speaking, the first of which focuses on groups while the second focuses on the individual body. The first form, Foucault explains, can be called a "biopolitics of the population." Starting from at least the eighteenth century, he claims, power manifested in the attempt "to rationalize the problems posed to governmental practice by phenomena characteristic of a set of living beings forming a population: health, hygiene, birthrate, life expectancy, race" (Foucault, 2010, p. 317). From the nineteenth century to the present, these problems became increasingly important, manifesting in any number of political and economic issues. Focusing on the biological life of the group, this form of biopower produces biometrics to monitor the population as an integrated organic totality (e.g., life expectancy and birthrate), imposes administrative requirements aimed at preserving the social body (e.g., vaccination campaigns), and promotes the health of the population in general. These measures preserve a collective human resource or "biocapital" that preserves the productivity of the social whole (Rose, 2007). The other form of biopower, however, takes as its primary object the living bodies of individual subjects. Rather than managing populations, it encodes itself in the behavior of each body. This "anatomo-political" power, as Foucault calls it, is "centered on the body as a machine: its disciplining, the optimization of its capabilities, the extortion of its forces, the parallel increase of its usefulness and its docility, its integration into systems of efficient and economic controls, all this was ensured by the procedures of power that characterized the disciplines: an anatomo-politics of the human body" (1978, p. 139). Production regimes, for example, extort the most basic biological competencies, shaping the ways we walk (or shuffle along) and talk (or mutter under our breaths). This aspect of biopower, then, concerns the body's affordances for productivity. Together, these dispose the body-machine to perform various kinds of labor. As Brian Pronger recognizes, in this sense biopower represents the "political dispositions towards the body that render it a useful resource" (2002, p. 103). It approaches the subject as a stock of organic resources that can be augmented and trained. The operation of this form of biopower is thus not a question of "treating the body, en masse, 'wholesale,' as if it were an indissociable unity, but of working it 'retail,' individually; of exercising upon it a subtle coercion, of obtaining holds upon it at the level of the mechanism itself – movements, gestures, attitudes, rapidity: an infinitesimal power over the active body ... The human body [enters] machinery of power that explores it, breaks it down, and rearranges it" (Foucault, 1995, pp. 137–8). In this matrix of biocapital, the simplest actions – how we move our fingers and eyes over the screen and the products it displays – are managed in order to extract value.

These "breakdowns" and "rearrangements" take on special significance when articulated as a function of liberal biopower. Critics of biopower typically treat biopolitics as a collectivist project aiming at the level of population or targeted subgroups therein (Agamben, 1998). Liberal regimes may shield individuals' medical privacy to some degree and prevent vaccine mandates or other manifestations of population-biopower. However, biopower can still target individuals in Foucault's second form. A liberal iteration of biopower's defining tendency isolates the body and its capacities for productive labor. Liberal biopower and its "instrumental conception of life," Roberto Esposito argues, breaks the subject apart into an assemblage of potentialities for a given assignment (2012b, p. 91). On this view, this "division of man's nature ... allows the biopower of the individual to be more easily captured by either the State or, today, the market through the mediation of the neoliberal subject intent on augmenting his own biopower" (2012b, p. 77). As a locus of diverse capacities, the dividuated subject labors under the pressures of command-and-control protocols that originated outside the self. Biopower articulates the body according to the operations that put body parts *to use*. The fingers dial, the feet pedal, the mouth reports to the ears in the meeting, and the brain calculates. While value is extracted from these embodied capacities, other parts of the body remain operationally dormant and superfluous. From Foucault's perspective of anatomo-politics, "reduc[ing] human life to mere biology" coincides with individual subjects becoming laboring body-machines defined according to the technologies and operations that articulate them (Esposito, 2012a, p. 18). Go-to examples of such cog-like bodies may be found in factories, hospitals, schools, and the like, as well as call and contact centers, logistics facilities, and the many fleets of vehicles deployed by freight and wholesale trade companies.

From Han's perspective, however, biopower and biopolitical control are inadequate heuristics for understanding the technology of power under neoliberalism, much less for diagnosing its various psychopathologies. For all Deleuze's Foucauldian apologetics – "Foucault agrees with [William S.] Burroughs who claims that our future will be controlled rather than disciplined" (Deleuze, 1992, p. 164) – Han thinks Foucault's inability to discern domination beyond discipline is his major shortcoming. Han insists, "Foucault did not see that *the neoliberal regime utterly claims the technology of the self for its own purposes*" (P 27–8). That is to say, for Han, Foucault could not anticipate how neoliberal strategies of power would divest themselves from biopolitical disciplinary techniques. Foucault could not imagine the subversion of "practices by which men not only fix rules of conduct for themselves but seek to transform themselves, to change themselves in their particular being, and to make their life an *oeuvre*" (Foucault, 2005, p. 61). This oversight, Han argues, stems from Foucault's inability to see beyond biopower, which conceptualizes domination only in terms of a disciplinary orthopedics targeting the body. What Foucault did not envision is a system of rule where the ways that people *wish* to optimize their biomechanics in order to reach a "state of happiness, purity, wisdom, perfection, or immortality" would co-opt anatomo-politics (Foucault, 1988, p. 18). But, according to Han, this is precisely how neoliberalism operates in effecting processes of subjectivation: it seizes the psyche and subtly controls it, such that it misidentifies technologies of objectivizing power as technologies of self-determination (IS 77–8).

Han's term for the current regime's technology of domination is *psychopower* or *psychopolitics*. Instead of targeting human groups or individuals from the outside, or externally, psychopolitics intervenes "in psychological processes themselves" (IS 78). It thereby "stabilizes and perpetuates the prevailing system by means of psychological programming and steering" (P 79). For instance, whereas liberal biopower assumes an ergonomic and physical point of view for the differential training of docile bodies and bodily/communicative capacities – disciplining bodies to perform the job of a worker in, say, the chemical or textile industry – psychopolitics adopts an affective-cognitive perspective, infiltrating the mind (or spirit or soul) of the subject. Rather than modulating physical gestures, abilities, and performance, as in the case of industrial labor, psychopolitics aims for the systematic technosocial engineering of human thoughts, needs, and desires. It thus bypasses localized disciplinary apparatuses such as the factory, relying instead on digitally governed automated media, from social media news feeds and AutoPlay to smart cars and the Internet of Things. These technologies, which piggyback on and extend the scale, scope, and architecture of the internet, can reach into, reconfiguring, and, in some ways, constituting inner subjective life (as well as daily lived-in environments). Unlike the localized factory, digital media make possible virtually unlimited surveillance, nudging, and control capabilities.[2]

If neoliberalism engineers societies of control along psychopolitical lines, then it does so, Han argues, primarily by way of digital media technology. During the industrial era, heavy, automated, mechanical machines technologized and exploited the basic productive elements of the body's material labor – arms, legs, eyes, vocal cords, mouth, etc. The "extortion" of such labor power occurred at geographically discrete locations such as the factory and during strictly demarcated working hours. Workers may have been oppressed, but the compulsion to work was limited in space and time. Han argues that the incorporation of digital apparatuses into processes of production and economic exchange opens a completely new perspective on labor, a new *gaplessness*. To begin with, the content of labor becomes mental and immaterial. As Michael Hardt and Antonio Negri observe, "The central role previously occupied by the labor process of mass factory workers in the production of surplus value is today increasingly filled by intellectual, immaterial, and communicative labor power" (2000, p. 29). Furthermore, productivity becomes more difficult to define in terms of labor time. Compare the wage for a factory worker who produces $x$ saleable units per hour to the labor time of a laptop class that multitasks, perhaps working remotely to produce spreadsheets that are *thought to* make the company more efficient or advertisements that are *thought to* increase sales. Second, "digital devices have mobilized work itself," transforming the workplace, in Han's words, "into a portable labor camp from which there is no escape": "Because of their mobility, they make possible exploitation that proves even more efficient by transforming every space into a workplace – and all time into working hours. The freedom of movement is switching over into a fatal compulsion to work everywhere" (IS 34), at all times, a transformation that effectively "totalizes a belabored temporality." "Today," he argues, "we know time only as time for working" (IS 33). The same could be said about space. From here on, the gaplessness of the same pertains not only to our nonrelations to the Other but also to the maximal extension of the workspace.

After capturing work inside a network, digital apparatuses disseminate labor "into different productive islands, formally autonomous but actually coordinated and ultimately dependent on a platform infrastructure" (Berardi, 2009, p. 88). Indeed, all digital platforms – whether incorporated by powerful tech companies, dynamic start-ups, industrial leaders, or agricultural conglomerates – are positioned as intermediators that bring together different types of users: producers and consumers, advertisers and service providers, and even physical commodities. No disciplinary techniques, or very few, are needed to ensure the integration of informational, bodily, and procedural flows, since most people are always and everywhere plugged in, connected via mobile (and increasingly wearable) devices to a labyrinthine material infrastructure designed to extract immaterial labor. Within these communicative networks, the time and space of labor becomes coextensive with the time and space of everyday life. The result is a confusing space-time that, following Yves Citton, we could appropriately interpret as an *intra-structural*, rather than merely infrastructural, effect: digital subjects are "crisscrossed, opened up, reoriented, and redeployed by the same flows that pass through" both human subjects and media channels. In a Moebius effect of mutual inclusion, each one of us is constituted in our digital media; "they are constituted in us; and we are constituted collectively in the relationship they establish between us" (Citton, 2019, pp. 42, 43; see Lévy, 1995, p. 22).

Invoking Flusser's notion of the fingertip revolution (2011b, pp. 23–32; 1997, p. 188), whereby, thanks to digital apparatuses and infrastructures, human beings will no longer be defined as workers but as players of and with information, Han acknowledges that work approaches play and increasingly resembles a game. Digitality replaces the hand, "the organ of work and action," with the finger, "the organ of choice" (N 9). What Flusser's forecasting overlooks, for Han, is "the principle of *performance*" or *achievement*, which effectively drains away the playfulness so that we are left with work once more. "Playing the game," Han argues, "amounts to yoking oneself to the compulsion to perform optimally and achieve maximally" (IS 33). Because cognitive, immaterial, or communicative labor develops within the frame of neoliberalism, its limits or imperatives are the same as those characterizing essential capitalistic forms. Cognitive labor, which manifests itself as info labor, is essentially "communication put to work," where cooperation means "transferring, elaborating, and decoding digitized information" and doing so not freely but compulsively (Berardi, 2009, pp. 86, 88). "*Here, too,*" Han writes, "*freedom is switching over into compulsion and constraint*" (IS 34; cf. 48–9). Only superficially could digital play be considered an enriching experience. At its core, it is an impoverishment: digitally augmented forms of production install new constraints, the cumulative effect of which is an immaterial dystopia of continuous achievement and exploitation. The opportunity to work on ourselves, and even to reinvent ourselves, is the freedom of "can" that achievement society offers, and which neoliberal psychopolitics and their agents so effectively exploits – as exemplified in the remark from WeWork's former CEO Adam Neumann at the beginning of a 2021 Hulu documentary about the company directed by Jed Rothstein: "Show them your heart. Show them your truth. Never give up. Work until you drop."[3] In contrast to the tech industry's promotional hype, present virtual reality more closely resembles the Matrix, which harvests energy from unwitting humans absorbed in a simulation, than a world of unrestricted leisure and play. In just a few short decades, "the development of digital technologies and their miniaturization has led to a ubiquitous and all-pervasive infiltration of the material networks of intermediation in our most everyday actions and our most intimate thoughts." Such intrastructural networks constitute a whole tangled web of "positioning and juxtapositioning systems" by which we are situated, identified, and ceaselessly cross-referenced, our attentional resources harvested and controlled as so much usable (and sellable) data fuel (Citton, 2019, p. 38; see also Thrift, 2004).

The new topology of the fingertip revolution lacks a command hierarchy that imposes controls on a population. As we saw in chapter 1, Han's disciplinary society, now understood as a combination of Foucault's analyses of disciplinary techniques in schools and factories and the biopolitics of the population, gives way to achievement society. Foucault's anatomo-political power, the second aspect of biopower, becomes immanent in horizontal and transversal processes in a way that he did not or could not foresee. Biopower is deterritorialized and permeates the simplest bodily functions down to fractions of seconds of labor time, which is increasingly indistinct from what was formerly time for life as opposed to work. Control, in other words, is incorporated in digital networks as the "compulsion to produce, elaborate, distribute, and decode signs and informational units of all sorts," so that these can be endlessly rearranged in more efficient combinations. If in the late twentieth century it became an increasingly common practice for workers – especially so-called white-collar workers – to bring their work home with them, in an era of Web 2.0 and digital collaboration work is already at home and leisure is an asymptote, a figment of the imagination that is only ever available to one's future self. The smartphone is "probably the technological device that best illustrates this kind of network dependency" (Berardi, 2009, p. 89). "The smartphone promises more freedom," Han writes, "but it radiates a fatal compulsion – the compulsion to communicate" (IS 34). Most people leave their devices on during leisure time or even when playing with their children, and even when they are sleeping, meaning that "at every moment and place they are reachable" ("networkable") "and can be called upon to perform a productive function." As members of teams on platform infrastructures that process information around the clock, workers cede their lifetime to their employers (though they are "paid only for the moments when their time is made cellular)," while "preparing their nervous systems as active receiving terminals for as much time as possible" – compulsively checking their phones and reaching for it as soon as notifications ding or buzz. Neoliberalism manifests in workflow notifications and reminders rather than in bosses and firings. The new anatomo-political networks are markedly transversal and comprehensive. Perhaps the information systems measure how much downtime each worker needs and generate performance evaluations accordingly. "The entire lived day thus becomes subject to a semiotic activation but one that becomes directly productive only when" expedient (Berardi, 2009, p. 90).

Even so, in the digital infosphere, limitless freedom and communication predominate. "Everyone feels free," and this *feeling of freedom*, Han argues, is the problem: "Now, communication and control have become one, without remainder. Now, everyone is his or her own [warden]" (P 40). This is in fact *the* ploy of digital psychopolitics, the preeminent bait-and-switch scheme of neoliberalism. It amounts to a digitally updated version of Baudelaire's line about the Devil's loveliest trick: if "the cleverest ruse of the Devil is to persuade you he does not exist ..." then the greatest trick of digital psychopolitics is to convince the world that it is free – free to communicate and consume, free to connect, to recombine, to elaborate, to distribute, and to decode, to the point of burnout for the individual and to the great benefit of government and corporations (1919, p. 82). In this regard, while Han's analysis in many ways dovetails with Shoshana Zuboff's in her important 2019 study *The Age of Surveillance Capitalism*, he ultimately thinks Zuboff overestimates the likelihood of the widespread resistance to digital surveillance she calls for towards the end of her book: "We are too intoxicated by our digital drugs, by communication, to raise the voice of resistance and cry 'No more!' There is simply no place here for any romantic notion of revolution" (N 25; cf. Zuboff, 2015). The reason for this is as plain as it is vexing: much of today's exploitation is possible without any domination at all, relying as it does on self-entrepreneurial achievement subjects who believe themselves to be free.

Here, Han's thought links up with the recently developed field of surveillance studies, particularly David Lyon's concept of surveillance culture. Emphasizing the unprecedented shift in surveillance practices of the last twenty to thirty years, from discrete monitoring via cameras and microphones to the generalized surveillance of ubiquitous networking devices, surveillance culture refers to subjects' active participation in surveilling ourselves and others. Han calls this "auto-surveillance" (P 61). As a *culture*, surveillance "is no longer merely something external that impinges on our lives. It is something that everyday citizens comply with ... and, in novel ways, even initiate and desire" (Lyon, 2017, p. 825). Gone are the anxiety-ridden days of fearing, avoiding, and resisting surveillance, of concerns about privacy; yesterday's wary surveillance targets have been displaced by today's willing, even eager, performers. Digital media users freely produce and share all manner of private data, and they do so in total awareness that their data are being stored, transmitted, and processed.

Han thinks that what is most important in the inversion of freedom and control is the compulsion for transparency as guided by the principle of positivity. Whereas biopolitical regimes – both collectivist and liberal – were defined by the principle of negativity, by discipline, neoliberal psychopower encourages everyone to communicate and consume. Insofar as this enticement works, it effectively strips people of their interiority, transforming them into positivized things that, because they lack inner space, *"can circulate independently, free from any and all context"* (P 9). As depleted un-persons, digital users come to resemble more and more informational beings – transparent, open, and subject to processes of quantification, measurement, and steering. "Pure positivity – pure exteriority – is what defines information" (IS 40). In an age of digital psychopolitics, it is also what defines the self – now rendered as a proliferating formless mass of the same. "Utter exteriorization" amounts to "more information," and more information means "more productivity, acceleration, and growth" (P 9). Transparency and positivity thus do not merely expel the Other while instituting the gaplessness of the same but constitute the essential characteristics of the new technologies of power. By refashioning freedom as a form of "compulsion and constraint," digital media bring about a kind of *"subjectivation and subjugation,"* which is more efficient than biopolitical administration and control. In fact, Han argues, "The freedom of *Can* generates even more coercion than the disciplinarian *Should* ..." (P 1, 2). Unlike *Should*, *Can* has no limits, and its compulsion knows no bounds.

## All Work and All Play Makes Jack a Self-Exploiting Entrepreneur of the Self

For Han, the crux of psychopolitical subterfuge is the digital instrumentalization of freedom into a means of coercion and compulsion. Psychopolitics is thus shorthand for *digital* psychopolitics, the technical mode of governmentality that, according to Han, is "taking over the social behavior of the masses by laying hold of, and steering, the unconscious logic that governs them" (IS 80). The possibility that one *can* be "on" and "connected" everywhere, at all times, conceals the expectation that one *ought* to be, thereby serving as a switch for the transformation of "allo-exploitation into auto-exploitation" (P 6). Han's reasoning, here, seems to follow the technical axiom, identified by Ellul, that, "if a machine can produce a given result, it must be used to capacity," a tendency which only intensifies when there is an environmental inducement, as in the case of neoliberalism (1964, pp. 80–1; cf. p. 99). As Nick Srnicek argues in *Platform Capitalism* (2017), the digital economy and digital infrastructures (platforms) are increasingly essential to much of today's economy, having become central to a wide cross-section of traditional economic sectors and capitalist firms, from manufacturing, services, and transportation to mining and telecommunications. Nevertheless, the combination of technical possibility/necessity and infrastructural interdependence falls short of providing a sufficiently compelling account of psychopolitical control. The spatio-temporal totalization of work can still be experienced as an imposition and is likely to be experienced as one in the absence of other psychopolitical stratagems. Something else is needed for the neoliberal system of rule to grasp, penetrate, and subtly control the human psyche. Otherwise, there is no crisis of freedom, only a digitally updated form of disciplinary biopolitics.

To move beyond the shadow of biopolitics requires a more focused consideration of capital's relationship to affect and desire. Concretely, it calls for pursuing a line of thought similar to that which grounds the critical media theory of Franco Berardi: namely, "how did it happen that work," since the 1990s, "regained a central place in social affectivity and why did society develop a new affection for work?" (2009, p. 83).[4] Berardi's answer, which offers a useful supplement to Han's concept of psychopolitics, centers on his notion of semiocapitalism, a form of capitalism based on immaterial labor (sign-value) and the proliferation of digital technologies (see Stoneman, 2023). Developing the insights of contemporary autonomists such as Christian Marazzi (2011), Paolo Virno (2011), and Maurizio Lazzarato (2014), each of whom conceptualized the relation between language and the economy, Berardi argues that semiocapitalism "takes mind, language and creativity as its primary tools for the production of value."[5] At its core, he thinks, semiocapitalism marks the passage, opened up by the digitization of exchanges and the financialization of the world economy, from the industrial abstraction of work as conceptualized by Marx's theory of value to the dematerialization of the labor process and the emancipation of money – the financial sign – from the industrial production of things (Marx, 1990, p. 137ff.). Industrial "labor had a substantially interchangeable and depersonalized character" and for that reason "was perceived" by workers "as something foreign" (Berardi, 2009, p. 74). That all changes, however, in an age in which semiocapitalism takes over from industrial capitalism and the digitization of the labor process absolutizes the invisible goal of abstract valorization (Berardi, 2012, pp. 23–4, 135–8).

Once labor is digitally transformed into the ceaseless elaboration and communication of abstract signs or information rich with knowledge (algorithms, figures, digital differences), it becomes much "more specific," much "more personalized," and "therefore ever less interchangeable" (Berardi, 2009, p. 78). It becomes, in a word (Han's, not Berardi's), *positive*, no longer apart but a part of the isolated worker-subject. Cognitive workers of all stripes – from attorneys and architects to software developers and computer technicians – "may sit in front of the same screen and type on the same keys" or touchscreen, but they "could never trade places," not really: their knowledge, abilities, and performance "are completely different and cannot be easily transmitted" (ibid., p. 76). Consequently, Berardi argues, "while industrial workers invested mechanical energies in their wage-earning services according to a depersonalized [and disciplinarian] model of repetition, *high tech* workers invest their specific competences, their creative, innovative and communicative energies in the labor process; that is, the best part of their intellectual capacities" (ibid., p. 78). The digitalized labor process captures even the creative thoughts of workers' leisure time. Arguably, then, semiocapitalism captures what belongs most essentially to human beings: communication, creativity, affect, and imagination. For cognitive workers who perform the "highest levels of productive labor and valorization," "work tends to become the center toward which desire is focused, the object of an investment that is not only economical but also psychological" (ibid., pp. 78, 79). Workers are not simply connected to the Matrix as human terminals. Once labor is bound up with their thoughts and feelings, workers come to identify their work with their life's purposes and goals. This is the birth of Han's achievement subject.

This positive identification with one's work – what the literary critic Kenneth Burke refers to as a feeling of consubstantiality – serves as the affective fulcrum, the digital switch, by means of which biopolitics yields to psychopolitical control (1969, pp. 20–1,

25–6). One of the primary effects of this investment of desire is the disappearance of any opposition between labor and enterprise. This disappearance occurs simultaneously in social perceptions and in the consciousness of the individual subject. Berardi describes the resulting "ambiguity of enterprise" – that is, the development of the "human initiative of transforming the world, nature, and one's very relation with others" and the self "within the frame of the capitalist economy" (2009, p. 83). Enterprise is subordinated to capital. Berardi, however, stops short of following this exploitable ambiguity to its logical psychopolitical conclusion. What for Berardi is an exploitable ambiguity becomes for Han the crux of the "dialectic of freedom which turns into its opposite" (IS 49). Here, too, we see the appearance of the gaplessness of the same. Within a neoliberal system of rule, the positive identification between workers and enterprise leads to an overidentification such that workers are transformed from subjects into narcissistic projects, from entrepreneurs into entrepreneurs of the self.

There is an intoxicating sense of liberation when the subject is freed to become a project who can refashion and reinvent herself at will. All the same, Han argues, this projection is ultimately *the* psychopolitical technique of "compulsion and constraint"; indeed, he thinks it amounts to "a *more efficient kind of subjectivation and subjugation*" (P 1). We can reinvent ourselves; now we must reinvent ourselves. "Compulsion and constraint" now operate predominately under the banner "of performance, achievement, self-optimization, and self-exploitation" (IS 48):

> perpetual self-optimization – as the exemplary neoliberal technology of the self – represents nothing so much as a highly efficient mode of domination and exploitation. As an "entrepreneur of himself," the neoliberal achievement-subject engages in auto-exploitation willingly – and even passionately. The self-as-a-work-of-art amounts to a beautiful but deceptive illusion that the neoliberal regime maintains in order to exhaust its resources entirely. (P 27–8)

Compelled from within, self-achieving, performance-oriented subjects voluntarily subtend the neoliberal system of rule, providing psychosocial grist for the digitally updated satanic mills of control society. What is more, by ensuring that "people subordinate themselves to the system of rule voluntarily," this "system-preserving" technique of power traverses divisions not only between work and leisure, home and office but also between classes (CDD 17). "Today," writes Han, "everyone is a self-exploiting worker in his own enterprise. Everyone is both master and slave. The class struggle has been transformed into an internal struggle against oneself." Consequently, "Those who fail blame themselves and feel ashamed. People see themselves, rather than society, as the problem" (CDD 16). And so, what we see emerge for the first time is self-exploitation, "a singular phase of history when freedom" is not taken away from the people but "itself entails pressure and coercion" (IS 48). For Han, the creation of the free entrepreneur of the self is the particular intelligence defining the neoliberal regime and a further manifestation of the principle of positivity. In our present media ecology, this intelligence is perhaps best embodied in the Microsoft-owned, business and employment-oriented platform LinkedIn. Turning the Facebook page that first appeared in college dorm rooms into a transparent set of professional connections, the online service effectively blurs the line between social media and what can feel like a continual interview process. We proudly list our publications on Academia.edu or ResearchGate, pleased to imagine how many people are reading them around the world, expanding our future sphere of influence.

Central to the transition from subject to project are, of course, digital media as well as their various self-harmful psychopathologies. Both are ecologically interpolated in the classless positivity of semiocapital's technologies of power. While Han is careful to acknowledge that this transition was underway before the advent of digital technology (entrepreneurial consciousness probably gets it start at the turn of the twentieth century with the development of modern advertising and public relations), he maintains that today's forms of life increasingly "depend on prevailing media."[6] "Now," he argues, "digital media are completing the process whereby the subject transforms into a projection." The digital so completely takes on the role of facilitating "entrepreneurs of the self" that Han thinks it constitutes "a *medium of projection*" (IS 45). Just as our digital infrastructures permit the technician working for an oil company or the manager of an Amazon distribution center to perform their immaterial labor at any time, from the "comfort" of their mobile screens or sensors, so too can internet users work on perfecting their simulated selves with the mere touch of their fingertips or the sound of their voice – in the early hours of the morning, on their commute to work, whenever and wherever they can "make the time" (which is of course, potentially, any time). The only real restriction is the connection (wired or wireless) to a network. This free labor, as Tiziana Terranova (2000) calls it, is free in the double sense of both voluntary and unpaid. Unlike the remunerated labor of the technician or manager, free labor may take as its object the self as an ever-incomplete work-in-progress.

That this type of work may look and feel *like* play makes no difference. Or, rather, the difference consists in the dialectic ruse whereby play itself becomes its own form of labor. The French media theorist Yves Citton employs the neologism *playbor* to describe this phenomenon: *"an inextricable combination of playful pleasure and productive labor,"* playbor transforms *"the internet into an unstable and disconcerting mixture of playground and factory"* (2017, p. 65). The process of creating and maintaining a "likable" online persona – on blogs, fan sites, dating apps, and so on – and of transforming that work into an ideal profile, is an unending self-designing project. Not everyone may be an influencer or social media marketer with thousands of followers, but every user who posts on Snapchat, Instagram, TikTok, Twitter, and the like *is* a self-marketing influencer, whether they identify as such or not. The anonymity of certain profiles does not alter this reality: anonymous users are merely self-marketing and self-designing somebodies whose anonymity serves only to qualify the projection. While the playbor of self-optimization may elicit pleasurable feelings of empowerment, neoliberalism is organized around the parasitic capture of this free, distributed productivity. Such emotional management, Han argues, "reaches deeper into a person" than rational management and is therefore more effective: "Under the neoliberal regime, a person is not only exploited during working hours; rather, the whole person is exploited" (DR 12). As with the positive identification with one's work, the freedom to self-exploit is immanent to psychopolitics, which sustains playbor even as it exhausts it.

There are real psychological limits to self-optimization from which no achievement subject is immune. Just as the expulsion of the Other results in self-erosion, with classless exploitation and the illusion of unlimited self-production, people turn their aggression against themselves. Under the neoliberal regime of self-exploitation, the exploited are inclined not to revolt so much as to depression and burnout, maladies that represent the psychic cost of the crisis of freedom. In the manner of "the bigger they come, the harder they fall," the auto-exploiting self is psychically driven to wire the explosives for its own demolition: "The achievement subject exploits itself until it collapses. It develops autoaggressive traits. Often enough, they lead to suicide. As a beautiful project, the self turns out to be a *projectile* that it now turns on itself" (IS 49;

cf. 34, 60–1). Today, most cognitive workers are perfectionists, self-optimizers on the way to their next collapse.

People may be more efficiently controlled, and more effectively subjugated, if psychically steered rather than molded from the outside. Digital technology heralds the beginning of psychopolitics because it perfects the means of intervening in psychological processes themselves, of fashioning a subjectivity that continues to confuse freedom and play with their opposites. This stratagem of control is made all the more powerful in connection with the surveillance capabilities of digital media and Big Data. Combined with the distance-destroying transparency of ubiquitous interconnectivity, the positivity of classless self-exploitation culminates in the transformation of persons into transparent, positivized (non-) things – observable, quantifiable, measurable, and predictable.

## A Life Logged in Full

Perhaps the most conspicuous example of self-entrepreneurship, which also serves as one of Han's preferred examples of digital surveillance, is the notion of the quantified self. Combining the positivity of self-exploitation with the transparency of self-*illumination*, the quantified self refers to "[the] quest to instrument the body, monitor its behavior and derive actionable insight from these soundings" (Greenfield, 2017, p. 32). It encompasses both actual technologies for tracing and quantified biometrics and a loose global network of enthusiastic users whose slogan is "self-knowledge through numbers" (Ferris, 2013). Technically speaking, self-tracking devices are wearable biometric sensors, "devices that collect the various traces of our being in the world and submit them to the network for inspection and analysis" (Greenfield, 2017, p. 33). These range from simple networked digital pedometers, available now in inexpensive models that track or, to be more precise, estimate the user's total steps, cumulative distance, and burned calories for review and analysis, to more complex biometric sensors (ibid.). More elaborate trackers, such as Fitbit, the Apple Watch, and the Nike+ FuelBand, measure heart rate, breathing, skin temperature, perspiration, blood sugar levels, and fat content – from these often claiming that, when you are, say, sexually aroused or too anxious, it can be inferred by statistical comparison. We internalize these bionumbers and consult with our physicians in order to feel, as we say, "back to normal." Perhaps the pinnacle of such numerical tracking is "lifelogging," where the days themselves become chronicled and often meticulously measured, perhaps reduced to biometrics and other quantitative registers.[7] This "life logged in full," as Han describes it, is undertaken in the service of achievement, of course, as a means of continual, indeed neverending, self-optimization (P 61). It is thus a biometric, psycho-emotional extension of the auto-exploiting entrepreneur of the self. At the same time, because of its self-illuminative capabilities, "the recorded life" represents the merger of digital psychopower and pornographic self-monitoring. Wearing self-tracking devices and poring over blood or genomic testing results, the quantified self "transforms the body into a control-and-surveillance screen," dissolving it into data sets that are made available on the internet and exchanged. Observing the logic of psychopolitical efficiency, the transparent, *"data-compatible"* body signals the approach of the society of surveillance (SB 13).

For Han, however, psychopolitical surveillance differs from the surveillant technologies and practices belonging to the era of biopower. What is more, the use of digital apparatuses to store, transmit, and process behavior is essential to the accomplishment of neoliberal control. It therefore rounds out the prerogative of psychopower to exploit the whole person. To highlight the differences separating digital modes of surveillance from the analog forms it assumed during industrial modernity, Han draws a contrast between Jeremy Bentham's panopticon and what Han refers to as digital panopticons. The "panopticon is based on the dominance of the gaze," which "rests on a central perspective" (EO 48). As detailed by Foucault in *Discipline and Punish*, Bentham's panopticon is a prison design where cells, often stacked on top of each other several levels high, are arranged around a court yard and guard tower so that the cells' occupants are visible. This is a prison efficiency, according to Bentham, since it allows one guard to monitor all inmates. Even if the guard is not looking (or even if the guard is not there), the inmates always feel like they are being watched. Foucault notes that, when prisoners believe they may be under surveillance, but cannot confirm it, they internalize their surveilled status and police their own behavior (1995, pp. 202–3). Han acknowledges that "digital surveillance society evinces a particular panoptic structure" (IS 71): "Every click that one makes is stored. Every step that one takes can be traced. We leave digital tracks everywhere," all the time (IS 71). Yet Han also holds that the digital "is a *medium with no gaze*" (EO 48). This means that the digital panopticon is no longer an *opticon* at all but operates aperspectively, enabling illumination from all sides, even from within the self (P 61).

The exercise of this power is much more efficient than perspectival surveillance because it makes possible the storage, transmission, and processing not only of behavior but also of inner thoughts, needs, and desires. "Thoughts elude the gaze," writes Han, "but they do not escape the digital panopticon" (EO 49). The occupants of transparency society are not prisoners; they "do not feel gazed upon." They are not isolated from one another but "feel free and expose themselves voluntarily" (EO 49). This is the peculiarity, Han thinks, of the digital panopticon: that, by "exhibiting and exposing themselves" through hypercommunicative networks, "inhabitants actively take part in building and maintaining it" (CDD 39). At once perpetrator and victim, guard and inmate, transparent users willingly "feed the digital panopticon … by shining a light on every part of their lives" (IS 72), collaborating in their own surveillance, and voluntarily surrendering data as though out of an inner need. In a "digitalized, networked" society, everyone takes on "the task of conducting perpetual auto-surveillance," because the subject has become "a *panopticon of itself*" (P 61).

This transformation in surveillance technology simultaneously heralds a new form of power in which "individuals act on themselves so that power relations are interiorized and interpreted as freedom" (P 28). This "smart, friendly power," as Han calls it, is qualitatively different from but also more powerful and more efficient than the kind of repressive power envisioned in George Orwell's dystopian surveillance state. In place of torture chambers and telescreens, today's digital panopticon substitutes the internet, wearable self-tracking tools, smartphones, social media, and much else besides. "In the digital panopticon," Han writes, "the illusion of limitless freedom and communication predominates. Here there is not torture – just tweets and posts" (P 38). Big Brother is no longer a symbol of a repressive, threatening Other but wears a permissive, "*friendly* face." His ingratiating tactics are, in fact, "what make surveillance so efficient" (P 39).

A smooth and superficial friendliness characterizes achievement society, though, in fact, the very thing missing from our absolute projects of infinite self-fashioning are practices of friendly greeting, or anything that would allow deep friendliness to a world that is not enframed by our ever-changing individual life plans. Crucial to this "friendly" makeover are the technical biases (or neoliberal *dispositifs*) of transparency and positivity. Whereas Orwell's state and biopolitics more generally were defined by the principle of negativity, as well as by spatial and communicative isolation, today everyone is encouraged to communicate and consume, to make everyday life obscene through voluntary self-illumination and over-exposure. More information means more productivity, more acceleration, more growth. What one wears, reads, watches, visits, orders, and eats, as well as when and where and how one rates them – all comprise potentially exploitable data points for the economic panopticon of transparency society. "Exposure is exploitation," and the "fully exposed," digitally surveilled user-consumer-inhabitant "is subjected to limitless exploitation" (CDD 39). Stripped of its interiority, the transparent, positivized person *"can circulate independently, free from any and all context"* (P 9). The positivity of total communication, however, does not stop at the utter exteriorization of the subject. It also produces a "leveling effect" by tamping down deviation: "it is as if *everyone were watching over everyone else*," as if "everyone were Big Brother and prisoner – in one (P 10; IS 75). In contrast to *"secondary, extrinsic* surveillance," whether of intelligence agencies or secret services, the "democratized," lateral surveillance of digital panopticons is *"primary, intrinsic,"* and therefore "much more problematic" (P 10). In blurring the line separating Big Brother and inmates, primary surveillance replaces the big, scary authoritarian Other with invisible moderators, anonymous somebodies, and an environment of data-collecting sensors.

These three aspects of digital panopticons – "friendliness" (read: connectivity), voluntarism, and primacy – are exemplified in Samanta Schweblin's unnervingly contemporary science-fiction novel, *Little Eyes*. In the world of the novel, the kentuki is the must-have consumer item. A stuffed animal with a camera inside, the kentuki is little more than "a cell phone with legs": "The animal's camera was installed behind its eyes, and sometimes it spun around on the three wheels hidden in its base, moving forward or backward. Someone was controlling the creature from somewhere else, and they didn't know who it was" (Schweblin, 2020, pp. 112, 1). The kentuki is somewhere between a Furby, the fuzzy robot toy that set off a similar craze in 1998, and a nanny camera. However, the buyer ("keeper") cannot choose the identity of the nanny-like person connecting with the robot and observing the keeper from a remote location ("dweller"). Likewise, these dwellers have no control over where and with whom their kentukis are activated. Schweblin redeploys the cliché of toys come to life intent upon harm, as in Stephen King's "Battleground," but for a networked age. Cute stuffed animals are possessed by creepy stalkers who spy upon children, communicate with them, and harass them. Equally unnerving is the banality of the kentuki. The characters have freely chosen and paid for the experience of constant lateral surveillance – as a quick-fix means of compensating for feelings of abandonment, solitude, powerlessness, etc. What begins as commodity fetishism, however, gives way to Baudrillard's ecstasy of communication. What is fetishized is not the kentuki itself but the mode of communication it manifests, as well as the thrill of "the game of possibilities" represented by a furry-faced, one-way screen (2012, p. 13). The kentuki illustrates the seductive capacity of smart, friendly power to make use of freedom through mediated forms of voluntary, decentralized self-exposure: "Smart power with a [neo]liberal, friendly appearance – power that stimulates and seduces – is more compelling than power that imposes, threatens and decrees" (P 15). It is even more compelling, Schweblin suggests, when its appearance is as winsome and innocuous as a child's felt-covered toy.

The kentuki also represents a primitive aspect of what Han considers "the completion of the transparency society," which is "indistinguishable from a society of total surveillance" (CDD 28). What brings the society of control to completion, he claims, is the Internet of Things (IoT). The IoT refers to "ubiquitous computing infrastructures that promise to redouble the object world in the form of an endless array of data-gathering sensors" (Andrejevic, 2019, p. 10). For Han, this implies networked perception. The technologist Mike Kuniavsky characterizes networked perception via the IoT as a state of being in which "computation and data communication [are] embedded in, and distributed through, our entire environment" (2010, p. 3). "Sensors not only cover our bodies," as they do in the quantified version of the self; "More and more of them," Han argues, "can be found in our environment" (CDD 40). That is, all our appliances, spaces, tools – even urban and domestic environments (so-called smart cities and smart homes) – will continually collect and store data; that information will also of course be shared with parent companies. The IoT thus promises (or threatens) to transform the components of our everyday environments into increasingly powerful and broad-ranging sensors that capture, record, transmit, store, and analyze data, dissecting not just the body but life itself into measurable, quantifiable sets of digital data (Andrejevic and Burdon, 2015). In *Non-Things*, Han calls such "smart" objects "informatons" (N 3–5). A common example of the IoT is Amazon's smart speaker, the Echo. Alarms have been raised about employees listening in via smart speakers and spying via smart security cams, not unlike the kentuki. Mark Andrejevic predicts an additional range of sensors and sensor capabilities that Amazon or one of its competitors could add: "facial recognition, mood detection, and increasingly sophisticated forms of image classification" (2019, p. 33). Han notes that the "smart home" is actually a thoroughly surveilled "*smart prison*." The "informatons" in which it is decked out and "that free us from so much work turn out to be efficient *informants* that surveil and control us. In this way, we become incarcerated in the infosphere" (N 5).

Writing in the late 1980s, Virilio anticipated the then nascent colonization of everyday life by the digital processing of sensor-collected data. Invoking the Swiss-born German artist Paul Klee, Virilio writes, "Now objects perceive me." Virilio's forecasting of a world in which synthetic-perception machines "analyze the ambient environment and automatically interpret the meaning of events" now summarizes what is actually occurring in an era of total information capture (1994, p. 59). As Han writes, "Objects that we use day in and day out are keeping tabs on our every move. Without cease, they pass along information about what we do – and don't do. They are active collaborators in logging our lives down to the very last detail" (IS 74). Of course, IoT users/inhabitants are themselves active collaborators in the digital panopticon's operations. We are not coerced into surrendering our data but freely exteriorize our lives and bodies into transparent, positivized data; we willingly relinquish any and all information about ourselves to an immersive, all-seeing, sometimes wearable, network of interactive sensors. "This is a power," writes Adam Greenfield, "that Frederick Taylor never dreamed of, and Foucault would have been laughed out of town for daring to propose" (2017, p. 35). Yet data collection for every conceivable purpose – which, today, meets little to no resistance – accurately describes the reigning ideology of the day. As with every accepted technology, digitized, networked interactivity (digital surveillance) provides its own justification: "everything must become data and information" (P 57) – and so it does. IVAs are like blasphemous counterfeits of the icon through which the invisible God envisages believers (Marion, 2013, p. 191). If the smartphone is the rosary of achievement society, then Alexa is the icon of dataism.

This *dataism*, as Han calls it, constitutes a "second Enlightenment," wherein thoughts and actions are submitted to an operationalized, "*data-driven process* which takes place without any autonomy or dramatic orchestration of the subject" (SB 9). It is an age in which automated data collection and self-disclosure are so frenzied as to express something bordering on a new religious faith. This new faith, however, has all the trappings of a creeping nihilism, substituting, as it does, data for meaning and knowledge. And so we find ourselves, Han thinks, hovering in "a strange realm of meaninglessness." To compensate, we can only "throw ourselves into [more] hyperactivity and hypercommunication" (CDD 40–1). This torsion, in which the poison is indistinguishable from the cure, marks the vicious apogee of psychopolitics, the closure and ultimate ruse of total control.

## The Death of the Subject

Delivering his 1947 Presidential Address to the Royal Society of Canada, Harold Innis began by quoting the famously cryptic passage from the introduction to Hegel's *Elements of the Philosophy of Right*: "Minerva's owl begins its flight only in the gathering dusk" (2008, p. 3; cf. Hegel, 1991, p. 23). For both Innis and Hegel, this line functions as a cipher meaning that the crystallization of culture occurs during periods of decline and fall, that the flowering of a culture, its critical self-awareness, comes right before its disappearance or collapse. The philosopher of technology Albert Borgmann makes a similar observation but in connection to his concept of the paradigm of technology: "It is only when a pattern of procedure or a paradigm ... begins to fail and be questioned and perhaps challenged by a new procedure that the paradigm emerges as such" (1987, p. 35). This dilemma names the sticking point, but also the exigence, for all media theory in the technological tradition: namely, how to make an object of conscious reflection, how to bring to the fore, those conditions which constitute the invisible, taken-for-granted ground of social and psychic reality? This is, in fact, another meaning of McLuhan's aphorism "the medium is the message": pay attention to the invisible environment; observe what is going on and try to discern patterns in the chaos around you. It is at once a promising and improbable task. For even if Minerva's owl begins its flight before the onset of dusk, media as environments or ground are always exerting a shaping influence, to which we are often oblivious but to which we can nonetheless attend.

Lazzarato, whose observation about the economic production of subjectivity helped frame this chapter, provocatively suggests that, since the Great Recession of 2007, neoliberalism has failed to articulate a relation between the economic and subjective economy. In the current era of debt and machinic subjugation, "no new production of subjectivity takes place," only "the negative and regressive subjection" of indebted man (Lazzarato, 2014, p. 8). If over the course of the 1980s and 1990s the subjective economy was exemplified by the entrepreneur of the self, then with the recent series of financial crises it is "the 'indebted man' who appears instead to embody the subjective figure of modern-day capitalism. The condition of the indebted man … now occupies the totality of public space. All the designations of the social divisions of labor in neoliberal societies … are now invested by the subjective figure of the 'indebted man'" (Lazzarato, 2012, p. 38). On this view, the figure of the self-entrepreneur, whose successful deployment depends on the totalization of belabored spatio-temporality, is already a thing of the past. If it is visible today, then that is because, like the owl of Minerva, it belongs to a cultural formation that is at the cusp, or already in a state, of collapse. This is at least a convincing possibility and one that Han does not seem to consider explicitly.

However, what becomes clear in Han's writing is that neoliberalism no longer requires positive forms of subjectivation, whether of the entrepreneur of the self or some other figure (e.g., worker, communist, social-democrat, bourgeois subjectivity, etc.). It no longer requires subjects at all, only occupants of digital panopticons, subjects not of Big Brother but of Big Data. Perhaps Lazzarato is correct and the liberatory injunction to "work on the self" has been rendered void, "transformed into the imperative to take on the risks and costs that neither business nor the State are willing to undertake," viz., employability, debts, drop in wages and income, "the reduction of public services," and so on (2012, p. 93). What Lazzarato does not seem to account for is that, from the perspective of neoliberalism, the purported crisis of subjectivity is not a crisis at all. If there ever were such a crisis, it has since been solved by the widespread implementation of networked structures of interactive digital media. These do not depend on subjects, either autonomous or heteronomous, but on a range of micro-operations – clicks, searches, swipes, requests, commands – that submit thoughts and acts to computable and controllable processes. Dataism is not only a new faith but also a vision of a world in which sets of data are preferable to thinking, desiring subjects.

And so, Lazzarato is correct in his assessment about the absence of positive, twenty-first-century neoliberal subjectivation while also failing to grasp the reality, stakes, and power of digital psychopolitics. With the transition "from passive surveillance to active steering," neoliberalism now "facilitates intervention in the psyche and enables influence to take place on a pre-reflexive level" (P 10, 11). The ever-swelling deluge of high-speed data, which is nonetheless directed into databases for analysis, storage, and processing – so-called Big Data – is crucial in this process. A highly efficient psychopolitical instrument, it makes human behavior predictable, calculable, and thus seems to make the future controllable. This terminal transparency, Han argues, precipitates "a further crisis of freedom" by announcing "the end of the *person* who possesses free will" (P 12). The end of digital psychopolitics is thus not negative subjectivation but the automation and liquidation of the subject as an irreducible, unspecifiable point of non-totalizability. This terminus even goes beyond optimization and compulsive achievement. Here, too, the positivity of transparency pre-empts experience, forestalling desire by eliminating lack. As Andrejevic points out, in the digital era, "data-driven systems will know what we desire or intend before we ourselves know" (2019, p. 8). This could be an act of consumption, transportation, violence – any context "reliant on the logic of automated information capture and processing" (ibid., p. 37). The only limit to predicting human behavior is the available data set, which, thanks to the prodigious storage capacity of Big Data and the Internet of Things, is apparently limitless, or virtually so. While the promise of perfect pre-emptive prediction is impossible, what is achievable, what Han thinks we are in the midst of, is the disintegration of the world and ourselves into meaningless data – positivized, transparent things, at once quantified, measured, and steered. This is the way the world ends: not with the achievement subject or indebted man, certainly not with biopolitical disciplinarian regimes, but with predictive analytics and just-in-time Amazon delivery, with immaterial, objectless "non-things" (N 1).

For these reasons, Han does not hold out much hope either for revolutionary movements or reformist measures. On the one hand, while technical-legal proposals such as a "charter of fundamental rights for the digital age" or a comprehensive reduction in data collection and processing (i.e., "data disarmament") may be necessary, they are not enough to stem the tide of digital psychopolitics (CDD 24). On the other hand, there can be no revolution when system-preserving power takes on a smart, friendly form. Believing itself to be free, the subordinated subject exploits itself under the guise and through the illusory element of freedom. Enticements to communicate, "*Like*," and consume supersede coercive techniques to repress and inhibit. As Geert Lovink has recently observed, "What's to be done with workers that have nothing to lose but their Ray-Ban sunglasses ...? No matter how desperate the situation, the uprising simply won't happen" (2019, pp. 11–12).

If in the 1920s Fritz Lang's *Metropolis* could envision the possibility of a technologically repressed unconscious returning in the form of a chaotic and destructive force (see Rutsky, 2013), Christopher Nolan's *Inception* and Yasutaka Tsutsui's *Paprika* imagine a new digital unconscious in which technology can directly access the unconscious while escaping detection. Narratives such as these, where there is no repression but, rather, intervention in the realm of unconscious actions and inclinations, constitute the representative anecdotes for the era of digital psychopolitics. By highlighting the internal rather than external nature of neoliberal control, they put paid to the straightforward calls for transformative revolution of a pre-digital age while underscoring the practical necessity of seeking new and radical approaches to avoiding digital totalitarianism. Considering Han's critique of psychopolitics, they suggest that, in addition to any reformist proposals, "We must also bring about a change in consciousness and mindset" (CDD 23). This is ultimately the practical end goal of Han's media ecology, which itself is a propaedeutic to various practices aimed at restoring an open, indeterminable future that is worthy of and commensurate with free will.

One necessary practice, according to Han, is theorizing that can chart new directions and restore a sense of possibility. In some ways this is a very old practice, but it is important in particular ways, and must be pursued in particular ways, in a time when the sense of the possible is constrained by the biopolitical averages of Big Data. The collapse of grand narratives has cleared the way for the deluge of data. The dawn of the Information Age has taken on the authority of a grand narrative without providing orientation in time or a sense of deeper meaning.[8] Data displace theory and philosophical thinking; rather than giving an account of something, data only count, ceaselessly quantifying, measuring, and optimizing in the name of maximal efficiency and performance. Han points to Chris Anderson's 2008 article "The End of Theory," which holds "that the inconceivably large volumes of data now available have made theoretical models entirely superfluous" (AE 48). Anderson writes, "Google's founding philosophy is that we don't know why this page is better than that one: If the statistics of incoming links say it is, that's good enough. No semantic or causal analysis is required." Furthermore, data allow Google to "match ads to content without any knowledge or assumptions about the ads or the content." Data deal in patterns and correlations, promising an efficiency and accuracy that theory could never achieve. There is no need for hypotheses, seemingly no need even for analysis or interpretation (and here Anderson is far more hyperbolic than any scholar or even attentive student of data); all things cooperate in lockstep after the right algorithm has been deployed – or now, a decade and a half later, when the right prompt is given to the AI.

Against the widespread assumption of data's superiority and sufficiency, Han offers an emphatic theory. "Emphatic" thinking for Han stems from "a primary, primordial decision, which determines what counts and what does not – what *is* or *should* be, and what does not matter. As highly selective *narration*, it cuts a clearing of differentiation through untrodden terrain" (AE 49). In politics, for instance, where polling data have at times proven stubbornly resistant to transparency, data encourage politicians to watch, and game, the numbers that purportedly determine re-election rather than to deliberate and govern. Politicians often alternate between firing up the base and fearing their constituency, between imprudent rhetoric and extreme caution, with a constant eye on "likes" and polling numbers. With respect to public opinion polls, the situation is different but no better. As an informational tool, polls function cybernetically as an operational model or technical medium, one that, according to Baudrillard (1985), implies no end purpose or meaning, only the careful calibration, via feedback, of input–output, stimulus–response, encoding–decoding. In place of meaningful political participation, citizens enact a dream of communication. Han's emphasis on the theory of positive violence reveals us to be agitated spectators and servo-mechanisms heading for burnout.

Han's "*should be*" in the quotation above also suggests the blindness of data to questions of normativity, of what we *should do*. The algorithms curating social media content and ads are notoriously value blind in this regard (blind, that is, to any value that does not speak the language of efficiency and yield) and have contributed greatly to polarization. Anderson's vision of the end of theory is utopian. We cannot escape interpretation, and we cannot escape ethical discernment and judgment. That is, we cannot escape them if we want to escape the hell of the same. We might hear an echo in Han of Aristotle's claim in the *Poetics* that narrative lifts what is significant out of the flux of history. Theory lifts what is significant out of informational flows.

Han defends our need for theory further still. Theory relies on "an insight preceded by [transformative] *experience* [that] is capable of shaking up the status quo in its entirety and allowing something *wholly Other* to begin" (AE 51). It introduces the new and has a more robust sense of contingency and of what might be than a predictive model based on averages. As Abeba Birhane has argued, machine learning cannot bring us the "wholly Other" because it flattens out the ambiguity of *each* Other. It cannot "recognize that uncertainty, ambiguity, and fluidity, not static dichotomies, exemplify human beings and their interactions" (2021, p. 45). It identifies patterns and makes predictions based on this often stereotyped flattening out. Furthermore, we drown in a torrent of data that introduces its own, very different sort of ambiguity. Warring parties marshal their own data. Apart from emphatic thinking, data lend themselves to gridlock and inertia, to continual calculations and counting.

Unapologetically theoretical, Han thinks philosophers today must recover thinking that cuts new pathways through the deluge of data to make space for narrative, for our own *petits récits* rather than grand narrative (Lyotard, 1984, p. 60). Han insists that "Theory clarifies the world before it elucidates it" (AE 50). His theoretical interventions blaze through the world of digital bias in stark terms that make us rethink the absolute value of our own projects. Yet theory is not an end in itself for Han. *Theōria*, contemplative seeing, looks to renew philosophy and politics. Beyond theory, Han invites us to a world where things and others appear in their own light. To give the world a friendly look is to see ourselves in the light of what is so rather than to see the world in terms of our manifold tools, plans, and powers. Friendliness is both the promise of philosophical freedom, for Han, as well as the promise of freedom to others.

# 5

# *Duration: Finding Time*

## Steven Knepper

> As planet-bound animals, we live inside shortening and lengthening days; inside the weather, where certain flowers and scents come back, at least for now, to visit a year-older self. Sometimes time is not money but these things instead.
>
> Jenny Odell, *Saving Time*

### Whizzing Time and Contemplative Duration

There is no guardhouse to attack at the center of the digital panopticon because it is routed through each of our desires, goals, and habits. Resistance to psychopolitics, then, must begin in the psyche, in the soul. This chapter and the next turn from Han's critique of the digital control society to his proposed remedies. While responsive to contemporary challenges, these remedies draw upon perennial practices of contemplation. If the title *The Burnout Society* sums up the cause of our present malaise, then the title of the book Han published shortly before it, *The Scent of Time: A Philosophical Essay on the Art of Lingering*, suggests where a remedy may be found: in contemplation. He is not just offering us self-help through a few mindfulness practices, however, because his aim is to draw us out of self-enclosure in our projects altogether. Han returns to the roots of philosophy in contemplative *theōria* to counter the restless hyperactivity of the burnout society.

In Han's turn to contemplation, two major and complementary aims emerge: experiencing time as duration and encountering the

Other. Different modes of life allow us to achieve these aims: the friend, lover, artist, collector, listener, dweller, wanderer, gardener – the philosopher, as well. Crucially, these modes of life cannot be pursued instrumentally, in the spirit of the achievement subject, or else they will be counterfeited or at least compromised. Yoga and mindfulness meditation can be incorporated into the schedule of the highly regimented achievement subject. They may be offered by one's employer. They thus become a sort of contemplative band-aid or "hack" for increasing overall efficiency. Chase Padusniak (2018) likewise observes how "very often the prescription to stop, pause, and reflect comes from precisely the same culture of positivity that Han indicts. Mindfulness is popular with Silicon Valley, precisely because the system recognizes that its mandatory positivity burns people out." To avoid this, contemplative modes require a deep receptivity to and lingering with what is beyond the individual ego. But Han also presents contemplative practices as accessible. He is not a spiritual elitist recommending expensive retreats, weekly classes, or coaches. This chapter focuses on how contemplation allows one to linger attentively in the moment. The next focuses on how contemplation allows for a true encounter with the Other.

As noted in the previous two chapters, Han writes *The Scent of Time* before his turn to media theory. It thus downplays the role of technology in the sense of "whizzing," disorienting acceleration that marks contemporary experiences of time. But it also exposes another root cause that Han has never abandoned even as he gives technology far more attention. In *The Scent of Time*, he argues that time whizzes by for late-moderns because they no longer conceive time as having meaningful narrative patterns, with beginnings, transitions, tension, and endings.[1] Their time – *our* time – is instead empty "point-time," with one homogeneous second always ticking away to the next homogeneous second, one blank calendar square after another. This conception of time cannot provide, or at least rarely provides, the experience of time as rich, full duration. Han contrasts our digital-age "point-time," the time of late-, or post-, or hyper-modernity, with the mythic time of premodernity and the historical time of modernity (see also Flusser, 2002, pp. 117–24).

In mythic time, the gods "tell us about the way things and events are related to each other, and these narrated connections create sense." In mythic time, the world is an ordered, meaningful cosmos, so ordered and meaningful that "the world becomes readable, like a *picture*" (ST 12). Consider Achilles' shield in the *Iliad* as a mythic picture of the cosmos adorned with images of sea and land, war and peace, city and field, birth and death. The shield bears a microcosmic image of the embracing cosmological image of the epic itself, which in turn images a livable mythic world. Mythic time is marked by the "eternal return" of ritual, by pattern and type and analogy and symbol, which give time meaning and duration (ST 13; cf. Eliade, 1959).

Historical time does not fully displace mythic time until modernity.[2] In contrast to the eternal return of mythic time, historical time is always looking towards some future goal. It encourages restlessness, anticipation, and planning instead of attending to or enjoying the moment. Yet, even if it strains forward, historical time still has a structuring aim, albeit an "open-ended" one, namely the "progress of human reason" (ST 14, 15). This aim keeps modern subjects from feeling too disconcerted by accelerating time because time remains meaningful. Indeed, many welcome it: "Given the fact that the goal is in the future, the acceleration of the historical process now makes sense" to people (ST 16; cf. 29). When belief in progress falters, however, the perceived acceleration now tends to alarm and disconcert. When we begin questioning the worthwhileness of our collective projects, we undermine our fragile individual histories as well. The real temporal crisis thus begins when we are confronted with "a meaningless future," with the loss of an orienting goal that gives time structure and sense (ST 17). Han thinks this is the achievement subject's predicament.

Of course, Han (over-)generalizes here. The genealogy he offers at the beginning of *The Scent of Time* is painted in three broad, suggestive brushstrokes – mythic, historical, post-meaningful. He fills in detail across his other works. Many people still live, or try to live, in a religious temporality. Jewish and Christian narratives still at least residually shape Western societies. The Enlightenment optimism of progress-oriented "historical time" still has its advocates as well, such as Steven Pinker (2018) and Yuval Noah Harari (2017). Han notes how, in historical time, "technological progress is underpinned by a quasi-religious narrative which assigns it the function of accelerating the arrival of a future salvation" (ST 29). Such narratives of progress remain in play. They may even be having something of a renaissance today, over a decade after Han published *The Scent of Time*. A renewed sense of progress allows many to cheer on the latest from Silicon Valley even if it means addiction and total user information capture. Devotees of the singularity and digital immortality overtly fuse eschatology and technological progress. Here it is perhaps possible to say that belief in progress is not only like a messianic religion or residually shaped by it but actually becoming a new form of it. At the end of his recent work *The Palliative Society*, Han acknowledges that this transhumanist dream of tech-enabled immorality may even be realized in some form or another. The final words of his study offer an ominous warning in this regard. The "form" it takes is likely to shed not only the physical frailties but also the precious goods of human embodiment: "In order to survive, humans are abolishing themselves. They may succeed in becoming immortal, but only *at the expense of [human] life itself*" (PS 60).

More prevalent than the dream of digital immortality, however, is the hopeful promise, increasingly made through clenched teeth, that technology will save us from the worst of climate change, future pandemics, or resource depletion. This is not a grand hope for a technological utopia. It is a chastened hope that technology might just deliver us from dystopia. Indeed, there seems to be an increasing expectation that the future will be more or less dystopian, with screens and devices perhaps providing a new opiate for the masses. Ellul anticipated this future nearly seventy years ago, arguing that, in a pre-digital but increasingly post-industrial world, technology shaped preferences before it satisfied them: "It makes men happy in a milieu which normally would have made them unhappy, if they had not been worked on, molded, and formed for just that milieu" (1964, p. 348). This is the frank and unsettlingly upbeat vision of Tyler Cowen in *Average is Over* (2013), where the prominent libertarian economist imagines a world in which AI and attendant hyper-efficiencies render most workers redundant or superfluous, save for those, more servants than service workers, who cater to the whims of a productive cognitive elite of some 10 to 15 percent of the population. Cowen thinks that access to YouTube videos, games, and social media via cheap or publicly funded internet access, along with inexpensive food on the shelves of grocery stores, will keep the masses content – or at least content enough to prevent serious social upheaval. (We shall see if the era of cheap food continues.) Like Cowen, Han thinks we are already well on our way to this "form of rule," a digital age version of "bread and circuses" based around "universal basic income and computer games" (N 11; cf. EPI). However, for Han, as for Ellul before him, the prospect of a permanent and permanently distracted underclass is dystopian.

Increasingly, even the limited faith that technology will stave off the worst is shadowed by fear that technology is ushering in a future of surveillance and control, of addiction and isolation, that technology will render us redundant and then perhaps enslave or destroy us. This is pervasive in recent science fiction, which rarely shows the confident and calm *Star Trek* optimism of the mid-twentieth century. In a 2021 interview with Sergio C. Fanjul, for instance, Han meditates on the ultra-violent Korean television series *Squid Game*, which became a Netflix hit and offers a particularly dystopian spin on digital-age gamification. Han observes that "the characters are in debt and agree to play this deadly game that promises them huge winnings. *Squid Game* represents a central aspect of capitalism in an extreme form" (EPI). The first episode begins with the thrill of winning in games of skill and the get-rich-quick allure of games of chance, but it soon becomes clear that the "players" in the show, desperately or even hopelessly indebted, are driven by a lack of options rather than brash treasure hunting.

Other, older temporal orientations may continue to exist in our contemporary moment, but Han shows at a minimum how they cease to unify and orient developed societies. He also helps us understand that those who attempt to live out a different temporal narrative, individually or communally, do so under significant cross-pressures, with a strong sense of contingency, and often at best in a fragmented fashion. Han suggests, for instance, that those who hold to a narrative in a fanatical or fundamentalist fashion, whether it be religious or political or conspiratorial, often do so at least in part as a response to broader narrative loss. Conspiracy theories become remedial "*micro-narratives*," embraced as "*resources that provide identity and meaning*" (I 51). Extremism can come from a desperate search for stable meaning in a time of inundating dispersion.

Other factors contributed to the contemporary experience of "temporal dispersal." Han highlights modernity's privileging of action over contemplation, which is unsurprisingly pronounced in a time of future-oriented projects. He traces this privileging in a second genealogy at the end of *The Scent of Time*. Revisiting Max Weber's classic thesis about the Protestant work ethic, Han holds that Calvinists privileged work while denigrating the classical and medieval emphasis on contemplation, shaping modernity down to the present day (Weber, 1958).[3] Han notes, for instance, the double meanings of "industry" and "industrial," as both productive individual activity and a form of (non-artisanal) production (ST 91). Yet he also holds that the "inner-worldly asceticism of

Protestantism" retained important checks on emerging capitalism that were eventually removed (ST 89). Hence, as the Sabbath gradually loses its cultural grip, the weekend becomes merely a recuperation for renewed productive effort. As Protestant mores such as thrift, temperance, and simplicity give way, consumption swells alongside the emphasis on work. This deepens the temporal crisis since "the compulsion to consume does away with duration" (ST 93).

## The Ruins and the Incense Clock

Han largely agrees, then, with the diagnosis of the French philosopher Jean-François Lyotard (1984, 1991), who in the late twentieth century famously sounded the death knell of *grands reçits*, of structuring "metanarratives" and the meaning they offered in our emerging "postmodern condition." Han points out that Lyotard was no nihilist.[4] Lyotard in his own way was concerned with renewing our relationship to time. He hoped that the collapse of metanarratives – particularly the metanarrative of technocratic, rationalist progress – would free up time, being, and perception, that it would clear space for the arrival of "events" we would not ordinarily see due to how narrative blinders shape our view of past, future, and present. And he thought the collapse of grand narratives would thus open the possibility of a "turn towards *being*," towards a sort of deep immediacy. Lyotard, in Han's paraphrase, holds that, "when meaning retreats in the course of de-narrativization, being announces itself" (ST 50). He claims that amidst the ruins of the grand narratives we might newly, emphatically encounter being in its sublime *thereness*. We might recover an intensive relationship with being.

Yet, after a sympathetic exposition, Han ultimately concludes that Lyotard is too blithe. Even if Lyotard is no nihilist, there is nonetheless a "nihilistic dimension" to his account in that "the intervals between events are death zones. During these eventless in-between times, the soul falls into lethargy" (ST 53). Lyotard makes important points, ones which Han develops in his own key and to which we shall return in the discussion of beauty and the sublime in the next chapter. But the sublime event, according to Han, is not enough to recover duration amidst empty time. We need not only an openness to the exceptional but also a contemplative lingering that brings duration to the seemingly quotidian. Han suggests that

Western philosophy can learn much from Taoism and Buddhism in this regard. Writing of the ever-shifting but continuous "way" of the Tao, he concludes, "Ruptures or revolutions, however, are alien to the Chinese awareness of time. This is why Chinese thought does not appreciate *ruins*. It does not recognize the kind of identity that is based on a unique event" (S 3). This passage could be a response to Lyotard's emphasis on the sublime event.

The title of Han's book *The Scent of Time: A Philosophical Essay on the Art of Lingering* evokes how a scent, perhaps a candle or perfume, fills whatever space it is in, how it lingers in the air. A noise or a sight can sound or flash instantaneously, but a smell has duration. Contemplative lingering can thus give time a "scent" even in the absence of narrative frameworks that structure time. Han often uses "scent" as a metaphor for this experience of contemplative duration, but, in a lyrical chapter at the heart of the study, he explores the literal possibilities of "scent" as well. He describes the *hsiang yin*, the Chinese incense clock, in which "a template, which often includes written characters, is filled with pulverized incense" (ST 56). The patterned incense slowly burns out. Such a clock may measure time, but it does not count seconds and minutes. There is instead duration. Han notes a difference even from water clocks or sand-filled hourglasses: "Fragrant time does not flow or trickle away" (ST 57). The consumed incense, still tracing out its sign, lingers as ash. Han also observes the link between the incense clock and poetry, noting the template's sign and the poetic words that often adorn the box of the clock.

Han quotes lines from several poems about incense clocks. This is fitting since poetry is another contemplative practice, one that invites us to linger with the words, to savor the resonances of metaphors. A poem is meant to be read and re-read, meditating on the resonances between its words, the way its words resonate with each other, the way it spreads beyond itself via connotations and metaphorical connections. Poetic metaphor, like the burning incense, establishes rich, at times surprising, resonances between things. Both allow us to contemplatively linger within time.

## Dwelling (Nowhere)

Han claims that Lyotard's account of the post-narrative Event "altogether lacks the *space for dwelling*" (ST 54). "Dwelling" is, of course, a keyword for the late Heidegger, who returns as Han's main interlocutor in the middle chapters of *The Scent of Time*. In the late Heidegger, duration and the possibility of dwelling come from a renewed relationship with what is primordially given, the cyclical "facticity" of night, day, and the seasons. In a way, the late Heidegger calls us back to the realities upon which mythic narratives build. In touch with these primordial realities, Heidegger thinks we can dwell again as "mortals" with the "earth," "sky," and "divinities" (see Heidegger, 1975, 145–61). We can accept the vulnerability of being-in-the-world, of being among things in their radiance and never-fully-graspable mystery, rather than seeking to turn the world into a "standing reserve" for our endless death-dealing and death-denying projects. This is the late Heidegger's contemplative "releasement" that lets things be (see Heidegger, 1966).

A central image for this Heidegger is the path he walks while living as a peasant-philosopher in his cottage in Germany's Black Forest. On this path he enters the natural world. He sinks into the rhythms of the days and seasons: "The pathway represents a clearly delineated world of duration with its own natural oscillation" (ST 67). The rhythm of walking the pathway, the rhythm of dwelling with the primordial realities, is one of repetition with often subtle variation: "Again and again, Heidegger uses the trope of the 'back and forth' as a counter-trope to historical time. In the movement of the back-and-forth, time comes to stand still [*zum Stehen*], so to speak" (ST 66). Here we are clearly closer to cyclical, mythic time, with its ordered cosmos and continual returns. With his evocation of the providing "divinities," Heidegger perhaps reaches the threshold of myth. Yet Han claims that Heidegger does not fully cross this threshold (H 83). He writes: "As a place for contemplative lingering, the path symbolizes a dwelling that does not need a goal or purpose, one that can do without a theology or teleology" (ST 67). Hence Heidegger evokes his own possibilities for restoring duration after the loss of overarching narratives, one that awaits the revelatory event but also achieves duration via "releasement" on the Black Forest path.

The Heideggerian notion of dwelling resonates with Han. It pervades many of his writings. One story he tells about his life as a thinker begins with the sky. In a 2017 editorial written in response to rising xenophobia in Germany, Han explains why he abandoned his technical studies in Korea and moved to Germany to study philosophy. He claims that he simply found the sky "too beautiful" not to be a contemplative philosopher (CDD 65). Han would write his dissertation at Freiburg on mood [*Stimmung*] in Heidegger's thought, and it is hard not to hear an echo, or anticipation, of the late Heidegger in Han's comment about the beautiful sky. In "Building Dwelling Thinking," Heidegger writes that mortals live under the sky – sun, moon, stars, weather, seasons – but do not tend the heavens as they do the earth. "Mortals dwell in that they receive the sky as sky," he writes in his late poetic way. "They leave to the sun and moon their journey … they do not turn night into day nor day into a harassed unrest" (1975, p. 150; cf. HH). The sky is for contemplating. It gives ruminators the gift of duration. And, indeed, Han's instances of contemplation and duration are often drawn from the natural world. Stars are particularly prominent throughout his writings. Still, the earth is prominent as well. In 2018, Han published a strikingly personal meditation on gardening, *Lob der Erde*, which testifies to how he seeks to dwell.

Chapter 2 discussed how the poetic musings of the late Heidegger can be read as an evasion of political responsibility. The late Heidegger might also seem preciously impractical in his quaint evocations of peasant life and cottages and pathways that wend through the countryside. "There can be no doubt," Han acknowledges, "that the later Heidegger invokes the return of conditions of the archaic and premodern world through their romantic transfiguration, conditions whose overcoming has meant essential progress for mankind" (ST 76). Han thinks that the most important lessons of the late Heidegger, however, are not tied to his Black Forest cottage life. He is interested in the contemplative moods that Heidegger's pathway encourages. It allows for pauses, for "contemplative lingering," for silence and slowness and unexpected encounters, for a more poetic attunement to being. This, too, has been frequently dismissed as mysticism or obscurantism, especially by hardnosed philosophers looking for propositions and carefully laid out arguments. But Heidegger's aim, Han would say, is to evoke contemplative moods that widen the notion of truth beyond the proposition and the concept, beyond a notion wherein truth is *our* correlating determination. His intention is to call forth the more basic truth of the way being "unconceals" itself to receptive attention.

Such contemplative lingering has the potential to bring duration and a closer relationship to any environs, whether the countryside or the city. In *Lob der Erde*, for instance, Han tends a small flower garden in Berlin, one where he especially cultivates winter-blooming plants – perhaps symbolizing the possibility of contemplative dwelling and duration even amongst the "winter" of contemporary alienation. He notes how this gardening transformed his sense of time, giving it the shape of the seasons and the cycles of planting, tending, weeding, etc. What is more, since each plant has its own temporality, blooming at different moments and for different lengths of time, the garden offered a richly variegated experience of duration. Denise Levertov (1999, pp. 11–12), in her poem "The Métier of Blossoming," observes an Amaryllis closely, wondering at each unfolding blossom, and wondering too at what it would be like "If humans could be / that intensely whole, undistracted, unhurried." Jenny Odell points in the same direction in *Saving Time* (2023): "As planet-bound animals, we live inside shortening and lengthening days; inside the weather, where certain flowers and scents come back, at least for now, to visit a year-older self. Sometimes time is not money but these things instead" (p. xv). Similar sentiments abound in Han's *Lob der Erde*.

Han also brings dwelling out of the Black Forest in his early writings on Zen Buddhism. He claims that Heidegger is more a thinker of essence than of Buddhist emptiness (A 4). The latter allows for dwelling anywhere or, to be more precise, a "dwelling nowhere" (PZB 61). Han points to the wandering of Bashō, which does not follow a specific circuit through the countryside: "Bashō might also have said 'poetically man dwells.' For him, dwelling poetically would mean dwelling nowhere, like drifting clouds, *in every place sojourning* as a guest of the world, which is a guest house" (PZB 59). Bashō's wanderings are not a quest for a lost treasure or for a particular person. He does not seek out a special destination or a particular goal. Han contrasts him in this regard with great wanderers of the West and the Near East: Odysseus seeks a homecoming, a return after long decades of war and wandering to the Ithaca he left long ago; Abraham and Moses seek a "promised home." None of them are wanderers in the sense of Bashō, whose wandering "is without future. Bashō's wandering is *in the moment*; it rests in the presence of each moment. His wandering is free of any teleological or theological meaning" (PZB 64). This allows it to be a wandering that "dwells in every instant" (A 17).[5]

## *Vita Contemplativa* and Not-To

In chapter 2, we saw how Han critiques Heidegger for not seeing the *friendly* possibilities for releasement in boredom. Profound boredom and profound tiredness, two forms of "primordial ontological passivity," recur throughout Han's writings as starting points (VC 36). He calls us to Handke's "ultimate tiredness" that is "the best action" because it is a "beginning," and sets us on our way in freedom (Handke, 1994, p. 37). Han is not defending laziness or inactivity for its own sake but is, rather, attracted to the affordances in a receptive tiredness for beginnings, for what Arendt calls natality, for escaping predeterminations and preoccupations to think and to make new things (MCS 18:55; cf. Valls Boix, 2022).

It is important to differentiate this sort of original ontological passivity from three other forms of passivity in Han. First, it has nothing to do with compulsive hyperactivity. Han writes, "Paradoxically, hyperactivity represents an extremely passive form of doing, which bars the possibility of free action" because it cannot help but respond to every stimulus (BS 24). Second, it has nothing to do with burnout. Han explains, "No-longer-being-able-to-be-able leads to destructive self-reproach and auto-aggression" (BS 11). Depressive exhaustion is not completely passive, for Han, because there is this element of self-hatred or sense of heaviness amidst the burdens of life. Third, it is not the complete passivity of blank inertness. Han does not beckon us to an oblivious stupor on the couch in front of the television after a long workday. Unlike profound boredom and tiredness, these forms are not rich with creative possibilities for new beginnings, for freedom.

We must learn to be receptive to boredom and tiredness when they are bestowed upon us. It takes a certain discipline to embrace them. For instance, achievement subjects are likely to feel anxious and guilty over their boredom, inactivity, and tiredness. Han urges us to an askesis of this anxiety that will allow us to embrace these moods and the rich passivity they bestow. He shows that they are beginnings because they give us the contemplative freedom to linger. *Deep* boredom and *deep* tiredness have the depth for contemplation. They can give rise to contemplation. Yet contemplation proper is more disciplined than these basic moods from which it can emerge. Contemplation is both patient receptivity and disciplined attention: "It enables spirit to engage in still, contemplative lingering, that is, deep attentiveness" (N 82). Contemplation can even be strenuous, since it calls for a discipline of "not-to," a "negative potency" (BS 24; cf. N 76–85). "In Zen meditation," Han points out, "one attempts to achieve the pure negativity of not-to – that is, the void – by freeing oneself from rushing, intrusive Something" (BS 24). Contemplation calls for the capacity to resist certain stimuli. It involves the ability not to be waylaid by distracted thoughts or urges. This includes the restless itch to pull out one's smartphone. Contemplation involves the ability *not* to attend to some things in order to attend to others.

Contemplation can take many forms. Contemplative attention can be broadly focused, such as when one sits patiently at a wood line throughout the evening to observe wildlife. It can be narrowly focused, such as when one paints a still-life or reads a book on a bench at a busy bus stop (M 12:15). Han recognizes that contemplation has never been easy. As we discussed in chapter 1, Han is in a long line of thinkers who see restlessness as a defining mark of modernity. He acknowledges this and draws on many of these thinkers, but he also holds that the constant distractions and allurements of the digital age greatly intensify the issue. Ads and screens spread across surfaces like mold in a moist environment, filling airports and restaurants, appearing on gas pumps and even above urinals: "The world is polluted not only by excretions and material waste but also by junk communication and information. It is plastered with advertisements" (N 80). Smartphones and social media are, like digitally revamped slot machines, addictive by design and use self-refining algorithms to lure deeper into addiction (see Crawford, 2015, pp. 89–112). In this world of commodified and relentlessly pursued attention, contemplation becomes a mode of resistance, a way to fortify ourselves against the intrusions that new power structures make into our attention.[6]

Contemplation is crucial for art, philosophy, and politics. It gives one the thinking space to parse out what matters and to discover unexpected connections. It gives thought time to mature. Many philosophers, poets, mathematicians, and scientists have been ardent walkers. Han also notes how contemplative repose can lead to a deep sleep of fecund dreams, another possible source of inspiration or insight. While most philosophers champion a vigilant wakefulness against numb, oblivious slumber, Han is one of the few who champion the generativity of restful sleep. He juxtaposes such sleep against an anxious, restless insomnia on the one hand and an instrumentalized "power nap" on the other, both of which are common in achievement-cum-burnout society and neither of which allows for a deep visit to the "true internal world" of dreams. Han turns to Marcel Proust, who meditates on how both dreams and waking contemplation allow unbidden memories to resurface in epiphanic fashion (VC 9). Such sleep, like profound boredom, is a state of deep relaxation ready to receive such gifts. Contemplative silence, Han holds, "enables us to say something *unheard of*" (VC

# Finding Time

18; cf. Picard, 1988). In contrast with frenetic activity in which one continually reacts, contemplation prepares one to act decisively (VC 2).

In this regard, action needs contemplation. Han sees this as a central insight of premodern Christianity, which elevates the *vita contemplativa* over the *vita activa* but not in a way that spurns action.[7] Contemplation of God may be the highest vocation of humanity, but it also prepares one to act more purposefully and to serve less egotistically. Han points to the motto of the Benedictine monks, *ora et labora*, pray and work, and he frequently quotes Gregory the Great:

> Be aware: while a good plan for life requires that one moves from the active to the contemplative life, it is often useful if the soul returns from the contemplative to the active life, in such a way that the flame of contemplation which has been lit in the heart passes on all its perfection to activity. Thus, active life must lead us to contemplation, but contemplation must set out from what we inwardly considered and call us back to activity. (Quoted in ST 111; cf. BS 55, VC 84)

Contemplation makes it possible to act at the right time, in the right way, for the right reasons. Contemplation makes action responsible. It allows us to *respond* rather than react and to attend to others rather than to automatically advance our own projects.

Han defends premodern contemplative traditions and practices against Arendt (see BS 16–20; ST 101–10; VC 60–85). In *The Human Condition* (1958), she criticizes the medieval emphasis on contemplation and an otherworldly fixation on the afterlife, both of which leave consideration of the *vita activa* undeveloped. Arendt instead wants to recover "heroic actionism" (BS 16). But Han insists that Arendt neglects the necessity – recognized in the Christian tradition – for contemplation to infuse action with deeper purpose. Without contemplation, decisive action often dissipates into merely reactive activity.

While Arendt critiques the Christian emphasis on contemplation, she simply elides it from her preferred Greek polis. She recognizes that the medieval Christian tradition draws upon and reworks the classical emphasis on contemplation, but she claims it does so in a way that loses the decisive place of the *polis*. Yet Arendt's antiquity is one without either *theōria*, the engaged contemplation of the sacred festivities, or *temenos*, the sanctuaries, shrines, and temples: "There are no divine festivals in Arendt's *polis*. Festivals, rituals and games have no place in her thought, which is dominated by the *pathos* of action" (VC 64). Therefore, Han charges Arendt with missing the political lesson of Plato's *Apology*. The *polis* may need a daimonion-guided gadfly given to contemplative reveries and drinking parties to save it from complacency and corruption, to speak truths that it does not want to hear. Arendt rightly distinguishes between the frenetic, routinized activity of *animal laborans* and true action, but Han contests her genealogical claim that *animal laborans* emerges when modernity inverts the medieval hierarchy of contemplation and a hollowed-out action (see Arendt, 1958, pp. 313–21). Han claims instead that *animal laborans* emerges with the loss of contemplation-inspired, purposeful action. Arendt's *The Human Condition* ends with a counterintuitive claim (via the elder Cato) that thinking is actually "the most active of all human activities" (VC 84; cf. BS 20; Arendt, 1958, pp. 324–5). Han is unconvinced by this attempt to align thinking and the *vita activa*. Hence, Arendt "inadvertently closes her book on the *vita activa* by praising the *vita contemplativa*" (VC 84). Arendt needs contemplation to secure the kind of action she champions.

An interesting contrast can also be drawn between Han's turn to contemplative practices and the turn to practices in Peter Sloterdijk's *You Must Change Your Life* (2013). Both stress the importance of recovering practices to address contemporary ills. They do so, however, in very different ways. Sloterdijk follows his Nietzsche, who is far more active than Han's. Sloterdijk calls for a renewed spirit of the Greek gymnasium, an athletic-spiritual practice of self-transformation in the pursuit of excellence. His title comes from Rainer Maria Rilke's "Archaic Torso of Apollo," and this is the interpretation that he gives to the statue's famous injunction at the end of the sonnet: "Hear the voice from the stone, do not resist the call to get in shape! Seize the chance to train with a god!" (2013, p. 28). Sloterdijk exhorts his readers to heed this call, to commit themselves to rigorous practice.

Contemplation is not a major concern of Sloterdijk's study. He tends to recast contemplative or meditative practices in terms of athletic training. Writing of Buddhism, for instance, he claims: "Verbal paradoxes are all projections of the basic ascetic paradox whereby one conveys to the adept the message that there is 'nothing to attain' – but that to understand this, they must first of all sit in meditation for ten years, ideally for fourteen hours a day" (2013, pp. 283–4). Ultimately, Sloterdijk does not see much of a future for the traditional practices of the world religions, claiming that, "for a contemporary philosophical psychology, the only path that remains is the middle one, equidistant from the Hindu[/Platonist/Christian] and Buddhist over-non-animation; it would therefore advise neither a leap into being nor a leap into nothingness. Instead of promoting self-sacrifice on one side or the other, it argues for the connection between effort and self-experience" (2013, p. 285). Sloterdijk likely sees Han's turn to practices as too passive and not sufficiently athletic. Han, for his part, might see Sloterdijk as skirting close to a spiritualization of the achievement subject.

## Stabilizing Things

Things can also help us dwell. Heidegger's famous example is a jug, formed of the earth's clay, holding either water that has fallen from the sky or wine pressed from grapes. It is central to the daily meal as a serving pitcher or as a sacral vessel with which to pour a libation to the gods. Heidegger's jug gathers the "four-fold" and thus gathers us in dwelling: "In the gift of the outpouring earth and sky, divinities and mortals dwell together all at once" (Heidegger, 1975, p. 173). Once more, Han draws lessons from Heidegger's hut and then leaves the Black Forest.

If Han rejects Arendt's critique of the *vita contemplativa*, he ultimately takes his bearings from her more than Heidegger with respect to things. In *The Human Condition*, Arendt discusses "durable" things that we "use" repeatedly rather than "consume" for our daily needs. Such things "have the function of stabilizing human life, and their objectivity lies in the fact that – in contradiction to the Heraclitean saying that the same man can never enter the same stream – men, their ever-changing nature notwithstanding, can retrieve their sameness, that is, their identity, by being related to the same chair and the same table" (1958, p. 137). Things prevent our dispersion over time, a point Han makes in *The Scent of Time*: "The human being can linger on things because things *make* the world relations *linger*." He gives a kind of Arendtian spin to Heidegger's jug, underscoring how it "is a con*tainer*" from which "*nothing trickles or flows away*." This makes it "a place for contemplative lingering" (ST 71).

Arendt's stabilizing thing is brought to the fore in Han's *Non-Things*, originally published in 2021, in which Han gives this insight its fullest development yet in his writings. Arendt's preferred examples of things are a table and chair rather than a jug. The table in our home gives us stability amidst daily vicissitudes and the daily grind. It usually does so without our conscious awareness. It nonetheless plays an important role. The table gathers us in a literal sense when we sit at it to eat or converse or read, but it also gathers us out of the dispersals of time and subjectivity.[8] The great Chilean poet Pablo Neruda's "odes to common things," such as an Arendtian table and chair, a bed, a pair of scissors, a guitar, often bring this gathering, grounding durability to view. Neruda's odes stir a sense of wonder at how we have neglected the crucial roles "common things" play in life. In his poem on the guitar, for instance, its hollow form becomes a sky full of stars. It holds within it past joys and pains, the memories of wedding celebrations and kisses and goodbyes and loneliness (Neruda, 2017, pp. 313–15).

Though perhaps humbler and more ubiquitous gatherings than the solemnities of Heidegger's fourfold, common things are worthy of reflection. Neruda's odes attest to this, and Han agrees. In the documentary *Müdigkeitsgesellschaft*, Han visits a claustrophobic "junk shop" in Berlin. He claims the junk store is a kind of stronghold, resisting, and presumably under siege from, "consumer culture" (M 9:15–10:30). The cluttered shop rescues things from the landfill or the incinerator. The visitor to the shop can do the same by rescuing, say, a jewelry box from the usual consumerist cycle of purchasing novelty and then quickly disposing of it. The rescued thing can rescue in return. It can become a durable, stabilizing companion in one's life (N 15–17).

One can imagine Heidegger at a rural market or fair, but it is hard to imagine him in a crowded Berlin junk store (or the Goodwill shop on the outskirts of your average American town). Again, Han is closer to Arendt in considering the wide range – indeed the ubiquity – of stabilizing things. All three do recognize a difference, however, in the things produced by an artisan rather than by mass production. Heidegger and Arendt would both nod in agreement with Han's claim that "beautiful crafted things warm the heart. The *warmth of the hands* is passed on to the things" (N 51). In "The Question Concerning Technology," Heidegger returns us to Aristotle's four causes to describe a silversmith who "gathers together" everything that is "responsible" for a silver sacrificial vessel. He is not simply a maker, but a receiver. Heidegger argues that it is "thanks to" the silver, thanks to "chaliceness," and thanks to "the realm of consecration and bestowal" (the *temenos*?), and finally thanks to the silversmith himself that the silver chalice comes to be a sacrificial vessel (2013b, pp. 8–9). We might consider humbler kin to Heidegger's jug and silver sacrificial vessel: a coffee mug turned on a potter's wheel, a unique mug unlike any other in that both the potter's craft and slipups, its making's intricacies and peculiarities, are all there in the glazed clay. The mug reflects the potter's close attention to the practicalities of daily use: the right heft and balance, a stable pedestal on the bottom, perhaps a thumb grip on the handle if it is a large mug. But it also reflects an aesthetic imagination: an image of an owl, tree, leaf, spider's web, or child perhaps adorns the mug. Use and adornment thus unite. The potter's initials carved into the bottom give it a sense of history, of originating from someone, somewhere. There is a warmth here that does not radiate from a mass-produced mug or a disposable service-station coffee cup. Handwork, for Han and Heidegger, is thinking in a deeply receptive, contemplative sense (N 66). Potters do not just assert their designs for mugs upon the matter of clay. The relationship is warmer because the potter cooperates with the earth in the making of the mug.

Extreme danger and disorientation can reveal the stabilizing power of things. Consider the title story of Tim O'Brien's *The Things They Carried*, where American soldiers during the Vietnam War carry mementos from home. These are more or less successful attempts to prevent a sense of dispersal during seemingly directionless missions within a seemingly directionless war often amidst deep jungle. One soldier, Dobbins, winds "his girlfriend's pantyhose … around his neck as a comforter" (2017, p. 24; cf. pp. 163–5). He thinks they grant him charmed protection, but the image of them wound around his neck also suggests they hold him together, that they prevent dispersal. Kiowa, another soldier, carries a Bible, gifted by his father. At one point, Kiowa lays down on the open Bible as a sort of pillow so he can smell it. This underscores the stabilizing power of its tangible thinghood, "the leather and ink and paper and glue, whatever the chemicals were" (ibid., p. 36). O'Brien often emphasizes the soldiers' sensory experience of their treasured things' materiality throughout the story – smells, textures, tastes.

Mass-produced goods, Han claims, are harder to bond with in a lasting way than artisan goods. The potter's mug is discretely unique, but it is also "discreet." It has a certain reserve and at the same time a certain receptivity to relationship. This allows us to form "intensive libidinal ties" to it as we use it day after day, at times without much thought, at times while contemplating it. The mug can thus become "close to the heart." A mass-produced mug, on the other hand, will likely be emblazoned with ads, logos, jokes, or scenes from a recent movie. Perhaps it is a designer mug from the latest seasonal line. Regardless, "today's consumer goods" tend to be "indiscreet, intrusive and over-expressive. They come loaded with prefabricated ideas and emotions that impose themselves on the consumer. Hardly anything of the consumer's life enters into them" (N 15). Still, this is not a blanket condemnation of mass production. One can easily imagine a mass-produced mug given as a gift that is treasured over time and held close to the heart. Indeed, Han does not categorically condemn them at all. Recall once more his interest in the Berlin junk store. Here he turns from Heidegger and Arendt to the aphoristic curios of the philosopher Walter Benjamin, who held that the "collector" perusing the stalls and shops of the Parisian Arcades has the power to free things "from the drudgery of being useful," to allow the fleeting commodity to become a beloved thing preserved in a collection (1999, p. 19; cf. pp. 203–11).

Perhaps unsurprisingly, one of Han's most prominent examples of a thing close to his heart is a mass-produced object, one that is close to the heart of modernity itself. It is the physical book, well-thumbed and annotated. The book-collecting Benjamin (2007) is again an influence. Han recalls an important book from his youth:

> Among all the books of philosophy on my bookshelves stands a book by Paul G. Shewmon, *Transformations in Metals*. It is the last book I read before I decided to drop metallurgy for philosophy. I keep it as a memento. Had I read it as an e-book, I would own one less thing that is close to my heart, that I can pick up again to remind myself of past times. Things make time graspable … The book's yellowed pages and its smell warm my heart. (N 95; cf. M 35:57–36:25)

Returning to a book that one has read before can be an uncanny encounter with one's earlier, at times quite different, self, but the physical book can also provide a sense of continuity, bridging memories of when and where one read the book before with when and where one is now. Layered marginal annotations inscribe this continuity in the book itself.

Han's concern with physical books versus e-books hints at his general concern, examined in chapter 4, that digitization and "smart technology" are ushering in an age of "non-things." The speedy cycles of a throw-away society already work against the stabilizing power of things. But the intangible ephemerality of e-books and digital media erases it altogether. Han contrasts the familiar teddy bear or doll as "transitional objects," which help children develop a sense of their own and others' durability and encourage a nascent sense of relationality, with the digital babysitting of a smartphone or tablet that displays ever-shifting content (N 25–7). He also points to how smart devices continually bombard us with shifting information that destabilizes rather than stabilizes. Things saturated with information become "non-things." The traditional watch may not invite lingering like an incense clock, but it is relatively unobtrusive and can be a companion for years. It can be an heirloom. The smartwatch, on the other hand, floods us with information and quickly goes out of date.

Smart technology also undermines agency and responsibility: "In a smart home, we are not autonomous conductors. Instead, we are *conducted* by various actors, even invisible actors that dictate the rhythm" (N 5). Han points to Matthew Crawford's interpretation of the children's show *Mickey Mouse Clubhouse*, where the clubhouse is always ready to smooth out any difficulty that arises for Mickey and his friends: "The Handy Dandy machine has a ready solution for every problem" (N 47; cf. Crawford, 2015, pp. 70–3). Smart things continually surveil, gathering information that feeds "personalized" algorithms that in turn routinize, even manipulate, the "user's" behaviors more thoroughly. "Things do not spy on us," Han states (N 23). Non-things do so by design.

The final chapter of *Non-Things* offers a lyrical homage to another mass-produced thing that warms Han's heart: a jukebox. He recalls happening upon a small Berlin shop selling jukeboxes. (Again, Han suggests this is a store for collectors rather than consumers.) The shop becomes a portal into an enchanted "fairy-tale world of wonderful things," one in which "things ... shone with an alien beauty" (N 86). He ends up buying one for his apartment. It shares a room with Han's grand piano. At night, Han listens to its music in a room darkened except for the jukebox's lights. His early studies in metallurgy and interest in gadgets contribute to his love for the chrome-plated, mechanical jukebox. He loves its whirs and hums and brushing sounds. He loves its materiality: "In the course of digitalization, we have lost any awareness of materiality" (N 96). Note the implied friendliness between the "high culture" of the grand piano and the "low culture" of the jukebox, how both can act as paradigmatic things, how both are remarkable pieces of technology. The jukebox is very far indeed from Heidegger's jug: "I can follow Heidegger's critique of technology only up to a certain point. Heidegger would certainly not have wanted to include the jukebox in his collection of things" (N 93).

## Restlessness and Ritual

As we have seen, *The Scent of Time* tries to recover contemplative lingering without insisting upon a return to narrative moorings. Han acknowledges concerns that narratives can obscure and limit (ST 51). Even in that study, though, Han continually notes the affordances of narratives and the consequences of their loss. Narratives afford temporal shape and tension. In seeking duration without narrative, *The Scent of Time* addresses itself to a time when narratives have collapsed, a time of narrative dearth. Han may also think that the recovery of contemplation should precede the recovery or development of narratives. Narratives without contemplation could easily become another project of the achievement subject, pseudo-, or counterfeit narratives that do not bring duration, narratives that are acted out online rather than lived out.

Regardless, it is clear in later works that Han thinks that narrative remains necessary even in an age of narrative collapse. In *The Disappearance of Rituals*, originally published in 2019, Han considers how rituals stabilize time via repetition, duration, and closure. Liturgies and festivals give narrative shape to the year. Rites of passage give narrative shape to a life. Han calls rituals *"symbolic techniques of making oneself at home in the world … They are to time what a home is to space: they render time habitable"* (DR 2). In some chapters, Han attends to living ritual traditions, such as the Japanese tea ceremony, the Jewish Shabbat, and the Catholic Mass.[9] In others, he draws examples from the past.

In a brief "Preliminary Remark," Han claims that his study "is not animated by a desire to return to ritual. Rather, rituals serve as a background against which our present times may be seen to stand out more clearly" (DR vi). Much of Han's study, then, is diagnostic. It is structured around trenchant oppositions of ritual and post-ritual existence. Han notes the "symbolic perception" of rituals, where deep, sustained attention is given to inexhaustible symbols (DR 2). One might think of meditation on or veneration of statues and icons in Buddhism, Hinduism, and traditional Christianity. Sacred texts are also the sites of symbolic perception, of intensive reading, re-reading, and meditation (SB 30). Han juxtaposes such deep perception with the rampant "serial perception" of today, which is defined by "shallow attention" and "is incapable of producing the experience of duration." We swipe from image to image. We give way to *"comatose viewing"* as episode leads on to auto-played episode (DR 7).

Han also juxtaposes ritualized repetition with routine. "Repetition," he claims, "stabilizes and deepens attention" (DR 8). It allows for deepening intensity, for bridges between past and present, for duration. Contemporary society, however, is marked by a chronic itch for the new. One continually wants new clothes, new things, new experiences. Acquiring them offers only momentary satiation. The itch for novelty quickly returns. Without "fulfilling repetition," we can only scratch the itch and make it worse (DR 10).

While Han's bracing oppositions often rightly preserve the qualitative chasms between such experiences, at other times they seem overdrawn. Most notably, Han frequently reduces concern with inwardness to self-absorption. He is perhaps at his most "postmodern" here, wary of the inward turn as a step towards the modern self. Yet premodern thinkers often conceive of inwardness in ways that explicitly counter narcissistic self-enclosure. Consider Augustine. Praised by some scholars and castigated by others for "inventing" the modern self, Augustine also describes sin as "man ... turned toward himself" – *inclinatus ad se ipsum* (1998, p. 609). Yet there is an inwardness that is not closed off in this way, an inwardness that is not self-enfolded but receptive. Augustine discovers an inner opening to God in prayer. His conception of inwardness is thus far removed from the static, sealed self of modernity. This inward turn in prayer ultimately opens one to others. It plays out according to the dynamic of *vita contemplativa* and *vita activa* that Han, as we have seen, endorses. Judaism, Christianity, Islam, Hinduism, Buddhism – all offer nuanced practices of inward askesis (Flood, 2013). Many of these are ritual practices. Han seems more attuned to the possibilities of a porous inwardness in other volumes, and there are passages in *The Disappearance of Rituals* that suggest a suppler dynamic in how, for instance, rituals shape communal feelings (DR 11–13). By and large, though, Han focuses on pernicious interiority. He is not wrong to warn against navel-gazing, but perhaps we need ritual both to draw us out of ourselves and to rediscover inwardness beyond the ego.

Han returns in *The Disappearance of Rituals* to distinctions introduced in earlier works between ritual "sites" and tourist "sights," between "cult value" and "exhibition value" (S 60–9). Ritual sites are places of deep attention and duration that draw people together as a community. Tourist "sights" are meant to be consumptively visited, viewed, and left behind. Han contrasts the temple and the museum in this regard (DR 45). He notes contemporary economic pressures to turn ritual sites into tourist "sights," to allow "exhibition value" to displace "cult value." In *Shanzhai*, Han points to the Shinto Ise Shrine in Japan. He notes how, for much of the shrine's long history, its old treasures were ritually destroyed when a new set was fashioned. Now, though, the old set is kept and "put on display in a museum" so that tourists can get a close look at them in "exhibit." The old treasures "owe their rescue to their increased exhibition value," Han notes. "However, their destruction belongs to their cult value itself, which is clearly disappearing more and more in favor of their museum exhibition value" (S 62). In short, maintaining the old set for display drains them of cultic value and, arguably, relativizes the new set that remains in cultic use. Consider likewise the pressures not only to restore but to "modernize" the Cathedral of Notre-Dame after its partial destruction by fire in 2019, to give it more exhibition value and make it more tourist "friendly."

In *Shanzhai*, Han's point about ritual sites is part of a broader attempt to unsettle Western, post-Renaissance notions of artistic "originals" (S 10–31). He does so by juxtaposing them against some Eastern conceptions wherein a highly accomplished reconstruction of an ancient painting by a contemporary artist would be considered "of equal value to the original" (S 60). Hence the subtitle of the study: "Deconstruction in Chinese."[10] But Han also points out that contemporary Western notions of the "original" and the "genius" are of relatively recent provenance. He notes that the Ise Shrine was stripped of its World Heritage site designation because it is continually rebuilt, yet the Freiburg Minster is under continual renovation as well due to the fragile sandstone from which it is constructed (S 60–6). Han's point is that this does not affect the cult value of either site. There is no ship of Theseus problem for ritual sites.

The distinction between "sites" and "sights" relates to one of Han's more provocative claims in *The Disappearance of Rituals*. He holds, against Agamben and many other thinkers, that capitalism is not a religion. At first, this seems to land Han in a contradiction. As noted earlier in this chapter, he claims that "technological progress is underpinned by a quasi-religious narrative" (ST 29). He notes how Calvinist theologies of work and salvation clear space for the contemporary achievement subject. By claiming that capitalism is not a religion, however, Han is not necessarily denying these secularized theologies and their new enchantments (see McCarraher, 2019). Recall from chapter 2 that religion for

Han means friendliness (WP 57). In *The Disappearance of Rituals*, he links religion to ritual practices of deep attention, duration, and community formation. In these areas, Han sees a crucial break between religion and capitalism. Indeed, the latter becomes something of an anti-religion, even if it closely mimics religion in some ways and feeds on a misplaced religious yearning. Money is not a unifying religious symbol: "It increases my individual freedom by liberating me from any personal bond with others" (DR 43). Religion is a matter of "the sacred and the profane," while capitalism seeks to commodify everything, thereby "totalizing the profane." In the liturgical calendar of Judaism or Christianity, "Every day is given a narrative tension, is made meaningful, by the overall narrative," while capitalism "does not narrate anything" but "merely counts" (DR 44). Along these lines, Han notes how religious rituals of initiation and life transition allow for maturation, whereas we now "age without growing *old*, or we remain infantile consumers who never become adults" (DR 35).

Han also notes that capitalism is hostile to the "contemplative rest" at the heart of religion. "Capital," he argues, "never rests. It is its nature that it must always work and continue moving. To the extent that they lose the capacity for contemplative rest, humans conform to capital" (DR 44). Here Han joins a wide range of thinkers claiming that modernity has largely lost touch with the festival and the Sabbath.[11] The prioritization of work reduces the weekend, holidays, and vacations to pauses in which we catch our breath, extended "break time" from otherwise ceaseless labor. The oscillation of work with contemplative, festive rest gives way to endless production and burnout. Han notes,

> If rest becomes a form of recovery from work, as is the case today, it loses its specific ontological value. It no longer represents an independent, higher form of existence and degenerates into a derivative of work. Today's compulsion of production perpetuates work and thus eliminates that sacred silence [of festival and Sabbath]. Life becomes entirely profane, desecrated. (DR 39)

The "cult value" of the religious festival or holiday increasingly gives way to consumerism. At its best, the festival "is characterized by both the intensity of life and the intensity of contemplation," by a synthesis of action and contemplation, whereas today we are given to bouts of "hyperactivity" that eventually lead to a crash or burnout (DR 38).

This is perhaps the main point that Han wants to make in *The Disappearance of Rituals*. Against the widespread view that the loss of ritual is "an emancipatory process," he holds that it has allowed for the more complete commodification of contemporary life (DR vi). Without ritual grounding, people are more pliable consumers. Without Sabbath and festival, the whole calendar is devoted to frenetic production and consumption. Han draws on thinkers as different as Rabbi Abraham Joshua Heschel and Georges Bataille to help make this point. The contrast with ritual thus allows him to sharpen his critique of our current crisis of time, atomization, and burnout. Han acknowledges that rituals can be bent to harmful ends. They can inculcate an exclusionary mindset and foment violence (DR 32). Elites and demagogues can use them for social manipulation. Yet Han argues that many contemporary problems result from the collapse of ritual. His preliminary remark in *The Disappearance of Rituals*, in which he claims that he is not calling for a nostalgic return, is an attempt to get readers beyond common knee-jerk assumptions about rituals to consider this possibility.

But is there a constructive upshot to Han's turn to ritual?[12] When he discusses contemplative practices elsewhere, he clearly offers a way for his readers to counter contemporary ills. This is less clear in his work on ritual. The "Preliminary Remark" heads off charges that he is animated by "nostalgia" for the world of premodern ritual, but it also makes the reader wonder what, if anything, is to be done (DR vi). Han does not seem to believe that a religious revival is imminent in the West, and he is not directly preaching one (NI). His study does, however, invite its readers to take a second, and more appreciative, look at living religious traditions. In a 2022 interview, Han also suggests that it is important to recover secular rituals weakened by the COVID-19 pandemic:

> After the pandemic, what is most in need of recovery is culture. Cultural events such as theater, dance and even football have a ritual character. The only way in which we can revitalize community is through ritual forms. Today, culture is held together solely by instrumental and economic relations. But that does not found communities – it isolates people. Art, in particular, should play a central role in the revitalization of rituals. (NI)

Han's philosophy cautions against digital counterfeits of these rituals. Watching the opera or a football match (or Mass) on a screen is not the same kind of community-forming ritual as watching them – indeed contemplatively participating in them – as part of an in-person group. Still, Han claims that he is "not completely pessimistic. Perhaps we shall develop new narratives, ones that do not presuppose a hierarchy. We can easily imagine a flat narrative. Every narrative develops its own rituals for the purposes of making it habitual, embedding it in the physical body" (NI). In short, the "Preliminary Remark" of *The Disappearance of Rituals* does not close the door on ritual. The book instead invites renewal and the new. Han notes, for instance, how we can attempt to ritualize the activities of our daily lives. As is always the case with Han, his diagnosis is not meant to leave us in despair. It is meant as a departure point. And as is often the case, Han unsettles ideological complacencies. If *The Disappearance of Ritual* challenges the left to look past emancipation narratives that are too simple, it challenges the right to attend to capitalism's role in the destruction of ritual and community and to be open to the new.

# 6

# *Eros:*
# *Finding the Other*

## Steven Knepper

> To experience the world gently, as if our senses were raw.
> Anne Dufourmantelle, *Power of Gentleness*

### The Hell of the Same

This chapter takes up a second of Han's remedies for contemporary ills: the recovery of the Other. This is more a shift of emphasis from the last chapter than a change in topic. Time remains important. Contemplative lingering can open us to the Other; the relationship with the Other can grant duration. The early sections of the present chapter focus on a trio of works published in the wake of *The Burnout Society*: *The Agony of Eros* (2012), *Saving Beauty* (2015), and *The Expulsion of the Other* (2016). They form a sort of loose trilogy on the Other and on the potential of eros to draw us out of ourselves. Han distinguishes the self-centered, market-stoked "wants and needs" of the ego from eros (AE 37; cf. CDD 93–103). He defines eros as desire that "pulls the subject out of itself, toward the Other" (AE 3). Eros can draw us towards many others, including the things of the world and the transcendent. But eros is also strongly associated with romantic desire for the Other, with romantic love.

The final section of this chapter returns to contemplative "friendliness" towards others and the world, friendliness that we called "deep cosmopolitanism" in chapter 2. This friendliness can take different forms. In his early works, Han focuses on the friendliness of Zen Buddhism. Over the past decade, however, he has also worked towards a form of friendliness developed primarily from Western philosophical and artistic sources. This most recent phase involves rehabilitation of concepts such as dialectic, the ethics of the Other, and eros, culminating in a renewed Romantic "friendliness," addressed to a time of social and ecological crisis, in Han's 2022 book *Vita Contemplativa*.

Han repeatedly claims that we live in the "hell," "inferno," or "terror" "of the same." This claim may seem strange, even counterintuitive. After all, a city such as Berlin or Seoul or London or New York is from one angle a rich tapestry of individuals, neighborhoods, cultures, religions. People from all around the world can be found there. Han's claim does not contradict this. Indeed, throughout his works, and especially in the early work *Hyperculture*, he stresses the modern city's cosmopolitan promise, but he also notes the homogenizing powers of globalization and consumption, where diversity can be reduced to commodified and fused styles, musics, and cuisines. As more and more areas of life are commodified, their otherness is obscured by the price tags placed on them. The values on the tags differ, but all are nonetheless subordinated to a scale that reduces worth to consumption value. All are subsumed into the global market. Relentless commodification denies, or is at least blind to, inherent worth, to personal or local worth outside of the market, even to a long-term usefulness that cannot yield near-term profits (for instance, the short-termism of deforesting the Amazon): "Globalization has an inherent violence that makes everything interchangeable, comparable and thus the same" (EO 10). The market offers a product to suit every preference, but it does so by subjecting everything to a logic of equivalence, to the hell of the same. Those who do not have enough money find themselves on the outskirts, or altogether outside, of this world of value.

Commodification facilitates an instrumental approach to things, an approach based on the consumptive hunger of the ego. As we have seen, the smartphones occupying our pockets or handbags ramify this effect. The infinitely malleable and algorithmically tailored world of the digital device, with its near instantaneous responsiveness to our wishes and whims, transforms how we see the shared world of non-virtual reality. "People" online are swiped between and exited out, to be followed, liked, and muted. They are mediated on the terms of the user – used by the user. This shapes in turn how people are approached, or not, offline. (As we saw in chapter 3, there is a dark side to this too, when those who seek affirmation online find themselves at the mercy of the often cruel whims of other users or of the "swarm.") We increasingly do not encounter people or the world outside the projections and projects, the fantasies and furies, of the ego: "The Other is bent into shape until the ego recognizes itself in them. The narcissistic subject perceives the world only in shadings of itself. This results in a disastrous consequence: the Other disappears" (EO 21). Here, too, we find ourselves in the hell of the same.

We can only recover the Other when we leave behind the distortions of our ego – or when our ego is pierced by some encounter or event. This is risky because it makes us vulnerable, and achievement society seeks to be risk-free. Yet the relationship with the Other is ultimately worth the risk for Han. It promises meaning, a fuller sense of time and a fuller validation, a sense of belonging to a richer world. It can provide the lasting satisfactions and joy that prove elusive in the achievement society and are often pursued via the dead end of redoubled achievement. Leaving behind the ego is also a precondition for offering these same gifts to the Other. It is a precondition of hospitality and responsive care.

When we truly see others, we see them in their singularity. We do not see them according to the scale of use value, or in terms of abilities or characteristics that relativize them vis-à-vis others – we see them in their incontrovertible mystery. The Other is, like the paradigmatic Socrates, always *atopos* (AE 2–3). We may draw near to the Other, but we know that we can never fully fathom them. As the contemporary French philosopher Luce Irigaray writes, "I recognize you means that I cannot know you [completely] in thought or in flesh. The power of a negative prevails between us. I recognize you goes hand in hand with: you are irreducible to me, just as I am to you" (1996, p. 103).

When we recognize that we cannot fully fathom the Other, we afford them a hospitable space. Han cites Martin Buber (1965), a twentieth-century philosopher and religious thinker, who calls this distance "primal" and suggests it is present whenever we recognize the Other as existing apart from our ego. This is the distance that, paradoxically, allows a real relationship to emerge, a relationship *with* the Other, though the grasping for a relationship on one's own terms can easily collapse the prerequisite distance. In the event of such a collapse, we have a relationship no longer with the Other but with an instrumentalized "it." Buber explains that "one can enter into relation only with being which has been set at a distance, more precisely, has become an independent opposite" (1965, p. 60). Thus, even when "near" to one another, even in the case of lovers in bed, any real relationship with the Other involves this recognition-granting distance (AE 12–13).

Consider listening, to which Han devotes the final chapter of *The Expulsion of the Other*. True listening, like contemplation, is not a state of blank passivity: "It is distinguished by a special activity: first I must welcome the Other, which means affirming the Other in their otherness. Then I give them an ear. Listening is a bestowal, a giving, a gift" (EO 70).

Listening involves both "patience" and "exposure," an opening of the ego and a silencing of one's own thoughts and concerns to receive the Other's words (EO 72). This is why listening is so difficult amidst the contemporary "hell of the same," in which the ego tends to mediate all. We become a new Narcissus whose distorted hearing turns the Other's voice into our own echo (EO 70). Once more, there is a parallel with Han's account of contemplation. "Hospitable" listening involves the power of "not-to" as well, the power not to allow the ego to distort the Other.[1]

The listening that interests Han in *The Expulsion of the Other* is not one of conversation, where a friend perhaps listens attentively then gives spoken advice or encouragement. He is interested in a listening that remains silent but clearly hears. "The hospitable listener," Han claims, "empties themselves to become the resonance chamber of the Other, saving the Other to themselves. Simply listening can heal" (EO 71–2). The "expulsion" of the title and opening pages of the book, with its connotation of vomiting, is here countered by the welcoming of the Other, by respiration of the Other, in which the listener "breathes in" the Other so as to breathe out the gift of healing resonance (EO 72). Han sees political significance in such listening: "It is an act, an active participation in the existence of Others, in their suffering too. It is what joins and connects people to form a community in the first place" (EO 75).

## The Relationship with the Other

The relationship with the Other offers duration and narration. It does so via a paradoxical gift: it both opens a future and grants closure. The closure it offers is not a definitive endpoint. Instead, the relationship is an end in itself: "Friendship is an end unto itself. Love is an absolute end unto itself" (AE 22). Recall from chapter 1 that the open-ended self-optimization of the achievement subject forecloses any bestowal of what, or whom, should be the ends that orient our lives. Achievement itself thereby becomes an end rather than a means to an end. The relationship with the Other can bring closure to the restlessness that plagues achievement society. One is not trying to achieve via the Other, to use the Other as a stepping stone, but to "be-with" the Other. Consider how reuniting with a good friend after a long separation is often marked by both an excitement to catch up and a being-at-rest together, as if one has reached port amidst the storms.

Neither does this closure render the relationship static, for it opens a future (AE 15–16). There is an unfolding inexhaustibility about it. The contemporary philosopher Alain Badiou, a major interlocutor of Han's, writes of relationships of romantic love: "The enigma in thinking about love is the duration of time necessary for it to flourish … We could say that love is a tenacious adventure" (2012, pp. 31–2). There is an unfolding story in a relationship, often one made up of shared experiences of duration. Here again, Han challenges a certain late-modern common sense about what provides freedom and meaning. Han challenges the "keep all options open" mentality that prevents one from committing to a place, a lover, even a friend (PS 30–3). Without denying the risk involved – the risk is real and there are no guarantees – Han insists, "The late-modern achievement-subject, with a surplus of options at its disposal, proves incapable of *intensive bonding*" (BS 43). In doing so, they struggle not only to attain duration and meaning but to offer true recognition and care to the Other.

Furthermore, the relationship with the Other is not static because it mutually transforms. Again, there is risk in opening oneself to such relationships: the risk of hurt and manipulation, of the "bad faith" relationships so trenchantly analyzed by the existentialist Jean-Paul Sartre (2021). In a healthy relationship with the Other, however, there is "the surrender, the giving up, of one's own self," but the Other gives something richer in return, a transformed self that carries within it something of the Other. We are transformed by the meeting, by the relationship. This is not "violent appropriation" but "the *gift of the Other*," one that can be offered to the Other in turn (AE 23). This transformation delivers us from the ego's hell of the same in which we remain trapped in our fixations. Think of the transformations that can happen over the course of a friendship and its many conversations, its shared moments and ventures and struggles. Such relationships, according to Han, afford real self-esteem beyond the fragile recognition grasped at by the ego, which often compulsively seeks affirmations that never quite satisfy or put at ease. Writing out of concern for rising rates of self-harm, especially among youths, Han explains, "To have a stable self-esteem, I am dependent on the notion that I am important for other people, that I am loved by them" (EO 23; cf. CDD 43–8). The need to be important to others can make one easy prey for manipulation, for being used, but in a true friendship one is important *qua* Other to the friend. To switch to the language of Aristotle in his famous discussion of friendship in the *Nicomachean Ethics* (2011), the highest form of friendship is one of "reciprocated" goodwill where friends want "the good things" for each other (1156a–b). In the contemporary hell of the same, "friendship" is often an attenuated digital form of Aristotle's lesser friendships: utility friends, who are useful to one another, or pleasure friends, who gratify one another. Contra the latter, goodwill towards the friend can involve disagreement and conflict, Aristotle's *parrhesia* or frank speech: "Conflicts ... produce relationships and identities. A person grows and matures by dealing with conflict" (CDD 47). The Other's wound to the ego can smart; the transformative gift of the Other can be painful. Yet it can also offer real growth and, again, a steadier self-esteem beyond fragile narcissism.

There are some Aristotelian echoes in Han's account, then, and he also has clear affinities with recent thinkers – such as Buber, Levinas, Irigaray, and Badiou – who stress the decentering, transformative encounter with the Other. Readers of Hegel will also hear some familiar notes in Han's account of the transformative gift of the Other. Indeed, he explicitly reworks Hegel's dialectic. As we saw in chapter 2, Han's early work *Hegel und die Macht* critiques how the dialectic ultimately folds back into the self, how it risks turning the Other into a dialectical means for the expansion and augmentation of one's own power. Han's post-*Burnout Society* works draw another possibility out of Hegel so that the Other is never fully mediated by the dialectic, so that the Other's otherness is preserved and recognized rather than fully sublimated into self-mediation. This is a dialectic of gift exchange rather than power augmentation. Han rightly holds that the dialectic of master and servant is one form rather than the paradigm of all relations in Hegel (AE 23). Like Irigaray (1996), or the contemporary Irish philosopher William Desmond (2012), Han "opens up" Hegel's dialectic: "If one takes Hegel's thought out of the corset of subjectivity, or breaks off the tip of subjectivity, it reveals some interesting aspects" (SB 51; cf. Hegel, 2010, p. 539). This open Hegel, he claims, proves "receptive to the Other like no other thinker" (AE 21). One can perhaps see Han drawing a constructive reading out of Hegel in *The Agony of Eros* without dismissing his earlier critical reading. He continually returns to thinkers to explore different interpretative perils or promises. Still, there seems to be a broader rethinking of the possibilities of dialectic in Han's later writings.

It is important to note that, for Han, the relationship with the Other allows one to see things from a shared perspective, a perspective that includes within it a sense that the Other sees things similarly *and* differently. Such a relationship "enables us to re-create the world from the perspective of the Other and leave behind the habitual" (EO 69). Giorgio Agamben, in his reading of Aristotle's account of friendship, claims that Aristotle makes a similar point when he calls the friend an "other self" [*alter ego*] (Agamben, 2009; cf. Aristotle, 2011, 1170a–1171b).[2] Friendship is an existential experience of "being-with." In Agamben's words, it "divides, disseminates, and renders sharable (actually, it has always been shared) the same sensation, the same sweetness of existing" (2009, p. 35). In friendship we realize, or are reminded, that we *share*, that the world is not ours alone. Badiou, writing of romantic relationships, makes a similar point: "Love involves Two" (2012, p. 28; cf. AE 44–6, EO 69–70). Love reveals the world beyond the ego in this perspective of two-ness. This perspective unfolds across time in a way that can bring duration. Lovers "engage in the extended experience of the constant (re)-birth of the world via the mediation of the difference in their gazes" (Badiou, 2012, p. 41).

The relationship to the Other should result in a broadly transformed approach to the world. One should not simply open oneself to a single Other but to a world of Others, to the otherness of the world. One should cultivate receptivity to all Others. This, as we have seen and will return to again, is what Han calls friendliness. Despite his clear affinities with Levinas and Buber, and his affirmative turns to them in both *The Agony of Eros* and *The Expulsion of the Other*, Han suggests in his earlier works that they frame the relationship to the Other as too exclusive, as not being broadly "friendly" enough (PZB 94–100; A 97–8). In the early work *Tod und Alterität* (103–19), Han raises the question of whether Levinas's emphasis on responsibility towards the Other leaves out too much of the world – the lay of landscapes, for instance, and the richness of colors. Receptivity towards otherness should make one "friendly" to these as well.

Han is especially concerned with our openness to nonhuman otherness, to how, when we step beyond the deadening ego, we find ourselves in a world of gazes and presences (EO 40–65; N 45–98; ARI). He notes how reading is not something we perform on an inert text. Books "gaze" at us in return (EO 44–5). They too can give the gift of transformative otherness. Han points out that "Sartre does not limit the gaze to the human eye; rather, *being gazed upon* is the central aspect of Being-in-the-world. *World is gaze.* Even the rustling of branches, a half-open window or the slight movement of a curtain is perceived as a gaze" (EO 47; cf. Sartre, 2021, p. 353). Han concurs, though such gazes are more salutary for him than for Sartre, whom they unsettle. Things not only "stabilize" our world with their durability. We are also affected by their tangible "presence." The child who senses a disconcerting or reassuring presence in the furniture, who perhaps wonders what that dresser gets up to when she closes her eyes or leaves the bedroom behind for school, does not merely have an overactive and anthropomorphizing imagination but also a heightened sensitivity to the effect of the furniture on the room as a space, to its creaks and cracks and groans, to the textures of its surfaces and the sharpness of its corners, to its sticky or smooth drawers. The child is attentive to what Hans Ulrich Gumbrecht (2004) would call the embodied presence of things. (Like Gumbrecht, Han calls us to be present to such presence.) The child is also attentive to what Jane Bennett calls the "vitality" of things, which we notice when we do not view them simply as "dead" matter, to "the capacity of things ... not only to impede or block the will and designs of humans but also to act as quasi agents or forces with trajectories, propensities, or tendencies of their own" (2010, p. viii).[3]

The child's response to things is also marked by a sense of metaphysical mystery, of wonder at the strange uncanny *thereness* of things being there at all, of *this* thing being there.[4] For Han, this is the metaphysical wonder at the heart of epiphanic encounters with things (N 56–60). Art is especially associated with such epiphanic wonder because it so emphatically asserts its *thereness* against our habituated perception and instrumentalist tendencies. This makes it "uncanny" (EO 61). Indeed, if one is skeptical that things have a gaze, stand before a painting (it need not be a portrait or depict any humans at all) and see if one's own gaze isn't met, see if one isn't addressed by the artwork. The same is true in a contemplative meditation on a poem: "To the poem, everything appears as a *you*" (EO 63). It is part of the vocation of art to restore the language of things, to reveal the expressive mystery of things beyond their reduction to utility. As should already be apparent, certain artworks may do so by depicting things, but all artworks do so through their own expressiveness.

Han's recent meditations on gardening in *Lob der Erde* are also crucial in this regard. He does not merely describe many varieties of flowers in this book. He poetically evokes their differing presences and how they address him. The book is a chronicle of how gardening changes him. This is again not simply a matter of the practices involved, though these are important. It is also a matter of how his nearness to the plants themselves, his attentive receptivity to them, transforms him. Reflections on music are woven throughout *Lob der Erde*, something else which is close to Han's heart, subtly underscoring the music of the growing and blossoming and wilting plants. Han would concur with Buber. A tree, a flower, can be a "thou" (1958, pp. 7–8).[5]

## Eros and the Other

All real relationships that involve openness to the Other involve risk, but the romantic relationship with the Other is particularly perilous. Note Han's title: the *agony* of eros. The title's primary meaning is the loss of eros amidst the hell of the same, but there are multiple meanings at play (AE 41). Han notes the sweet agony of an eros that leaves one yearning for the next encounter with the Other. But there is also eros that is unrequited or betrayed. There are counterfeits of eros that turn out to be selfish or even cruel. There is the possibility of manipulation, especially if one is open while the other instrumentalizes (or vice versa). As Sartre (2021) points out, one can land in a bad-faith relationship. One can land in an unhealthy relationship. Writing out of her extensive experience as a practicing psychoanalyst as well as a philosopher, Anne Dufourmantelle notes, "Above all, [love] can be reversed into hate" (2021, p. 97). The lover wounded in the vulnerability that love entails, the lover betrayed in commitment, can become vengeful. This is a terrifying theme of Euripides' *Medea*, the chorus of which makes Dufourmantelle's warning explicit: "There is no bitterness to be compared / With that between two people who once loved" (1990, p. 324). There is an agony that is anything but sweet.

Yet Han – and Dufourmantelle also – warns against an approach to relationships that tries to control all variables and remove all risk. This is especially on evidence in contemporary approaches, especially on dating apps, that look for perfect matches and try to bring risk down to zero. There is no eros in risk-free relationships, no movement towards the Other as Other, no "existential poetry" (Badiou, 2012, p. 8). Furthermore, a relationship of mutual risk-reduction and convenience cannot provide solace in hard times. Whenever one needs care, the implied "contract" is broken due to inconvenience. Here again, the relationship has been reshaped by a logic of consumption and disposability. It has become what Zygmunt Bauman (2003) calls "liquid love." At times, disappointment in the Other may come not from a betrayal, or even a shortcoming, but precisely from the ways in which the Other does not fit the ego's prefabricated fantasy. The dispelled fantasy may offer the possibility of a real encounter, but it is instead often dismissed as a disappointment.

A different sort of fantasy is proper to eros. It grows from a sense of the Other as *atopos*, as ultimately ungraspable. The fantasy does not grow out of projections but instead honors the irreducible mystery of the Other: "Thresholds and transitions are zones of mystery and riddle – here, the atopic *Other* begins. When borders and thresholds vanish, *fantasies of the Other* disappear too" (AE 41). The closing of eyes is important for Han, as is the caress that does not grasp but "reaches for what is vanishing into the future without end" (AE 16; cf. Levinas, 2003, pp. 89–90). Seduction is as important as well. It need not be manipulative trickery. It can instead be a playful way in which the Other draws one out of the ego in an experience of duration (DR 84–9). Dufourmantelle writes of "gentleness" as what preserves the otherness of the Other in romantic eros: "Gentleness is one of the sources of eroticism; it may reach its most savage lands, its most liberated lands. Without it, there would be no more space laced with shadows and light, no more drawing near, no more letting go, no more play, no inventions, no mirages" (2018, p. 57). The closeness to Han's own account can be seen in the seemingly paradoxical mix of passivity and action, a "drawing near" that allows for a "letting go," the recognition of the Other's otherness alongside the play of fantasy, the sense of duration which is suggested by Dufourmantelle's long second sentence and its anaphora.

In Han's account of eros, lovers are not desired because of their comparative sexiness, the way their attributes can be stacked up against those of others. They are desired precisely as *atopos*, as singular, incontrovertible, and mysterious. This is the heart of Han's critique of the pornographic as a counterfeit of the erotic. If the latter draws one towards the Other, the former remains in the compulsive wants of the ego:

> The body – with its display value – has become a commodity. At the same time, the Other is being sexualized into an object for procuring arousal. When otherness is stripped from the Other, one cannot love – one can only consume. To this extent, the Other is no longer a person; instead, he or she has been fragmented into sexual part-objects. (AE 12)

For Han, not only the consumption of porn but also a pornographic approach to sex is masturbatory and entails no real encounter with the Other. Porn dismembers the *atopic* Other into interchangeable body parts. Han's position is not one of prudery, though. He contrasts pornographic images with erotic photographs (SB 27–8), a hyper-clean pornography of waxing and airbrushing with a "dirty eroticism" of negativity (SB 8–9). He agrees with Bataille that eros can become madness to the point of self-dissolution (AE 24; cf. Bataille, 1986). Han is not averse to sex but to how the erotic is burned away in the pornographic hell of the same.

## Eros and Beauty

Han's account of eros draws inspiration from Plato. In the *Phaedrus* (250e–252a), beauty punctures the ego and gives the soul wings. In the *Symposium* (201c–212c), beauty stirs an erotic desire to create art, laws, and philosophy. To recover this power of beauty, however, Han must first address how it has been counterfeited in the hell of the same. He must recover a beauty with real otherness, a beauty that can wound and can draw one out.

In championing beauty, Han breaks with the mainstream of aesthetics from at least the early twentieth century onward. Beauty has been dismissed as so much tacky kitsch, as indulgently bourgeois, as escapist, as saccharine or simply boring. The sublime, with its power to shock our senses and sensibilities, has displaced beauty at the heart of aesthetic concern. Yet Han claims that this preference for the sublime over the beautiful relies on a mistaken opposition with roots in foundational works by Edmund Burke and Kant (SB 15–22). It opposes the sublime's power to shock with beauty's power to soothe. It opposes the "negativity of the sublime" with the "pure positivity" of beauty (SB 15). Ancient accounts did not make these stark oppositions. In Plato, "beauty inheres the negativity which is characteristic of the sublime. The sight of beauty does not cause pleasure, but shocks" (SB 16).[6] Han holds that this is a more accurate phenomenological account of beauty. It captures the way beauty draws us out of ourselves, the way we can experience beauty as a disastrous "event" that *"expropriate[s]* the ego" (SB 42).

Han points to a series of "inconspicuous" examples that modern aesthetics would situate safely in the tame environs of the beautiful, far from the crags and cataracts of the sublime: "white dust swirled up by a drop of rain, snow falling silently in the morning twilight, or a scent coming off a rock in the summer heat." Yet such events, like those that are more overtly shocking, can still "empty the ego, de-subjectify it" (SB 42). The problem for Han is not simply that aesthetics tends to privilege the sublime over the beautiful. The problem is that it dualizes them in the first place.

Han joins a minority report of recent thinkers who similarly attempt to "save" beauty from its relegation to the innocuous and the soothing (see Knepper, 2022, pp. 45–71). Most take some bearing from the Platonic insistence that beauty wounds and stirs. This is not to downplay the still significant difference between thinkers who wish to recover beauty along these lines. Consider the influential philosopher and Plato translator Alexander Nehamas. His study *Only a Promise of Happiness: The Place of Beauty in a World of Art* offers a provocative pairing of Plato and Nietzsche. Nehamas begins by recovering the "shudder" of beauty in the Platonic tradition from the banal "aesthetic" realm to which modern thought relegated it (2017, p. 2). There is much in this account with which Han would agree: the role Kant plays in reducing beauty to the "aesthetic" and in prioritizing critical judgment; the unsalutary trends over the course of modern thought to narrow the aesthetic to first the remarkable in art and nature and then to the artwork alone. But Han would demur from Nehamas's repeated insistence that beauty stirs a possessive desire (albeit one that vulnerably desires "sometimes" to be possessed in return) and the Nietzschean turn at the end of the study to aesthetics as a matter of "individuality" that somewhat mutes the otherness of beauty (Nehamas, 2017, pp. 57, 102–38).

Han focuses on how beauty hasn't simply been misunderstood in modern thought. Instead, a "smooth" counterfeit of beauty that consists in "pure positivity" displaced the wounding beauty of the Platonic tradition and now dominates the digital age. Han's account of beauty is thus important to his broader critique of positivity and the digital medium. This is part of what makes his account distinctive from other recent thinkers who wish to recover beauty. Han once again sees this counterfeit emerging at the origin of modern aesthetics. In his dualization of the sublime and the beautiful, Burke especially associates the latter with smoothness (SB 16–19; cf. Burke, 1998, pp. 113–14). Kant, too, equates beauty with "positive pleasure" (SB 19; cf. Kant, 1987, pp. 61–3). They thus set the coordinates for modern thought about aesthetics.

Yet this paradigm shift is not consummated until the twenty-first century, with a new era of digital smoothness. The smooth "connects the sculptures of Jeff Koons, iPhones and Brazilian waxing" (SB 1). Many people today find the smoothness of these sculptures, smartphones, and waxed bodies beautiful, but Han would hold that their shared aesthetic counterfeits beauty, robbing it of otherness, depth, and resistance. He notes that even the disturbing, ugly, and grotesque are "smoothened out into a form for consumption" (SB 8). The hell of the same, then, is aesthetically smooth.

The smartphone is probably the most pervasive and formative instance of the smooth in the twenty-first century (see N 18–28). It offers endless smooth transitions from tab to tab, app to app, image to image. The transitions are compulsively haptic, effected by the stroke of a fingertip over the perfectly smooth, perfectly responsive screen. They are frictionless in both their physical design and the digital access they provide. We become self-absorbed in the smartphone's mirror screen – a desire-mirror in its algorithmic tailoring but also a mirror as a picture-taking device. Han points to the selfie as the most (in-)famous form of smartphone photography. The face in the selfie is dramatized to get likes. It is merely exposing itself or, perhaps, attempting *"to produce itself"* (SB 12).[7]

But, of course, the smooth world of the internet is not always a world of likes. It is also a world of anxiety and vitriol, of destruction and self-destruction. It can seem less a world of the self's frictionless positivity than a chaotic bombardment of the self. As we saw in chapter 3, Han does not neglect these dynamics in his writings on the internet. In *Saving Beauty* he does not seem to have in mind the "doom scroller" who cannot stop looking at what will anger or cause despair. Yet there is something "smooth" about even this phenomenon of seeming negativity. For there is nothing to stop the doom scroller from continuing to scroll and click. The algorithm happily facilitates self-destruction. Here an encounter with negativity, if it brought resistance and redirection, would be salvific (the power going out, a knock on the door, a frustrated glare from a significant other). Indeed, if Han, à la Dante, would descend into the "inferno of the same," perhaps with Baudrillard as his Virgilian guide, he would undoubtedly encounter the doom scroller in some circle, oblivious to their arrival, brow wrinkled at the smoothly (self-)tormenting screen.

Han insists that beauty and the sublime are a manifestation of the Other. He insists that the artwork should give "a push" of otherness (SB 6). This he contrasts with Koons's polished balloon sculptures, which become artistic avatars of the smooth that never challenge our self-enclosure (SB 2–7). Han again criticizes a pernicious tendency of modern aesthetics: a tendency towards subjectification. Kant claims that the effects we ascribe to the beautiful or sublime object are more properly ascribed to ourselves. The pleasure taken in the dew-jeweled spiderweb discovered in a tree crook is not due to the web so much as to "the harmonious interplay of the cognitive faculties" (SB 19; cf. Kant, 1987, 44–95). Kant manages to privilege the subject even in the shocking sublime. The raging gale makes "the subject initially [feel] powerless," but "it takes refuge in the inwardness of reason and its idea of infinity," which is what is truly sublime instead of the external otherness of wind and rain and thunderclap (SB 20, cf. Kant, 1987, 97–126). To ascribe the sublime to their otherness is a mistaken "subreption." The web or the gale become occasions to reflect on the subject. Because Kant ultimately turns away from the external reality and back to the subject, Han deems his an "*autoerotic,*" a masturbatory aesthetics (SB 21).

Aesthetic subjectification reinforces the modern preoccupation with the self. The experience of beauty, beyond its modern theorization, nonetheless promises escape from the hell of the same. The negativity of beauty can open us up and slow us down. Beauty wounds our ego. It breaks us open. This is, in a sense, "the death of the autoerotic subject which clings to itself" (SB 42). This is one reason why beauty, eros, and death are so frequently linked.[8] But the wound caused by beauty is ultimately salutary. It lances the autoerotic subject's festering self-enclosure, opening it to the air and light of otherness. The pain that beauty inflicts on the ego is mixed with the pleasure of this renewed openness. There is pain in being displaced from the center of a small world of one, but there is potential joy in joining a much larger world among others. Han points to a childhood experience of the novelist-philosopher Maurice Blanchot when "the infinity of the empty [night] sky," which obliterates an egocentric universe, nonetheless offered the youngster "a 'devastating joy'" (SB 42, cf. AE 7–8; Blanchot, 1986, p. 120). Han tends to emphasize the wound of beauty, perhaps to the point of over-emphasis, likely because modern aesthetics neglects it, but he also notes that beauty offers joy.

Beauty is also paradoxical in that it frequently stills self-interested desire while stirring self-transcending eros. It stills one sort of desire while stirring another. Beauty wounds the ego but also brings peace to its grasping and calculative willing. Such willing constantly rushes us along and reduces the Other to a means to some end. Here Han gives a nod to Kant, who points to how beauty is "disinterested" (SB 46). In an article on Han's aesthetics, Francesca Teltscher Taylor observes how, despite their significant differences, "Kant and Han share a desire for the un-consumable" (2017, p. 48). The aesthetic tradition frequently, and rightly, points to how beauty transcends personal or societal utility. Yet modern aesthetics rarely attends to how beauty brings rest to the grasping will while stirring a yearning, ecstatic desire. Here Plato is again a better guide. The *Phaedrus* and the *Symposium* note how the wound of beauty gives rise to eros. Again, this is desire for the *atopic* Other that cannot be reduced to utility. Hence, beauty's mix of peace and longing, of release and desire.

Beauty's connection to eros is crucial for Han. For this is what allows beauty to be truly transformative rather than fleetingly palliative. Han points to the famous injunction that ends Rilke's "Archaic Torso of Apollo": "You must change your life" (SB 6; Rilke, 2000, p. 33). The eros of beauty can lead to ethical commitment and care for the Other. Han recalls the philosopher Elaine Scarry's influential account of the relationship between beauty and justice:

> In the face of beauty, the subject takes a side (*lateral*) position; it steps aside instead of pushing to the fore. It becomes a *lateral figure*. It takes itself back in favour of the other. This aesthetic experience in the face of beauty, Scarry believes, extends into the ethical. The retraction of the self is essential to justice. Thus, justice is a *beautiful* state of being together. (SB 61; cf. Scarry, 1999)

The closing lines of *Lob der Erde* make a similar point: the beauty of the earth obliges us to care, to be beautiful in turn instead of destructive (LE 153).

Han's declamation in *Lob der Erde* perhaps echoes the priestess Diotima's famous claim in Plato's *Symposium* (206b) that we give birth in beauty, a claim which Han explicitly discusses in the earlier work *Saving Beauty*: "Faced with beauty, the soul is driven to create something beautiful itself" (SB 77–8). The eros stirred by beauty is not "consumptive" but "generative" (SB 77). It can inspire new works of art and philosophy, even "beautiful laws" (SB 78). All these are eros-inspired gifts in return for the gift of originating beauty. The interplay described in the *Symposium* amounts to a beautiful gift exchange. There is utopian promise in the eros inspired by beauty. It points to a politics beyond calculation, machinations, self-interest, and tyrannical impulses. This is a politics of erotic *thumos*, of inspired courage "to bring forth beautiful deeds" (AE 44). It is a politics of "being-with" where beautiful novelty is possible.

Beauty also stirs an eros for truth. For beauty is "the advent of truth." It is disclosive, revelatory. The distorting cataract of the ego does not allow us to see things in their otherness. Beauty removes this cataract and allows us to perceive things in their truth. It allows us to see the web as web, the gale as gale, the night sky as night sky, the beloved as beloved. This perception allows us to see more of the Other, the specificities and singularities that the egotistical look neglects, but it also chastens our pretentious assumption that we can see all. We note the limits of our perception, the mystery of the Other, the *atopos* of the Other. Heidegger is again Han's guide at this juncture. Beauty does not entail truth as correspondence but truth as revelatory disclosure: "The advent of truth defines anew what *is* real. It brings forth *another Is*" (SB 79).

In the Platonic tradition, eros often leads to ascent. It makes the soul grow wings. It leads up the ladder of earthly beauty towards the form of beauty. It leads us towards the Good, the One, God. Does Han's eros lead us out of ourselves and towards the divine? While Han studied Catholic theology as well as philosophy, his discussions of religious rituals and festivals are often sociological or anthropological rather than explicitly theological.[9] In most of his works, God-talk is ascribed to the thinkers and traditions under discussion, as when *The Scent of Time* criticizes Heidegger for willfully misreading the Christian contemplative tradition as "categorizing" and "analytic seeing" rather than "a *lingering with God in loving attentiveness*" (ST 110, 111).

Still, there has always been a mystical note in Han, especially the kind of immanent mysticism of wonder that emerges when one fully attends to things. A more explicit religious mysticism comes to the fore in recent writings. This is especially true of *Lob der Erde*, where Han claims that gardening renewed his sense of God (LE 10, 106). In a 2021 interview, Han talks about visiting the churches of Rome by bicycle and how one "bestowed a now very rare experience of presence" of the holy spirit as "nothing other than the other" (ARI). *Non-Things* touches on the stillness of prayer and how, "only in stillness, in the *great silence*, do we enter into a relation with the *nameless*, which exceeds us and in the face of which our efforts at appropriating the name seem feeble" (N 83). This is a mysticism presented in the language of negative theology, hesitant to put a name or concept to the exceeding otherness. Han uses some language of transcendent ascent in the 2021 interview, but writings such as *Lob der Erde* and *Vita Contemplativa* show that his mysticism remains rooted in a sense of awe at the earth. In Christian theological language, it is a sacramental sense of the goodness of creation.

## Slow Beauty

Recall Han's criticism, noted in the previous chapter, that Lyotard does not solve the problem of "whizzing time" because he fixes too much on anticipation of the event's arrival. Given the prominence of the event in *Saving Beauty*, *The Agony of Eros*, and *The Expulsion of the Other*, Han's point is not that events do not arrive or that they are not important. He notes how the wound of the sublime or the beautiful can "be disastrous events, namely *events of emptiness* which empty the ego, de-subjectify it and take away its inwardness, thus making it happy" (SB 42). Han's concern with Lyotard is that he does not provide a contemplative lingering that brings duration to the time between events (ST 49–54).

Given this, it is unsurprising that Han attends to a slowly unfolding beauty. This is another distinctive trait in his account of beauty, and it is also where his account of beauty builds on his earlier concerns about profound boredom, lingering, and contemplation. Once more, contemplative practices come to the fore: "The contemplative immersion in beauty … produces a state in which time, so to speak, is at a stand-*still*" (SB 68). Sometimes the work of art will instantaneously knock us back, but every work of art reveals more – while intimating what it withholds or conceals – if we linger with it contemplatively. The same is true of any landscape (see Handke, 1985b, pp. 71–3). This lingering with the beautiful Other also grants duration.

Does such slowly disclosed beauty wound? There seems to be some tension between Han's emphasis on Platonic wounding and his prioritization of what we might call slow beauty. Nehamas claims that "both experience and a long philosophical tradition stand behind the idea that the effect of beauty is immediate" (2017, p. 16). Slow beauty cannot startle in the same dramatic way as, say, the storm's first searing blade of lighting against the purple twilit sky. Han's claim in the *Expulsion of the Other* that "beauty only reveals itself to the long, contemplative gaze" is overstated (60). But surely there are beauties that unfold, or deepen, only slowly – beauties that we "sink" into. Furthermore, contemplative lingering and the event-character of beauty should not be pitted against each other either, as Nehamas seems to do. Han encourages the cultivation of a "vulnerable" seeing that risks "exposing oneself to injury" (SB 34). Slowly disclosing beauty, our slow immersion in it, can gradually undo us. There may be a slow *askesis* of the ego, then, that brings one into relation to the Other and "suspends the *violence of time*" (SB 68). Consider once more Han's example of "disastrous events": "white dust swirled up by a drop of rain, snow falling silently in the morning twilight, or a scent coming off a rock in the summer heat" (SB 42). These could possibly wound in their initial immediacy, but these are also examples that invite contemplative lingering and may not disclose themselves as significant, let alone "disastrous," unless one is in a contemplative mood. They may not disclose themselves unless one follows Dufourmantelle's injunction "to experience the world gently, as if our senses were raw" (2018, p. 93).

Beauty offers duration. The beautiful work of art gives us pause. It invites contemplative lingering. We dwell on its nuances, ideally in silence. As noted earlier, the work of art gives an image of otherness – it would be better to say that the work of art is an Other – that cannot be readily instrumentalized or consumed. It invites us, often compels us, to acknowledge and linger with this otherness. In this regard, "the task of art is the *saving of the other*" (SB 68). But this in turn saves us from "whizzing time" as we tarry with the artwork. Any critical response to the artwork that does not emerge from such an experience of "contemplative immersion" will likely neglect the work's otherness. The art critic can participate in, or at least preserve, art's "*saving of the other.*" The critic can also easily betray it.

The experience of beauty is also often one of resonance, of affinities, of recollections. Seeing the glistening spider web in the tree crook recalls a childhood memory of a web stretched just beyond the bedroom window, making the familiar backyard vista beyond the web beautifully strange. Later still, an encounter with Vija Celmins's *Web #1* is deepened by its resonance with these prior experiences with luminous webs, and the artwork's intricate beauty in turn re-illumines and indeed re-collects them. It thereby offers a different experience of time, one rich with poetic connections. "It is not the immediate presence and contiguity of things that is beautiful," Han claims. "Essential to beauty are rather the secret correspondences between things and ideas that take place across vast spaces of time" (SB 74). Scarry makes the further point that dwelling with the beauty of one thing tends to open us more broadly, since "attention to any one thing normally seems to heighten, rather than diminish, the acuity with which one sees the next" (1999, p. 18). This is an especially important point for Han's approach to beauty. It suggests that beauty draws one towards friendliness, towards broad openness.

## Friendliness

In contemplative receptivity to slow beauty, then, we come again to Han's key concept of friendliness as "unlimited openness" to others and the world – to all others (PZB 88).[10] A telling example: while Han recognizes Heidegger's affordances for an ecological ethic, he notes that there are hardly any insects in the latter's writings (perhaps only a sole cricket?) (PZB 12; LE 75). In *Lob der Erde*, Han recalls playing as a child near a polluted river in Seoul. He fondly remembers the dragonflies that lived there, especially the red ones (LE 62). The "unlimited openness" should extend to plants and insects, to rocks and landforms as well.

Zen Buddhism has been friendlier to these than many forms of Western religion and philosophy, which have often relegated them to insignificance unless they have use value (or unless they annoy us). As noted in chapter 2, friendliness is an explicit concern of Han's early works, where he often juxtaposes Buddhist friendliness with Western ethical thinking, though he also finds friendliness in certain Western artists, composers, and writers, such as the Dutch still-life painters, Cézanne, John Cage, and especially Peter Handke. Friendliness is less prominent and does not receive sustained thematization in many of Han's works from the middle years of the 2010s onward, but it never disappears. In *The Scent of Time*, "Contemplative lingering is also a practice of friendliness" (113). The hospitable listener at the end of *The Expulsion of the Other* is a friendly listener. Friendliness is there whenever Han evokes Handke's "we-tiredness," in which the tired soul opens benevolently to the world.

Han's writings on Buddhism attempt to recover, we might even say decolonize, it from Western misconception. This is a major goal of *Absence, The Philosophy of Zen Buddhism,* and *Shanzhai*. Han criticizes the dismissive approaches of Hegel and Martin Buber to Buddhism. He highlights the subtler misunderstandings of appreciative Western thinkers such as Schopenhauer and Heidegger who draw on Eastern thought or claim to be its kindred. Han does not simply mount a defense of Buddhism. He corrects misunderstandings, but he also uses Buddhism to advance a blistering critique of the egotistic tendencies of Western philosophy. In particular, he takes aim at the Western fixation on the monadic self within its closed-off interior world.

The Buddhist notion of emptiness or absence (*śūnyatā*) is often particularly difficult for Westerners. In Western thought, emptiness tends to be viewed as blankly privative or simply as space to be filled. When emptiness is grappled with existentially, it is often given a negative valence. It is bleak to be "empty inside." An empty world or universe is a nihilistic one devoid of meaning and value. Indeed, one common knee-jerk Western reaction to Buddhist *śūnyatā* is to see it as nihilistic.[11] Han suggests that this reaction stems from the Western emphasis on substance and the ego (TA, A, PZB). Buddhism challenges the latter. It aims at the "great death" of the ego (PZB 69–82). This ego-death is "catastrophic" in that "it negates all subjecthood or I-hood" (PZB 79). But there is a second movement in Buddhism. The great death of the ego clears the way for a new self: "The self empties itself out by filling itself with a world-like vastness. This unique kind of death leads to the emergence of a self that is filled with vastness, a selfless self" (PZB 79). This kind of ego-death is what allows one to become an open "guest house." Zen emptiness is ultimately not nihilistic, then, but "a *medium of friendliness.*"

> In the field of emptiness, there are no strict demarcations. Nothing remains isolated in itself or within itself. Things nestle up to one another, reflect each other. Emptiness de-*internalizes* the I into a *rei amicae* that opens up like a guest house. Human being-with-one-another can also be understood in these terms. (PZB 83)

The last line in this quotation, the claim that "human being-with-another" can be a hospitable "guest house," shows why, in chapter 2, we called Han's friendliness a deep cosmopolitanism. It also underscores the contrast between *śūnyatā* as the "medium of friendliness" and the narcissism of the digital medium discussed in chapter 3. And here we also perhaps get another way of understanding what is so rich about such states as profound boredom and we-tiredness. They dilate the ego in a way that attunes one to this rich, open sense of emptiness.

As with the self that has gone through the great death, forms are not dissolved in Zen emptiness. Instead, "Form and emptiness are situated on the same level of being" (PZB 26). This is the "emptiness" that Han sees in Zen landscape paintings. These are not stuffed with the artist's ego, and "nothing delimits itself or closes itself off" (PZB 27). Han describes Yü-Chien's *Eight Views of the Xiao-Xiang*: "The river sits in its place, and the mountain begins to flow. Earth and sky snuggle up to one another" (PZB 27; cf. Hui, 2021, pp. 131–206).

Another common Western misconception of Buddhism is that it results in callous or blithe indifference. It aims to free the self of attachment and desire. It aims to move beyond an ethics of "I" and "Thou" (PZB 83–100). But the result is a friendly "in-difference," a friendly "being-with." This is what allows Buddhist compassion and "unlimited openness." Again, the latter is central to Han's ethical sensibility across his writings. He claims, "Original friendliness is *older* than the good, *older* than any moral law. It may be understood as a ground-providing ethical force" (PZB 89).

Han does not simply use Zen Buddhism to diagnose the ills of Western philosophy and culture. He presents it in its own integrity. But Han does suggest that Zen and other traditions of Eastern thought, such as Taoism, when truly encountered and listened to, can challenge Western thought to recover this "ground-providing ethical force." This is no small task. Han points to "egocentric" tendencies in Western thought from Plato and Aristotle onward. The difficulties become greater in modernity, as nature is increasingly treated as an exploitable resource, as the self is conceived more monadically, as the porous inwardness cultivated by Christianity gives way to narcissistic self-absorption.

As we have seen, Han draws some resources for this recovery from Western contemplative traditions and art.[12] His endorsement of a neo-Romantic friendliness at the end of *Vita Contemplativa*, however, may seem like a particularly bold – or suspect – move (86–99). After all, Romanticism has been charged with cultivating a "bad infinity" of inwardness, of bloating the "I" in unprecedented ways. Romanticism has been pointed to as the very origin point of modern narcissism. As we saw in chapter 2, Han criticizes these strands in Romantic thought in his earlier works. In *Vita Contemplativa* he wishes to take up another, more promising strand of early Romanticism that he associates especially with Novalis and Friedrich Hölderlin. Here he finds a desire to overcome the opposition, the rift, between humans and the rest of nature. Compared with Zen, this is a friendliness of intensities and eros, with all the attendant dangers noted by the early Han and all the possibilities noted in the more recent Han of *The Agony of Eros, Saving Beauty,* and *The Expulsion of the Other*. To realize these possibilities, Han stresses in *Vita Contemplativa*, this Romantic friendliness must remain broadly open. The freedom yearned for in Romanticism, he notes, is often still one of "being-with." Hölderlin's *Hyperion* is a touchstone for Han: "To be one with all that lives, to return in blessed self-forgetfulness into the All of Nature – this is the pinnacle of thoughts and joys, this the sacred mountain peak, the place of eternal rest" (2002, p. 3). From Novalis (1997), Han draws a messianic desire for peace and for a world community. (Hölderlin's politics tend in a similar direction.) This friendliness, too, is a deep cosmopolitanism. It promises a "coming realm of peace, [where] humans and nature are reconciled with each other. Human beings are but *fellow citizens* in a *republic of the living* – of plants, animals, stones, clouds and stars" (VC 98). Of course, the contemplative solutions offered here and throughout Han's body of work are likely to frustrate some readers, since they seem to be a-political or, at least, not to involve direct political action. Han's brief discussions of a "politics of inactivity" in *Vita Contemplativa* will likely deepen this frustration rather than dispel it. But Han leaves little doubt in his concern for societal problems and democracy that he is not politically quietist and that he thinks the cultivation of contemplation can be politically transformative. This cultivation is meant to be countercultural, clearing new space and opening a new sense of possibilities, in individual lives but also in communities both small and large.[13]

As we have noted throughout this study, Heidegger has been a companion in Han's thought since his dissertation. Han is sympathetic to the late Heidegger of dwelling and releasement. But he is also critical. Heidegger has an admirable sense of the mystery of things, an openness to the world, but his friendliness is far from cosmopolitan. Han's two forms of friendliness can thus be read as a critique of Heidegger that also salvages the promise of his thought.

It does so, on the one hand, by progressing through Heidegger to the Buddhist friendliness about which he was curious (and perhaps to which he was more indebted than he let on). It also critiques Heidegger by returning to his Romantic touchstones and recovering a deep cosmopolitanism from them.

But we should not reduce Han's pursuit of friendliness to a matter of philosophical contention with Heidegger. It is the eros of Han's own philosophical thinking. Han provocatively claims that "praise" is the highest goal of language (VC 55). He is not done thinking, but his goal in recent works seems to have been to help us to "praise the earth" once more. We see this in the very title of *Lob der Erde* and the ecologically attuned Romanticism of *Vita Contemplativa*. Han invites us to this praise. He invites us into friendliness.

# *Coda*

This book does not have a summary conclusion about Han's thought because there are no signs that he is finished thinking. He continues to develop and at times revise his thought in light of some emerging problems we touch upon in this study: corporations and governments using our self-exploitation and self-surveillance on social media for disciplinary ends; the advent of artificial intelligence; the increasingly virulent reactions against global hyperculture both within and outside the West. Han undoubtedly foresees other emerging problems that we do not. He is a far-sighted observer. "Toxic positivity" is only now entering the mainstream (Goodwin, 2022; Cain, 2022), while Han theorized it more than a decade ago. Thanks to him, those who read *The Burnout Society* in the 2010s have been ahead of the curve in thinking through some of the afflictions of the digital age.

Han also has unresolved tensions within his body of thought to work through. We have shown how his early studies of German and East Asian philosophy inform his perspective on the crisis of self-exploitation. Han downgrades sociological accounts of the construction of the self – through psychoanalysts' parent–child relations, Marxists' ideology critiques, or Foucault's disciplinary networks – in favor of showing how Western philosophical and religious traditions have posited the spiritual freedom of the inward self from ancient times, culminating in Hegel's totalizing vision where the world is nothing other than spiritual freedom. Early on, Han aligns himself with Heidegger, Zen Buddhism, and other radical critics of what Nietzsche called the "soul atomism" of Western metaphysics (1989, p. 20). Subjective freedom is the road to self-abuse that the West has taken. Instead, Han exhorts us to a friendly contemplation, to ways of sensing that we are temporary guests in a world of impermanent things and assemblages of the same. Until the mid-2010s, Han takes a fairly firm post-subjectivist line against identifying the self with its "highest" spiritual desires. He has been wary of how such desires intensify a self that instead needs to dilate. In recent works, however, he has offered a constructive re-reading of concepts such as erotic desire (and even Hegelian dialectic), showing how they can also, when rightly understood and rightly experienced, open the soul beyond atomism. The highly confessional *Lob der Erde*, written around the time Han's father died, takes up big ontological questions about care, desire, God, and the soul. Throughout 2016 and 2017, Han senses that the flowers in his garden, always dying and blooming anew, command his care (LE 15). Gardening is friendliness. But, in a twist, the garden authorizes Han's own spiritual eros for resurrection and God. Romantic care for the earth thus appears alongside Zen Buddhism in later works, especially *Vita Contemplativa*.

This book has emphasized the depth of Han's philosophical thinking and its overall coherence with his psychosocial critique of modernity. Therefore, we think that, going forward, Han will offer clues about how he is rethinking these ultimate questions thrown open by *Lob der Erde*. Nonetheless, even as he revisits key thinkers and traditions, sifting out new possibilities and dangers, it has long been clear where Han wants to go. Here he is unwavering. He wants to go towards *thinking*, blazing unapologetically theoretical trails, rather than being informed by Big Data, towards *beauty* by lingering with what challenges us, and towards a deep-cosmopolitan *friendliness* that makes us more receptive to one another and to the earth.

# *Notes*

## Chapter 1 Burnout

1. The figure of the "self-made man" came in simpler or more nuanced forms in the nineteenth-century United States. Perhaps the most nuanced comes in a frequently delivered speech by Frederick Douglass. His self-made man is not an achievement subject because he feels external pressure in an "urgent, pinching, imperious necessity" (2018, p. 431).
2. Unless otherwise noted, emphasis within quotation is always in the original.
3. Drawing attention to such a continuum might enlist critical theorists to Han's concern for the seemingly "first-world problem" of achievement subjects' self-harm. Additionally, Han's denial that wealthy consumers really enjoy *freedom* from their greater powers of consumption and self-invention neutralizes neoliberal tradeoff arguments for oppressive conditions suffered by workers in the Global South.
4. Han also distinguishes power and violence from force or coercion [*Zwang*], even when other writers do not insist upon this further distinction (WP 3 and 115n48).
5. Keefe's *Empire of Pain* (2021) tells the story of Arthur Sackler and his journey from selling Valium in the 1960s to building Purdue Pharma and generating $35 billion in OxyContin sales. The mislabeling and misprescription of OxyContin and other opioids led to lawsuits from multiple states and a $4.5 billion settlement with the Sackler family in September 2021.

## Chapter 2 World-Friendliness

1. Han has a footnote that may give readers the distorted impression that he advocates for a return to Hegelian freedom: "Freedom, in an authentic sense, is tied to negativity. It is always freedom from constraint that the immunologically Other exercises" (BS 54n3).
2. Authors' correspondence with Byung-Chul Han.
3. Ibid.
4. All translations that indicate Han's original German texts are our own.
5. One of the few political theorists who begins from the late Heidegger is Reiner Schürmann (1987). Schürmann implies a more direct relationship between Heidegger and Arendt, arguing that the political upshot of Heidegger's thinking is *an-archic*, meaning that every foundational principle [*archē*] for action will expire once he makes self-concealment the essence of Being.
6. On Heidegger's thinking having "no room for political philosophy," Arendt's verdict is echoed by Leo Strauss (1971).
7. Heidegger's observation that *Ort* originally means "spear-tip" is significant for Han, because it shows how force "worlds" the observable world (PZB 40; WP 80–1). For Han we must relinquish this somehow.
8. A theologian and philosopher of religion influenced by Heidegger such as Jean-Yves Lacoste can therefore propose that boredom is the "principal mood" of "nocturnal experience" by drawing on Heidegger's language of ultimacy. This boredom is "an indispensable moment in the liturgical life," Lacoste suggests, because "the boredom felt before God is really part of the secret of nocturnal experience" (2004, pp. 148–9). More deflationary, Han does not think boredom requires anxiety about death or whether the gods or fate will appear.
9. We emend Han's Latin translation slightly here.
10. Han might say that to be philosophical here would also be a matter of practice and not just of words and concepts. If philosophy is only the latter, the Zen masters reject it: "The experiences of being or of consciousness that the practice of Zen Buddhism works towards cannot fully be captured in conceptual language" (PZB vii). As we shall see, Han also recovers the roots of Western philosophy in contemplative practice. On "philosophy as a way of life," see Hadot (1995).
11. This phrase "epic of haikus" is from Handke (1985a, p. 52).

## Chapter 3 Digital Bias

1. "Communicating ourselves to death" is the formula for domination which Han attributes to the information regime: "a form of domination

in which information and its processing by algorithms and artificial intelligence have a decisive influence on social, economic and political processes" (I 1). It is intended as an updated version of Neil Postman's famous epithet "amusing ourselves to death," which characterizes the twentieth century's regime of mass media (Postman, 1985).
2 McLuhan calls new media "anti-environments" that make the older taken-for-granted environments visible (2003, pp. 13–14).
3 For a useful historical overview of the rise of empirical media studies in the US and the configuration of the then new field of communication research as behavioral science, see Czitrom (1982, pp. 122–46).
4 For a critique of the critical-theoretical tradition from a technological lens, see Packer (2013).
5 Bernhard Siegert (2013), one of Germany's most prominent media scholars, contests whether so-called German media theory can even be understood as a theory of media.
6 The anthropologist and paleontologist André Leroi-Gourhan (1993), who placed emphasis on the essential technicity of human beings, is an important influence on the posthumanist turn in media studies.
7 Han resists the posthuman or anthropotechnical drift in early German media theory by continually returning to contemplative practices that cultivate our receptivity to the world and to closely related moods such as boredom and friendly tiredness.
8 According to Innis (2008), durable, time-bias media such as stone tablets, clay, or sculptures are biased towards the persistence of messages over time and favor decentralized but hierarchical societies. More ephemeral, portable media such as papyrus and paper are biased towards the rapid transmission of messages across space, favoring expansionist empires that are less hierarchical and maintained through the administrative efficiency of these lighter, less expensive media.
9 "Intelligent virtual assistants" are part of the Internet of Things, a vast computing infrastructure consisting of digitally networked, sensor- and technology-equipped "smart" objects that are continually gathering and sharing data. Such "smart" objects are not limited to such things as entertainment devices or wireless-enabled wearable technology but include everyday household objects such as kitchen appliances, camera-equipped doorbells, and thermostats. Han discusses Alexa and other "smart objects" throughout *Non-Things*.
10 On the swarm trope, see Galloway and Thacker (2007); Berardi (2012); Galloway (2014); Citton (2017); and Hayles (2017).
11 On the psychopolitical significance of rage, see Sloterdijk (2010, pp. 13–22).
12 For Han's discussion of the absence of bodily signs in digital communication (particularly those of the voice and the gaze), see EO 44–58.
13 Han frequently improvises on Schmitt's definition of sovereignty: e.g.,

"sovereign is he who decides on the flow of data in the network" (CDD 23); "sovereign is he who has control over the information on the web" (I 11).
14  In 2018, Asmodee, a French publisher of board games, card games, and role-playing games, released the boardgame *Nosedive*, based on the *Black Mirror* episode. After being assigned an initial social score, players use a mobile app to give other players challenging experiences and then assess them with a star rating (McWhertor, 2018).
15  China's social credit system, first piloted in 2009, gives citizens an overall rating based on continually gathered civic data. Scores affect citizens' access to a wide variety of social and economic opportunities, with low scores resulting in their being blacklisted. And, as with the score in "Nosedive," a person's overall score was also dependent on the scores of the people in their social circle (see Denyer, 2016; Kobie, 2019). For a sample of writers who have compared "Nosedive" to China's social credit system, see Bruney (2018), Hughes (2017), Leane (2016), Sayer (2017), Stern (2016), Urueña and Melikyan (2019), and Vincent (2017).
16  Barba-Kay notes how digital transparency requires us to make "obligatory rehearsal[s]" of the "misdeeds" of artists we commend and offers Handke and Wallace as examples of figures who come with an inevitable "asterisk" (2023, p. 34). The reader may consider this our asterisk.
17  Han's extended treatment on Jünger's reflections on pain connects modern algophobia to digital media (PS 42–54); see also Stoneman (forthcoming).
18  For commentary on Sloterdijk's heterodox media theory, including a brief contrast to Han's, see Stoneman (2021).

## Chapter 4 Digital Psychopolitics

1  Han also claims that "the digital produces the compulsion for transparency" – that is, the "imperative" that "everything must lie open, ready and available for everyone" at all times (IS 39). This would appear to contradict his assertion that transparency is, at root, an economic imperative. But here we may distinguish between proximate causes (the bias of transparency that inheres in the digital) and the more fundamental – because environmental – cause of neoliberal hypercapitalism.
2  To be fair, Han does not acknowledge Foucault and company's differentiation of a liberal form of biopolitics from a collectivist one. By eliding the former from his juxtaposition of biopower and psychopower, Han makes the gap between his position and Foucault's unnecessarily cavernous. Nevertheless, while the individualistic,

anatomo-political form of biopower marks a transition beyond a biopolitics of the population, it remains a biopolitical variant, which operates through a rational administration of disciplinary compulsion and control. At the same time, the accompanying fixation with exteriority leads Foucault to disregard the unique affordances of digital (or electronic) media in processes of subjectivation. This is an important component of Han's critique of biopower, even though it remains implicit.

3 Despite Han's mainly negative critique of Flusser's media theory, their approaches to the study of media are not mutually exclusive. Stoneman (2024) demonstrates how Han's work can even clarify, supplement, and extend Flusser's media theory.

4 For Berardi, the 1990s mark a fundamental mutation in modern-day capitalism, namely, the entrance of cognitive labor into the cycle of virtual production. From that point on, he argues, cognitive labor becomes enterprise, entering "the formation circuits of the Techno-Sphere and media-scape" (2009, p. 96). This mutational process also gives rise to the "first post-alphabetic generation" (the Xennials or, in America, the Oregon Trail Generation), those "exposed since birth to the electronic flows of technical images, whose perception was formed in a media environment where most experiences were the effect of simulation" (Berardi, 2015, p. 112).

5 Berardi's concept of semiocapitalism is also a close analog to Yann Moulier Boutang's (2011) cognitive capitalism and Shoshana Zuboff's (2015, 2019) surveillance capitalism.

6 One does not need to think too long or hard to come up with pre-digital examples highlighting the tendency towards self-designing projects. For instance, since at least the 1920s, modern advertising has relied on a variety of persuasive techniques (e.g., celebrity testimonial, snob appeal, bandwagon effect, etc.) to influence potential consumers to buy something. Many of these tactics attempt to convince consumers that using a product will enable them to achieve and maintain new levels of self-improvement. Special-interest magazines, as well, especially those focused on health, financial investment, fashion, and lifestyles, play to niches of self-optimization and design. Even the rarified world of academia includes projections such as Foucault's "care of the self" (2008, pp. 161–4) and Guattari's "aesthetic paradigm" (1995, pp. 98–118), which, while more politically engaged than run-of-the-mill advertising, still place emphasis on self-positioning and self-affirmation.

7 Martin Dodge and Robert Kitchin describe "lifelogging" as "a form of pervasive computing, consisting of a unified digital record of the totality of an individual's experiences, captured multi-modally through digital sensors and stored permanently as a personal multimedia archive" (2007, p. 431).

8 The rise of data could be read as the return of the kind of rationalistic metanarrative that Lyotard (1984) saw collapsing in the back half of the twentieth century, but a difference, Han suggests, is the fragmenting effect of the proliferation of data in all areas of life, and the far less robust or coherent account of reason behind it.

## Chapter 5 Duration

1 At the beginning of *The Scent of Time*, Han notes death-avoidance, the failure to take death "into life and into the present as a shaping and consummating force" (ST 3). Han briefly returns here to a central concern of early works such as *Tod und Alterität*. See the discussion of this concern in chapter 2 of this study.
2 Mythical time is cyclical, while historical time is linear. The messianic time of Judaism and the eschatological time of Christianity are frequently juxtaposed with the cyclical time of other traditional religions. The former is sometimes blamed for displacing the latter, contributing to the loss of meaningful time and a loss of meaningful relationships with natural cycles. Clocks, later used to measure the industrial workday, were first used in the West to count the hours of the daily office. See Odell (2023, pp. 3–42). Han notes how historical time *is* first "eschatological time," with the eschaton eventually secularizing into social progress or the progress of reason. But he also notes the "cyclical" rhythms of the Sabbath and the liturgical calendar that make the time of Judaism and Christianity cyclical as well as linear (ST, DR, VC). One might also add that "mythic religions" at times have more linear elements, such as different ages of the gods and of humanity.
3 Han also criticizes the loss of contemplation and the privileging of work in modern philosophy, namely in Hegel's dialectic of "master and slave" and Marx's revision of Hegel, in which the human becomes *"animal laborans"* and in which *"spirit is* [effectively] *labour"* (ST 97). Somewhat surprisingly, neither *The Scent of Time* nor *The Burnout Society* addresses how Kant restricts the scope of contemplation. This is a concern in Han's dissertation on Heidegger, however.
4 Lyotard is not taking aim at narrative *tout court*. His focus in *The Postmodern Condition* is the grand narratives of Han's "historical time," with their strong belief in progress underwritten by scientific reason. There is perhaps less distance between Han's ultimate position and Lyotard's than the exposition in *The Scent of Time* suggests. Lyotard explicitly juxtaposes the "metanarrative" of scientific rationality against a self-legitimating "narrative knowledge" that is marked by "internal equilibrium and conviviality" (1984, p. 7). The collapse

Notes to pp. 132–146

of the metanarratives of historical time might allow for the return of this kind of narrative knowledge. Lyotard discusses "little" narratives, often contested by each other and themselves suffering fragmentation in postmodernity but also offering pluralistic possibility. That said, the Lyotard of *The Inhuman* does often orient these narratives around the event, and he is concerned with the anxiety caused by the event-that-may-not-happen (1991, pp. 63–4).

5   Han notes antecedents to Zen wandering in the Taoism of Laozi (A 5-6).
6   Given omnipresent and insidious forms of advertisement, Crawford (2015) and Odell (2019) call for a politics of attention. Han can contribute to such a politics by helping us to see how "positive violence" is often mistaken for freedom.
7   Jennifer Summit and Blakey Vermeule also draw on premodern Jewish and Christian contemplative traditions to call for a renewed balance in *Action versus Contemplation: Why an Ancient Debate Still Matters* (2018, pp. 142–8).
8   Albert Borgmann, who also wishes to bring Heidegger's account of things out of the Black Forest, speaks of "focal" things and practices that bring people together in substantive and orienting ways. The meal prepared for and shared at the table is one of his key examples (1987, pp. 196–210).
9   It is somewhat surprising that Han does not draw more from Confucianism, given its emphasis on ritual.
10  Yuk Hui, who, like Han, is a prominent philosopher of technology, aesthetics, and the dialogue between Eastern and Western traditions, qualifies Han's suggestion in *Shanzhai* "that there's almost no question of authenticity in Chinese art" (Hui and Schwabsky, 2023). Hui (2015, p. 190) elsewhere builds upon Han's distinction between Heidegger's "way" [*Weg*] and the way in Taoism.
11  In *Saving Beauty* (70–1), Han briefly discusses festivity via Hans Georg Gadamer's "The Relevance of the Beautiful" (1987). In *The Disappearance of Rituals* (36–46), he takes some of his explicit bearings about festivity and liturgy from Franz Rosenzweig's *The Star of Redemption* (1985). In *Vita Contemplativa* (61–2), he offers reflections on Rabbi Abraham Joshua Heschel's classic work *The Sabbath* (2005). Han draws some quotations from one of Josef Pieper's studies on contemplation in the German edition of *Vita Contemplativa*, but there are also interesting parallels between Han's accounts of leisure and festivity and Pieper's. See Šokčević and Živić (2021).
12  Leslie Marmon Silko's 1977 novel *Ceremony* is a compelling work to consider alongside *The Disappearance of Rituals*. It tells of the Pueblo veteran Tayo's search for a renewed ceremony to provide stabilizing continuity and healing for himself and his people within a broader Western society that, via colonialism and its attendant

## Chapter 6 Eros

1 Elias Canetti (1990, pp. 29–30) provides the main example of listening in *The Expulsion of the Other* (see the extended discussion of Canetti in TA).
2 In contrast to Agamben, Han is more sensitive to the pernicious possibilities in reading the Aristotelian friend as an *alter ego* (PZB 89–91).
3 Han draws on both Bennett and Gumbrecht in *Non-Things* (96, 106). It would also be interesting to bring Han's account of things and non-things into conversation with the object-oriented Ontology (OOO) of Graham Harman. There are many possibilities here, but one would be to compare Harman's "hot" and "cold" things to Han's "informatons" and "discrete" things or to use this same McLuhan-inspired dimension of Harmon's account as an approach to some of Han's favored artworks (Harman, 2020, pp. 178–9).
4 Han encourages a friendliness that extends to the uncanny and strange. See his discussion of Franz Kafka's house-haunting thing-creature "Odradek" in *Non-Things* (53–6; cf. Kafka, 1988, pp. 160–1).
5 Regarding plants, Han would likely be intrigued by the bold queries about "plant thinking" of Luce Irigaray and Michael Marder (2016).
6 See Bartles (2021) on the importance of negativity in Han's aesthetics.
7 Han critiques the pervasive and superficial sort of picture snapping encouraged by smartphones, but photography can be a rigorous training in attention, and the photograph can preserve otherness. See his discussion of photography in *Saving Beauty*, where he discusses Roland Barthes's concept of the *punctum* (33–9; cf. Barthes, 1982).
8 Another reason they are linked is that the awareness of one's approaching death can paradoxically return one to life, make one more present, more receptive to beauty and eros. See Han's discussion of Lars von Trier's 2011 film *Melancholia* in *The Agony of Eros* (1–8). An impending catastrophic planetary collision stirs eros in the film's depressed protagonist Justine (Kirsten Dunst).
9 Scott Beauchamp, who often writes appreciatively about Han, critiques him in this regard: "But, the more Han you read, the stronger your suspicions grow that he has built a cargo cult of meaning, reverse engineering it from its physical and psychological components while ignoring the actual transcendent mystery which makes meaning live within the world" (2019). Beauchamp focuses mainly on Han's *Good Entertainment* in this piece.

10 We have cited Anne Dufourmantelle throughout this chapter. There is perhaps no recent thinker who is more of a kindred spirit. Han's work on transparency finds a compelling counterpart in her *In Defense of Secrets* (2021), his work on contemporary risk aversion in her *In Praise of Risk* (2019). Her notion of "gentleness" (2018) is close to his friendliness. (Han himself connects gentleness and friendliness in ST 113). Dufourmantelle, too, draws on Eastern thought: "The East has (revered this spiritual authority [of gentleness] earlier and more profoundly than the West" (2018, p. 43). Even stylistically, she too favors shorter, meditative books and chapters.

11 It is telling that "Is Zen Nihilistic?" is the title of the third chapter in D. T. Suzuki's *An Introduction to Zen Buddhism*, which was crucial to the twentieth-century reception of Zen in the English-speaking world (1991, pp. 48–57). The philosophers of the Kyoto School, in conversation with Western philosophy, are often precisely interested in the Buddhist nothing as an alternative or as a way through modern nihilism. See Nishitani (1982).

12 It is somewhat surprising that Han does not turn to St Francis of Assisi, his famous canticle, and the Franciscan tradition, though he does describe his visit to a Franciscan monastery (LE 138) and approve of Pope Francis's choice of a pontifical name (Bae, 2013). Dufourmantelle writes, "The proximity of this saintly figure's gentleness to the plant and animal kingdoms is rare in the West" (2018, p. 35).

13 Perhaps one can make an analogy to Taoism here, which Han sometimes discusses in his writings (A, PZB). Developed in a time of widespread war and political calculation, Taoism seeks to cultivate an alternative to the grasping that often plagues politics and intensifies conflicts. One could perhaps say Taoism involves a "politics of inactivity," especially because Taoists discourage the resolve to *do something* that often only worsens political crises.

# *Works by Han*

*Absence: On the Culture and Philosophy of the Far East*, trans. D. Steuer. Polity, 2023 [A].
*The Agony of Eros*, trans. E. Butler. MIT Press, 2017 [AE].
"All That Is Solid Melts into Information," interview by N. Gardels, *Noēma*, April 21, 2022 [NI].
*The Burnout Society*, trans. E. Butler. Stanford Briefs, 2015 [BS].
"Byung-Chul Han: 'The Smartphone Is a Tool of Domination. It Acts Like a Rosary,'" interview by S. C. Fanjul, *El País*, October 15, 2021 [EPI].
*Capitalism and the Death Drive*, trans. D. Steuer. Polity, 2021 [CDD].
*Digitale Rationalität und das Ende des kommunikativen Handelns*. Matthes & Seitz, 2013 [DRE].
*The Disappearance of Rituals: A Topology of the Present*, trans. D. Steuer. Polity, 2020 [DR].
*The Expulsion of the Other: Society, Perception and Communication Today*, trans. W. Hoban. Polity, 2018 [EO].
*Good Entertainment: A Deconstruction of the Western Passion Narrative*, trans. A. N. West. MIT Press, 2019 [GE].
*Hegel und die Macht: Ein Versuch über die Freundlichkeit*. Wilhelm Fink, 2005 [HM].
*Heideggers Herz: Zum Begriff der Stimmung bei Martin Heidegger*. Wilhelm Fink, 1996 [HH].
*Hyperculture: Culture and Globalisation*, trans. D. Steuer. Polity, 2022 [H].
"I Practise Philosophy as Art," interview by G. Borcherdt, *ArtReview*, December 2, 2021 [ARI].
*Infocracy: Digitization and the Crisis of Democracy*, trans. D. Steuer. Polity, 2022 [I].
*In the Swarm: Digital Prospects*, trans. E. Butler. MIT Press, 2017 [IS].
*Lob der Erde: Eine Reise in den Garten*. Ullstein, 2018 [LE].

*Martin Heidegger: Eine Einführung.* Wilhelm Fink, 1999 [MH].
*Müdigkeitsgesellschaft: Byung-Chul Han in Seoul/Berlin* (documentary film), 2015 [M].
*Non-Things: Upheaval in the Lifeworld*, trans. D. Steuer. Polity, 2022 [N].
*The Palliative Society: Pain Today*, trans. D. Steuer. Polity, 2021 [PS].
"Philosopher, Culture Theorist Byung-Chul Han's Commencement Speech," MOME: Moholy-Nagy University of Art and Design Budapest, 2022 [MCS].
*The Philosophy of Zen Buddhism*, trans. D. Steuer. Polity, 2022 [PZB].
*Psychopolitics: Neoliberalism and New Technologies of Power*, trans. E. Butler. Verso, 2017 [P].
*Saving Beauty*, trans. D. Steuer. Polity, 2018 [SB].
*Shanzhai: Deconstruction in Chinese*, trans. P. Hurd. MIT Press, 2017 [S].
*The Scent of Time: A Philosophical Essay on the Art of Lingering*, trans. D. Steuer. Polity, 2017 [ST].
"The Tiredness Virus, " *The Nation*, April 12, 2021 [NTV].
*Tod und Alterität.* Wilhelm Fink, 2002 [TA].
*Todesarten: philosophische Untersuchungen zum Tod.* Wilhelm Fink, 1998 [T].
*Topology of Violence*, trans. A. DeMarco. MIT Press, 2018 [TV].
*The Transparency Society*, trans. E. Butler. Stanford Briefs, 2015 [TS].
*Vita Contemplativa: In Praise of Inactivity*, trans. D. Steuer. Polity, 2024 [VC].
*What Is Power?*, trans. D. Steuer. Polity, 2019 [WP].

# References

Abbey, R. (2000) *Charles Taylor*. Princeton University Press.
Agamben, G. (1998) *Homo Sacer: Sovereign Power and Bare Life*, trans. D. Heller-Roazen. Stanford University Press.
—— (2009) "The Friend," trans. D. Kishik and S. Pedatella, in *What Is an Apparatus? And Other Essays*. Stanford University Press.
Anderson, C. (2008) "The End of Theory: The Data Deluge Makes the Scientific Method Obsolete," *Wired*, June 23.
Andrejevic, M. (2019) *Automated Media*. Routledge.
Andrejevic, M., and Burdon, M. (2015) "Defining Sensor Society," *Television and New Media*, 16(1).
Appiah, K. A. (2006) *Cosmopolitanism: Ethics in a World of Strangers*. W. W. Norton.
Arendt, H. (1958) *The Human Condition*. University of Chicago Press.
—— (1977) *The Life of the Mind*. Harcourt.
Aristotle (2011) *Nicomachean Ethics*, trans. R. Bartlett and S. Collins. University of Chicago Press.
Augustine (1998) *The City of God against the Pagans*, trans. R. W. Dyson. Cambridge University Press.
Badiou, A. (2012) *In Praise of Love*, trans. P. Bush. New Press.
Bae, Y.-D. (2013) "Restoring the Fragrance to Our Fast-Paced Lives," *Korea JoongAng Daily*, English edn, March 31.
Ballard, J. G. (2000) *Super-Cannes*. Picador.
—— (2006) *Kingdom Come*. Fourth Estate.
Barba-Kay, A. (2023) *A Web of Our Own Making: The Nature of Digital Formation*. Cambridge University Press.
Barthes, R. (1982) *Camera Lucida: Reflections on Photography*, trans. R. Howard. Hill & Wang.
Bartles, J. A. (2021) "Byung-Chul Han's Negativity; or, Restoring Beauty

and Rage in Excessively Positive Times," *CR: The New Centennial Review*, 21(3).
Bataille, G. (1986) *Erotism: Death and Sensuality*, trans. M. Dalwood. City Lights.
Baudelaire, C. (1919) "The Generous Player," in T. R. Smith (ed.), *Baudelaire: His Prose and Poetry*. Boni & Liveright.
Baudrillard, J. (1985) "The Masses: The Implosion of the Social in the Media," *New Literary History*, 16(3).
—— (1988) *America*, trans. C. Turner. Verso.
—— (1990) *Fatal Strategies*, trans. P. Beitchman and W. G. J. Niesluchowski. Semiotext(e).
—— (1994) *The Illusion of the End*, trans. C. Turner. Stanford University Press.
—— (1998) *The Consumer Society: Myths and Structures*, trans. C. Turner. Sage.
—— (2012) *The Ecstasy of Communication*, trans. B. Schütze and C. Schütze. Semiotext(e).
Bauman, Z. (2003) *Liquid Love: On the Frailty of Human Bonds*. Polity.
Beauchamp, S. (2019) "Byung-Chul Han's Sinking Cargo Cult of Meaning," *Church Life Journal*, November 5.
Bell, D. (2021) "J. G. Ballard's Surrealist Liberalism," *Political Theory*, 49(6).
Benjamin, W. (1999) *The Arcades Project*, trans. H. Eiland and K. McLaughlin. Belknap Press.
—— (2007) *Illuminations*, trans. H. Zohn. Schocken Books.
Bennett, J. (2010) *Vibrant Matter: A Political Ecology of Things*. Duke University Press.
Berardi, F. (2009) *The Soul at Work: From Alienation to Autonomy*, trans. F. Cadel and G. Mecchia. Semiotext(e).
—— (2012) *The Uprising: On Poetry and Finance*. Semiotext(e).
—— (2015) *And: Phenomenology of the End*. Semiotext(e).
Berners-Lee, T., Hendler, J., and Lassila, O. (2001) "The Semantic Web," *Scientific American*, May 17.
Birhane, A. (2021) "The Impossibility of Automating Ambiguity," *Artificial Life*, 27.
Blanchot, M. (1986) *The Writing of the Disaster*, trans. A. Smock. University of Nebraska Press.
Borgmann, A. (1987) *Technology and the Character of Contemporary Life: A Philosophical Inquiry*. University of Chicago Press.
Bourdieu, P., and Wacquant, L. J. D. (1992) *An Invitation to Reflexive Sociology*. University of Chicago Press.
Brown, W. (2005) *Edgework: Critical Essays on Knowledge and Politics*. Princeton University Press.
Bruney, G. (2018) "A 'Black Mirror' Episode Is Coming to Life in China," *Esquire*, March 17.
Buber, M. (1958) *I and Thou*. 2nd edn, trans. R. G. Smith. Charles Scribner's Sons.

―――― (1965) "Distance and Relation," trans. R. G. Smith, in M. Friedman (ed.), *The Knowledge of Man: Selected Essays*. Harper & Row.

Buongiorno, F. (2022) "Beyond Efficiency: Comparing Andrew Feenberg's and Byung-Chul Han's Philosophy of Technology," in D. Cressman (ed.), *The Necessity of Critique: Andrew Feenberg and the Philosophy of Technology*. Springer.

Burke, E. (1998) *A Philosophical Enquiry into the Origin of Our Ideas of the Sublime and Beautiful*, ed. A. Phillips. Oxford University Press.

Burke, K. (1969) *A Rhetoric of Motives*. University of California Press.

Bush, R. (2008) *The Citizen Audience*. Routledge.

Butler, J. (1990) *Gender Trouble: Feminism and the Subversion of Identity*. Routledge.

Cain, S. (2022) *Bittersweet: How Sorrow and Longing Make Us Whole*. Crown.

Campbell, R., Martin, C. R., and Fabos, B. (2011) *Media and Culture: An Introduction to Mass Communication*. Bedford/St. Martin's.

Canetti, E. (1990) *The Play of the Eyes*, trans. R. Manheim. André Deutsch.

Carey, J. W. (2009) "Mass Communication and Cultural Studies," in *Communication as Culture: Essays on Media and Society*, rev. edn. Routledge.

Chun, W. H. K. (2016) *Updating to Remain the Same: Habitual New Media*. MIT Press.

Citton, Y. (2017) *The Ecology of Attention*, trans. B. Norman. Polity.

―――― (2019) *Mediarchy*, trans. Andrew Brown. Polity.

Connolly, W. (2011) *A World of Becoming*. Duke University Press.

Corrao, M. (2019) "On B. R. Yeager's 'Amygdalatropolis,'" *Newfound*, 10(1).

Cowen, T. (2013) *Average Is Over: Powering America beyond the Age of the Great Stagnation*. Dutton.

Crawford, M. (2009) *Shop Class as Soulcraft: An Inquiry into the Value of Work*. Penguin.

―――― (2015) *The World Beyond Your Head: On Becoming an Individual in an Age of Distractions*. Farrar, Straus & Giroux.

Curran, T., and Hill, A. P. (2019) "Perfectionism Is Increasing Over Time: A Meta-Analysis of Birth Cohort Differences from 1989 to 2016," *Psychological Bulletin*, 145.

Czitrom, D. J. (1982) *Media and the American Mind: From Morse to McLuhan*. University of North Carolina Press.

Dallmayr, F. R. (1984) "Ontology of Freedom: Heidegger and Political Philosophy," *Political Theory*, 12(2).

―――― (1995) *The Other Heidegger*. Cornell University Press.

―――― (2004) "Beyond Monologue: For a Comparative Political Theory," *Perspectives on Politics*, 2(2).

Deleuze, G. (1992) "What Is a *Dispositif?*," in F. Ewald (ed.), *Michel Foucault Philosopher*. Routledge.

―――― (1995) "Postscript on Control Societies," trans. M. Joughin, in *Negotiations: 1972–1990*. Columbia University Press.

Deneen, P. (2018) *Why Liberalism Failed*. Yale University Press.

Denyer, S. (2016) "China's Plan to Organize its Society Relies on 'Big Data' to Rate Everyone," *Washington Post*, October 22.
Desmond, W. (2012) *The William Desmond Reader*, ed C. B. Simpson. SUNY Press.
Dodge, M., and Kitchin, R. (2007) "'Outlines of a World Coming into Existence': Pervasive Computing and the Ethics of Forgetting," *Environment and Planning B*, 34(3).
Douglass, F. (2018) *The Speeches of Frederick Douglass*, ed. J. McKivigan, J. Husband and H. Kaufman. Yale University Press.
Dufourmantelle, A. (2018) *Power of Gentleness: Meditations on the Risk of Living*, trans. K. Payne and V. Sallé. Fordham University Press.
—— (2019) *In Praise of Risk*, trans. S. Miller. Fordham University Press.
—— (2021) *In Defense of Secrets*, trans. L. Turner. Fordham University Press.
Ehrenberg, A. (2010) *Weariness of the Self: Diagnosing the History of Depression in the Contemporary Age*. McGill–Queen's University Press.
Eliade, M. (1959) *Cosmos and History: The Myth of the Eternal Return*, trans. W. Trask. Harper.
Ellul, J. (1964) *The Technological Society*, trans. J. Wilkinson. Vintage.
Esposito, R. (2012a) "The *Dispositif* of the Person," *Law, Culture, and the Humanities*, 8(1).
—— (2012b) *The Third Person*, trans. Z. Hanafi. Polity.
Euripides (1990) *Medea*, trans. M. Townsend, in R. W. Corrigan (ed.), *Classical Tragedy, Greek and Roman: 8 Plays*. Applause.
Ferreira, B. (2002) *Stimmung bei Heidegger: Das Phänomen der Stimmung im Kontext von Heideggers Existenzialanalyse des Daseins*. Springer.
Ferris, T. (2013) "The First-Ever Quantified Self Notes (Plus: LSD as Cognitive Enhancer?)," *The Blog of Author Tim Ferris*, April 3; https://tim.blog/2013/04/03/the-first-ever-quantified-self-notes-plus-lsd-as-cognitive-enhancer/.
Fisher, M. (2009) *Capitalist Realism: Is There No Alternative?* Zer0 Books.
Fitzgerald, D. (2021) "Review of *Amygdalatropolis*," *Heavy Feather Review*, December 7.
Fitzsimmons, W., McGrath, M. E., and Ducey, C. (2000) "Time Out or Burn Out for the Next Generation," *New York Times*, December 6.
Flood, G. (2013) *The Truth Within: A History of Inwardness in Christianity, Hinduism, and Buddhism*. Oxford University Press.
Flusser, V. (1997) *Medienkultur*. Fischer.
—— (2000) *Towards a Philosophy of Photography*, trans. A. Mathews. Reaktion Books.
—— (2002) *Writings*, trans. E. Eisel, ed. A. Ströhl. University of Minnesota Press.
—— (2009) *Kommunikologie weiter denken: Die Bochumer Vorlesungen*. Fischer.
—— (2011a) *Does Writing Have a Future?*, trans. N. A. Roth. University of Minnesota Press.

―― (2011b) *Into the Universe of Technical Images*, trans. N. A. Roth. University of Minnesota Press.
Foucault, M. (1978) *The History of Sexuality*, Volume 1: *An Introduction*, trans. R. Hurley. Vintage.
―― (1988) "Technologies of the Self," in L. H. Martin, H. Gutman, and P. H. Hutton (eds), *Technologies of the Self: A Seminar with Michel Foucault*. University of Massachusetts Press.
―― (1995) *Discipline and Punish: The Birth of the Prison*, 2nd edn, trans. A. Sheridan. Vintage.
―― (2005) *The Hermeneutics of the Subject: Lectures at the Collège de France 1981–1982*, trans. G. Burchell. Picador.
―― (2008) *The Courage of Truth (The Government of Self and Others II): Lectures at the Collège de France 1983–1984*, trans. G. Burchell. Picador.
―― (2010) *The Birth of Biopolitics: Lectures at the Collège de France 1978–79*, trans. G. Burchell. Picador.
Franklin, S. W. (2023) *The Cult of Creativity: A Surprisingly Recent History*. University of Chicago Press.
Freud, S. (1989) *Civilization and its Discontents*, ed. and trans. J. Strachey. W. W. Norton.
Freudenberger, H. (1974) "Staff Burn-Out," *Journal of Social Issues*, 30(1).
Gadamer, H.-G. (1987) "The Relevance of the Beautiful," trans. N. Walker, in R. Bernasconi (ed.), *The Relevance of the Beautiful and Other Essays*. Cambridge University Press.
Galloway, A. R. (2012) *The Interface Effect*. Polity.
―― (2014) "Love of the Middle," in A. R. Galloway, E. Thacker, and M. Wark, *Excommunication: Three Inquiries in Media and Mediation*. University of Chicago Press.
Galloway, A. R., and Thacker, E. (2007) *The Exploit: A Theory of Networks*. University of Minnesota Press.
Gawande, A. (2015) *Being Mortal: Medicine and What Matters in the End*. Picador.
Gertz, N. (2018) *Nihilism and Technology*. Rowman & Littlefield.
Girard, R. (1977) *Violence and the Sacred*, trans. P. Gregory. Johns Hopkins University Press.
Goodwin, W. (2022) *Toxic Positivity*. Penguin.
Graeber, D. (2011) *Debt: The First 5,000 Years*. Melville House.
Greenfield, A. (2017) *Radical Technologies: The Design of Everyday Life*. Verso.
Guattari, F. (1984) "La Crise de production de subjectivité," Seminar of April 3; www.revue-chimeres.fr.drupal_chimeres/files/840403.pdf.
―― (1995) *Chaosmosis*, trans. P. Bains and J. Pefanis. Indiana University Press.
Gumbrecht, H. U. (2004) *Production of Presence: What Meaning Cannot Convey*. Stanford University Press.
Gumbrecht, H. U., and Pfeiffer, K. L. (eds) (1994) *Materialities of Communication*, trans. W. Whobrey. Stanford University Press.

Habermas, J. (1990) *The Philosophical Discourse of Modernity: Twelve Lectures*, trans. F. G. Lawrence. MIT Press.
Hadot, P. (1995) *Philosophy as a Way of Life: Spiritual Exercises from Socrates to Foucault*, trans. M. Chase. Blackwell.
Handke, P. (1985a) *Die Geschichte des Bleistifts*. Suhrkamp.
——— (1985b) *Slow Homecoming*, trans. R. Manheim. Farrar, Straus & Giroux.
——— (1994) "Essay on Tiredness," in *The Jukebox and Other Essays on Storytelling*, trans. R. Manheim and K. Winston. Farrar, Straus & Giroux.
Harari, Y. N. (2017) *Homo Deus: A Brief History of Tomorrow*. Harper.
Haraway, D. (2016) *Staying with the Trouble: Making Kin in the Chthulucene*. Duke University Press.
Hardt, M., and Negri, A. (2000) *Empire*. Harvard University Press.
Harman, G. (2020) *Art and Objects*. Polity.
Hayek, F. A. (2011) *The Constitution of Liberty*, ed. R. Hamowy. University of Chicago Press.
——— (2018) *Studies on the Abuse and Decline of Reason*, ed. B. Caldwell. Liberty Fund.
Hayles, N. K. (2017) *Unthought: The Power of the Cognitive Nonconscious*. University of Chicago Press.
Hegel, G. W. F. (1977) *Phenomenology of Spirit*, trans. A. V. Miller. Oxford University Press.
——— (1991) *Elements of the Philosophy of Right*, trans. H. B. Nisbet. Cambridge University Press.
——— (1993) *Introductory Lectures on Aesthetics*, ed. M. Inwood, trans. B. Bosanquet. Penguin.
——— (2010) *Aesthetics: Lectures on Fine Art*, Volume I, trans. T. M. Knox. Clarendon Press.
Heidegger, M. (1962) *Being and Time*, trans. J. Macquarrie and E. Robinson. Harper & Row.
——— (1966) *Discourse on Thinking*, trans. J. M. Anderson and E. H. Freund. Harper Torchbooks.
——— (1975) *Poetry, Language, Thought*, trans. A. Hofstadter. Perennial Library.
——— (1980) *Hölderlins Hymne "Germanien" und "Der Rhein": Gesamtausgabe*, Volume 39. Vittorio Klostermann.
——— (1981) "Only a God Can Save Us," in T. Sheehan (ed. and trans.), *Heidegger: The Man and Thinker*. Precedent.
——— (1985) *Schelling's Treatise on the Essence of Human Freedom*, trans. J. Stambaugh. Ohio University Press.
——— (1989) *Beiträge zur Philosophie: Gesamtausgabe*, Volume 65. Vittorio Klostermann.
——— (1992) *Parmenides*, trans. A. Schuwer and R. Rojcewicz. Indiana University Press.

—— (1995) *The Fundamental Concepts of Metaphysics: World, Finitude, Solitude*, trans. W. McNeil and N. Walker. Indiana University Press.

—— (1998) "Traditional Language and Technological Language," *Journal of Philosophical Research*, 23.

—— (2000) *Vorträge und Aufsätze: Gesamtausgabe*, Volume 7. Vittorio Klostermann.

—— (2012) *Contributions to Philosophy (of the Event)*, trans. R. Rojcewicz and D. Vallega-Neu. Indiana University Press.

—— (2013a) *The Essence of the Truth: On Plato's Cave Allegory and Theaetetus*, trans. T. Sadler. Bloomsbury Academic.

—— (2013b) "The Question Concerning Technology," in *The Question Concerning Technology and Other Essays*, trans. W. Lovitt. HarperPerennial.

—— (2021) *The Metaphysics of German Idealism*, trans. I. A. Moore and R. Therezo. Polity.

Heschel, A. J. (2005) *The Sabbath*. Farrar, Straus & Giroux.

Hobbes, Thomas (1994) *Leviathan*, ed. E. Curley. Hackett.

Hölderlin, F. (2002) *Hyperion and Selected Poems*, ed. E. L. Santer. Continuum.

Hong, R. (2022) *Passionate Work: Endurance after the Good Life*. Duke University Press.

Hughes, W. (2017) "At Least One Black Mirror Episode Is Already Coming True in China," *The A.V. Club*, December 15.

Hui, Y. (2015) "Anamnesis and Re-orientation: A Discourse on Matter and Time," in Y. Hui and A. Broeckmann (eds), *30 Years after Les Immatériaux: Art, Science and Theory*. Meson.

—— (2021) *Art and Cosmotechnics*. University of Minnesota Press.

Hui, Y., and Schwabsky, B. (2023) "The Call of the Unknown in Art and Cosmotechnics: Yuk Hui and Barry Schwabsky in Conversation," *e-flux*, 136.

Innis, H. A. (2007) *Empire and Communication*. Dundurn Press.

—— (2008) *The Bias of Communication*. 2nd edn, University of Toronto Press.

Ionesco, E. (1963) *Exit the King*, trans. D. Watson. Grove Press.

Irigaray, L. (1996) *I Love to You: Sketch for a Felicity within History*, trans. A. Martin. Routledge.

Irigaray, L., and Marder, M. (2016) *Through Vegetal Being: Two Philosophical Perspectives*. Columbia University Press.

Jünger, E. (2000) *The Glass Bees*, trans. L. Bogan and E. Mayer. New York Review Books.

—— (2008) *On Pain*, trans. D. C. Durst. Telos Press.

Kafka, F. (1988) "The Cares of a Family Man," in *The Metamorphosis, The Penal Colony, and Other Stories*, trans. W. Muir and E. Muir. Schocken Books.

Kant, I. (1987) *Critique of Judgment*, trans. W. S. Pluhar. Hackett.

Kateb, G. (1992) *The Inner Ocean: Individualism and Democratic Culture*. Princeton University Press.

# References

Katz, E. (1987) "Communication Research since Lazarsfeld," *Public Opinion Quarterly*, 51.

Keefe, P. R. (2021) *Empire of Pain: The Secret History of the Sackler Dynasty*. Knopf.

Kittler, F. (1999) *Gramophone, Film, Typewriter*, trans. G. Winthrop-Young and M. Wutz. Stanford University Press.

—— (2017) "Real Time Analysis, Time Axis Manipulation," *Cultural Politics*, 13(1).

Knepper, S. (2022) *Wonder Strikes: Approaching Aesthetics and Literature with William Desmond*. SUNY Press.

Knepper, S., and Wyllie, R. (2020) "In the Swarm of Byung-Chul Han," *Telos*, 191.

Kobie, N. (2019) "The Complicated Truth about China's Social Credit System," *Wired*, June 7.

Kracauer, S. (1995) *The Mass Ornament: Weimar Essays*, trans. T. Y. Levin. Harvard University Press.

Kuniavsky, M. (2010) *Smart Things: Ubiquitous Computing User Experience Design*. Elsevier.

Lacan, J. (1988) *The Seminar of Jacques Lacan*, Book II: *The Ego in Freud's Theory and in the Technique of Psychoanalysis 1954–1955*, trans. S. Tomaselli. Cambridge University Press.

—— (1993) *The Seminar of Jacques Lacan*, Book III: *The Psychoses 1955–1956*, trans. R. Grigg. W. W. Norton.

—— (2006) *Écrits: The First Complete Edition in English*, trans. B. Fink. W. W. Norton.

Lacoste, J.-Y. (2004) *Experience and the Absolute: Disputed Questions on the Humanity of Man*, trans. M. Raferty-Skehan. Fordham University Press.

Lazzarato, M. (2012) *The Making of the Indebted Man: An Essay on the Neoliberal Condition*, trans. J. D. Jordan. Semiotext(e).

—— (2014) *Signs and Machines: Capitalism and the Production of Subjectivity*, trans. J. D. Jordan. Semiotext(e).

Leane, R. (2016) "How Black Mirror Series 3 Is Eerily Coming True," *Den of Geek!*, November 3.

Leroi-Gourhan, A. (1993) *Gesture and Speech*, trans. A. B. Berger. MIT Press.

Levertov, D. (1999) "The Métier of Blossoming," in *This Great Unknowing: Last Poems*. New Directions.

Levinas, E. (1998) *Otherwise than Being: Or Beyond Essence*, trans. A. Lingis. Duquesne University Press.

—— (2003) *Time and the Other*, trans. R. A. Cohen. Duquesne University Press.

—— (2017) *Entre Nous*, trans. M. B. Smith and B. Harshav. Bloomsbury.

Levine, M. (2006) *The Price of Privilege*. HarperCollins.

Levy, K. (2022) *Data Driven: Truckers, Technology, and the New Workplace Surveillance*. Princeton University Press.

Lévy, P. (1995) *Qu'est-ce que le virtuel?* La Découverte.

Lomasky, L. (1987) *Persons, Rights, and the Moral Community*. Oxford University Press.
Lovink, G. (2019) *Sad by Design: On Platform Nihilism*. Pluto Press.
Lukács, G. (1971) *The Theory of the Novel*, trans. A. Bostock. MIT Press.
Luther, M. (1960) *Three Treatises*, ed and trans. W. A. Lambert and H. J. Grimm. Fortress Press.
Lyon, D. (2017) "Surveillance Culture: Engagement, Exposure, and Ethics in Digital Modernity," *International Journal of Communication*, 11.
Lyotard, J.-F. (1984) *The Postmodern Condition: A Report on Knowledge*, trans. G. Bennington and B. Massumi. University of Minnesota Press.
—— (1991) *The Inhuman: Reflections on Time*, trans. G. Bennington and R. Bowlby. Polity.
Machiavelli, N. (1998) *The Prince*. 2nd edn, ed. H. C. Mansfield. University of Chicago Press.
MacIntyre, A. (2006) *Edith Stein: A Philosophical Prologue*. Rowman & Littlefield.
—— (2007) *After Virtue: A Study in Moral Theory*. University of Notre Dame Press.
Mahieu, E. (2021) "From the Iron Cage to Burnout," *L'information psychiatrique*, 97(6).
Marazzi, C. (2011) *Capital and Affects: The Politics of the Language Economy*, trans. G. Mecchia. Semiotext(e).
Marcuse, H. (1991) *One-Dimensional Man: Studies in the Ideology of Advanced Industrial Society*. 2nd edn, Beacon Press.
Marion, J.-L. (2013) "The Icon or the Endless Hermeneutic," in K. Hart (ed.), *The Essential Writings*. Fordham University Press.
Marx, K. (1990) *Capital*, Volume 1, trans. B. Fowkes. Penguin.
Mau, S. (2019) *The Metric Society: On the Quantification of the Social*. Polity.
McCarraher, E. (2019) *The Enchantments of Mammon: How Capitalism Became the Religion of Modernity*. Belknap Press.
McLuhan, M. (1962) *The Gutenberg Galaxy: The Making of Typographic Man*. University of Toronto Press.
—— (2003) *Understanding Media: The Extensions of Man*, critical edn, ed. W. T. Gordon. Gingko Press.
McLuhan, M., and McLuhan, E. (1992) *Laws of Media: The New Science*. University of Toronto Press.
McWhertor, M. (2018) "*Black Mirror*'s Nightmarish Social Media Episode Is Now a Board Game," *Polygon*, November 15.
Merleau-Ponty, M. (1962) *The Phenomenology of Perception*, trans. Colin Smith. Routledge & Kegan Paul.
—— (1964) "Cezanne's Doubt," in H. L. Dreyfus and P. A. Dreyfus (ed. and trans.), *Sense and Non-Sense*. Northwestern University Press.
Mill, A., and Jones, L. (2018) *Square Eyes*. Jonathan Cape.
Mill, J. S. (2015) *On Liberty, Utilitarianism, and Other Essays*, ed. M. Philp and F. Rosen. Oxford University Press.

Montesquieu (1989) *The Spirit of the Laws*, ed. and trans. A. M. Cohler, B. C. Miller, and H. S. Stone. Cambridge University Press.
Moulier Boutang, Y. (2011) *Cognitive Capitalism*, trans. E. Emery. Polity.
Mumford, L. (1967) *The Myth of the Machine: Technics and Human Development*. Harcourt, Brace, Jovanovich.
——— (1970) *The Myth of the Machine: The Pentagon of Power*. Harcourt, Brace & World.
Myerscough, P. (2013) "The Pret Buzz," *London Review of Books*, 35(2).
Nehamas, A. (2017) *Only a Promise of Happiness: The Place of Beauty in a World of Art*. Princeton University Press.
Neruda, P. (2017) "Ode to the Guitar," in *All the Odes*, trans. I. Stavans. Farrar, Straus & Giroux.
Nietzsche, F. (1974) *The Gay Science*, trans. W. Kaufmann. Vintage.
——— (1989) *Beyond Good and Evil*, trans. W. Kaufmann. Vintage.
——— (1996) *Human, All Too Human*, trans. R. J. Hollingdale. Cambridge University Press.
Nishitani, K. (1982) *Religion and Nothingness*, trans. J. V. Bragt. University of California Press.
Novalis (1997) *Philosophical Writings*, ed. and trans. M. M. Stoljar. SUNY Press.
O'Brien, T. (2017) *The Things They Carried*. Thorndike.
Odell, J. (2019) *How to Do Nothing: Resisting the Attention Economy*. Melville House.
——— (2023) *Saving Time: Discovering a Life beyond the Clock*. Random House.
Orgad, S., and Gill, R. (2022) *Confidence Culture*. Duke University Press.
Packer, J. (2013) "Epistemology NOT Ideology OR Why We Need New Germans," *Communication and Critical/Cultural Studies*, 10(2–3).
Padusniak, C. (2018) "Embrace Negativity or Risk Never Being Happy," *Church Life Journal*, August 21.
Perks, L. G. (2014) *Media Marathoning: Immersions in Morality*. Lexington Books.
Peters, J. D. (2015) *The Marvelous Clouds: Toward a Philosophy of Elemental Media*. University of Chicago Press.
Picard, M. (1988) *The World of Silence*, trans. S. Godman. Gateway.
Pinker, S. (2018) *Enlightenment Now: The Case for Reason, Science, Humanism, and Progress*. Viking.
Plato (1997) *Complete Works*, ed. J. M. Cooper with D. S. Hutchison. Hackett.
Poster, M. (2011) Introduction to V. Flusser, *Into the Universe of Technical Images*, trans. N. A. Roth. University of Minnesota Press.
Postman, N. (1974–6) "Media Ecology: General Semantics in the Third Millennium," *General Semantics Bulletin*, nos. 41–3.
——— (1985) *Amusing Ourselves to Death: Public Discourse in the Age of Show Business*. Penguin.
Pronger, B. (2002) *Body Fascism: Salvation in the Technology of Physical Fitness*. University of Toronto Press.

Rilke, R. M. (2000) "Archaic Torso of Apollo," in *The Essential Rilke*, ed. and trans. G. Kinnell and H. Liebmann. Ecco Press.

Robertson, N. G. (2021) *Leo Strauss: An Introduction*. Polity.

Robitaille, I. (2023) "Neoliberal Keywords: Creative, Passionate, Confident," *Public Books*, June 7.

Rosa, H. (2020) *The Uncontrollability of the World*, trans. J. C. Wagner. Polity.

Rose, J. (2006) Preface to P. Virilio, *Art and Fear*. Continuum.

Rose, N. (2007) "Molecular Biopolitics, Somatic Ethics, and the Spirit of Biocapital," *Social Theory and Health*, 5.

Rosenzweig, F. (1985) *The Star of Redemption*, trans. W. W. Hallo. University of Notre Dame Press.

Rousseau, J.-J. (1979) *The Reveries of a Solitary Walker*, trans. P. France. Penguin.

—— (1997) *The Discourses and Other Early Political Writings*, ed. V. Gourevitch. Cambridge University Press.

Rutsky, R. L. (2013) "Between Modernity and Magic," in J. Geiger and R. L. Rutsky (eds), *Film Analysis: A Norton Reader*. 2nd edn, W. W. Norton.

Ryan, B. (2014) *Kierkegaard's Indirect Politics*. Rodopi.

Sandel, M. (2020) *The Tyranny of Merit: What's Become of the Common Good?* Farrar, Straus & Giroux.

Sartre, J.-P. (2021) *Being and Nothingness: An Essay in Phenomenological Ontology*, trans. S. Richmond. Washington Square Press.

Sayer, C. (2017) "We Got Charlie Brooker to Rate Real Life 'Black Mirror' Events," *ShortList*, November 22.

Scarry, E. (2001) *On Beauty and Being Just*. Princeton University Press.

Schmitt, C. (1985) *Political Theology: Four Chapters on the Concept of Sovereignty*, trans. G. Schwab. University of Chicago Press.

Schürmann, R. (1987) *Heidegger on Being and Acting: From Principles to Anarchy*. Indiana University Press.

Schweblin, S. (2020) *Little Eyes*, trans. M. McDowell. Riverhead Books.

Scott, J. T. (1992) "The Theodicy of the Second Discourse: The 'Pure State of Nature' and Rousseau's Political Thought," *American Political Science Review*, 86(3).

Scudder, M. (2020) *Beyond Empathy and Inclusion: The Challenge of Listening in Democratic Deliberation*. Oxford University Press.

Senate Hearing 115-683 (2019) *Facebook, Social Media Privacy, and the Use and Abuse of Data*. U.S. Government Publishing Office.

Seymour, R. (2019) *The Twittering Machine*. Indigo Press.

Shively, W. P. (1991) *Power and Choice: An Introduction to Political Science*. McGraw-Hill.

Siegert, B. (2015) *Cultural Techniques: Grids, Filters, Doors, and Other Articulations of the Real*, trans. G. Winthrop-Young. Fordham University Press.

Silko, L. M. (1977) *Ceremony*. Viking Penguin.

# References

Sloterdijk, P. (2009) "Spheres Theory: Talking to Myself about the Poetics of Space," *Harvard Design Magazine*, 30.
—— (2010) *Rage and Time: A Psychopolitical Investigation*, trans. M. Wenning. Columbia University Press.
—— (2013) *You Must Change Your Life: On Anthropotechnics*, trans. W. Hoban. Polity.
—— (2016a) *Foams: Spheres Volume III: Plural Spherology*, trans. W. Hoban. Semiotext(e).
—— (2016b) *Stress and Freedom*, trans. W. Hoban. Polity.
Šokčević, S., and Živić, T. (2021) "Byung-Chul Han and Josef Pieper on Festivity: An Attempt to Rehabilitate the Culture of Festivity in the Time of Mere Survival," *Bogoslovska Smotra*, 91(5).
Srnicek, N. (2017) *Platform Capitalism*. Polity.
Stern, M. (2016) "'Black Mirror' Creator Charlie Brooker on China's 'Social Credit' System and the Rise of Trump," *Daily Beast*, October 27.
Stoneman, E. (2021) "Spheres Ecology: Peter Sloterdijk's Spatial-Analytic Approach to Media Environments," *Explorations in Media Ecology*, 20(1).
—— (2023) "Escape from the Digital Infosphere! Mutation and Disentanglement in Franco Berardi's Critical Media Theory," *Paragraph*, 46(2).
—— (2024) "Toward a Telematic Aesthetics: Vilém Flusser on the Dialogic Promise of Technical Images," *Angelaki*, 29(5).
—— (forthcoming) "The Anaesthetic Crisis of Work and Leisure: On Byung-Chul Han's *The Palliative Society*." Telos.
Storey, B., and Storey, J. S. (2021) *Why We Are Restless: On the Modern Quest for Contentment*. Princeton University Press.
Strate, L. (2008) "Studying Media *as* Media: McLuhan and the Media Ecology Approach," *Media Tropes*, 1.
—— (2017) *Media Ecology: An Approach to Understanding the Human Condition*. Peter Lang.
Strauss, L. (1971) "Philosophy as a Rigorous Science and Political Philosophy," *Interpretation*, 2.
Ströhl, A. (2002) Introduction to V. Flusser, *Writings*. University of Minnesota Press.
Summit, J., and Vermeule, B. (2018) *Action versus Contemplation: Why an Ancient Debate Still Matters*. University of Chicago Press.
Suzuki, D. T. (1991) *An Introduction to Zen Buddhism*. Grove Press.
Taylor, C. (2007) *A Secular Age*. Harvard University Press.
Taylor, F. T. (2017) "The Self as Experienced Aesthetically: The Reflective Relationship between Immanuel Kant, Heinrich von Kleist, and Byung-Chul Han," *Colloquy: Text, Theory, Critique*, 34.
Terranova, T. (2000) "Free Labor: Producing Culture for the Digital Economy," *Social Text 63*, 18(2).
Thrift, N. (2004) "Remembering the Technological Unconscious by

Foregrounding Knowledges of Position," *Environment and Planning D: Society and Space*, 22.

Tocqueville, A. (2010) *Democracy in America: Bilingual Edition*, ed. E. Nolla, trans. J. Schliefer. Liberty Fund.

Turkle, S. (2017) *Alone Together: Why We Expect More from Technology and Less from Each Other*. 3rd edn, Basic Books.

Urueña, S., and Melikyan, N. (2019) "Nosedive and the Anxieties of Social Media," in D. K. Johnson and W. Irwin (eds), *Black Mirror and Philosophy: Dark Reflections*. Wiley-Blackwell.

Valls Boix, J. E. (2022) *Metafísica de la pereza*. Ned Ediciones.

Villa, D. R. (1996) *Arendt and Heidegger: The Fate of the Political*. Princeton University Press.

—— (2008) *Public Freedom*. Princeton University Press.

Vincent, A. (2017) "Black Mirror Is Coming True in China, Where Your 'Rating' Affects Your Home, Transport and Social Circle," *Daily Telegraph*, March 19.

Virilio, P. (1994) *The Vision Machine*, trans. J. Rose. Indiana University Press.

—— (2005) *Negative Horizon: An Essay in Dromoscopy*, trans. M. Degener. Continuum.

Virno, P. (2011) *Convenzione e materialismo*. Deriveapprodi.

Wallace, D. F. (2011) *The Pale King: An Unfinished Novel*. Little, Brown.

Wark, M. (2012) *Telesthesia: Communication, Culture and Class*. Polity.

—— (2020) *Sensoria: Thinkers for the Twenty-First Century*. Verso.

Weber, M. (1958) *The Protestant Ethic and the Spirit of Capitalism*, trans. T. Parsons. Charles Scribner's Sons.

Weiner, J. (2010) "Is an Interwar German Philosopher the Inspiration for David Foster Wallace's New Book?" *Vanity Fair*, September 9.

West, A. N. (2017) "Media and Transparency: An Introduction to Byung-Chul Han in English," *Los Angeles Review of Books*, September 14.

West, C. (1989) *The American Evasion of Philosophy: A Genealogy of Pragmatism*. Macmillan.

White, S. K. (2000) *Sustaining Affirmation: The Strengths of Weak Ontology in Political Theory*. Princeton University Press.

—— (2009) *The Ethos of a Late Modern Citizen*. Harvard University Press.

—— (2011) "Contemporary Continental Political Thought," in G. Klosko (ed.), *The Oxford Handbook of the History of Political Philosophy*. Oxford University Press.

—— (2017) *A Democratic Bearing: Admirable Citizens, Uneven Injustice, and Critical Theory*. Cambridge University Press.

Winthrop-Young, G. (2011) *Kittler and the Media*. Polity.

Wolin, R. (1990) *The Politics of Being: The Political Thought of Martin Heidegger*. Columbia University Press.

Wyllie, I. (1954) *The Self-Made Man in America: The Myth of Rags to Riches*. Free Press.

Yeager, B. R. (2017) *Amygdalatropolis*. Schism Press.

Zuboff, S. (2015) "Big Other: Surveillance Capitalism and the Prospects of an Information Civilization," *Journal of Information Technology*, 30.
—— (2019) *The Age of Surveillance Capitalism: The Fight for a Human Future at the New Frontier of Power*. Profile Books.
Zuckert, C. (1990) "Martin Heidegger: His Philosophy and Politics," *Political Theory*, 18(1).
Zuckert, M., and Zuckert, C. (2014) *Leo Strauss and the Problem of Political Philosophy*. University of Chicago Press.

# Index

*Absence: On the Culture and Philosophy of the Far East* 48, 167
achievement society/subject 1–2, 3, 8–34, 54, 102, 103, 107, 110, 125, 133, 150
  abolishing of negativity 10, 11, 14–23, 53
  artists/writers sensitivity to shift to 12
  and competition with ourselves 23, 28
  and freedom 3, 6, 11–12, 14, 16, 17, 18–19, 20, 29, 30, 31, 33, 35, 97
  incapable of intensive bonding 152
  linking of to neoliberal meritocracy 3, 19, 27, 28
  pain as meaningless in 22
  political economy 20
  and positivity 1–2, 9–10
  power structure of 17
  reasons for emergence of 16
  self-optimization of 9, 12, 151–2
  temporality of 31, 123–47
action
  and contemplation 127–8, 135
adversity, disappearing of 4, 14, 22, 30

advertisements 134
aesthetics
  and neglect of beauty 7, 158, 159–60, 161, 162
Agamben, Giorgio 33, 154
*The Agony of Eros* 4, 7, 148, 154, 156, 164, 169
algorithms 74, 121, 134
alienation, digitalized 6, 87
allo-exploitation 13, 17–18, 106
analgesics 22
anatomo-political power 98, 99, 100, 103, 104
Anderson, Chris
  "The End of Theory" 120–1
Andrejevic, Mark 116, 119
*animal laborans* 136
anxiety 12, 27, 34, 36, 43, 133
  about death 5, 37, 41, 56
  lateral 28
Appiah, Kwame Anthony 58
Arendt, Hannah 17, 34, 43, 133, 135–6, 138
  *The Human Condition* 135, 136, 137
Aristotle 54
  and friendship 154
  *Nicomachean Ethics* 153
  *Poetics* 121–2

# Index

art/art works 53–4, 161, 164, 168
  and contemplative lingering 165
  and epiphanic encounters with things 155–6
  and Romanticism 53
  as saving of the other 165
Artificial Intelligence 43, 171
artists 1, 5, 7, 144
  and boredom 56
  and ethos of friendliness 38, 51, 54, 55, 166
Augustine 143
auto-exploitation 17–18, 106, 108, 110, 112
auto-surveillance 104, 113

Badiou, Alain 152, 153, 154
Ballard, J. G., *Super-Cannes* 23–4
Barba-Kay, Antón 19
Bashō 53, 55, 132
basic mood 40, 41, 42, 44, 45, 47, 53, 60, 133
Bataille, Georges 146, 158
Baudrillard, Jean 5, 17, 65, 70, 80, 81–2, 86, 90, 104, 121
Bauman, Zygmunt 157
beauty 4, 7, 33, 53, 57, 59, 128, 158–62, 172
  and contemplation 164, 165
  and eros 158–64
  and escape from the hell of the same 161
  and recollections 165–6
  slow 164–6
  and smoothness 159–60
  and sublime 158–9, 160
  and truth 163
beauty filters 88
Being 41–3, 49, 55, 63, 71, 128
Benedictine monks 135
Benjamin, Walter 17, 46, 81, 140
Bennett, Jane 155
  *Vibrant Matter* 60
Bentham, Jeremy 112
Berardi, Franco 88, 101–4, 106–8

Berlin junk store 138, 140
Berners-Lee, Tim 75
bias *see* digital bias
Big Brother 113, 114
Big Data 111, 118, 119, 120, 172
*Big Little Lies* (TV drama) 85
binge-watching 76–7, 95
biopolitics, 97–9, 103, 106–8
biopower 112
  and anatomo-political power 103
  body as machine 98, 99
  critics of 98–9
  and Foucault 97–100
  liberal 98–9, 100
Birhane, Abeba 122
Black Forest 30, 131, 132
*Black Mirror* (TV drama) 85–6
Blanchot, Maurice 161–2
body dysmorphic disorder 88
body-image disorder 88
body-machines 98, 99
Bolz, Norbert 69
books 140, 155
boredom 7, 24, 44–50
  and freedom 37
  friendly 5, 45–50, 52, 56, 57, 63, 132–3
  and Handke 45, 46
  and Heidegger 5, 44, 46, 47–8, 52, 55, 132
  profound 7, 45, 46, 132–3, 134, 164, 168
Borgmann, Albert 117
Brown, Wendy 17, 62
Buber, Martin 150–1, 153, 167
Buddhism 129, 136; *see also* Zen Buddhism
Burke, Edmund 158, 160
Burke, Kenneth 107
burnout 2, 8–34, 73, 110, 121, 133, 145
  abolishing negativity and 10, 11, 14–23, 53
  as a crisis of freedom 11–12
  and excess positivity 9–10, 29–34

burnout (*cont.*)
  political response to 35–9
  strategies for resistance to 6, 123–47
*The Burnout Society* 1, 2, 3, 4, 6, 8–34, 35, 36, 38, 45, 46, 49, 53, 55, 123, 171
Burroughs, William S. 99
Butler, Judith 62–3

Cage, John 51, 54, 55, 166
Cain, Susan, *Bittersweet* 9
Calvinism 144
Canetti, Elias 38, 51
capital 19, 20
capitalism 18
  crony 13
  Han's critique of neoliberal 19–20
  as not a religion 144–5
  semiocapitalism 106–7, 109
*Capitalism and the Death Drive* 66
Catholic theology 163–4
Cézanne, Paul 5, 44, 51, 54, 55, 166
Christianity 51, 168
  and contemplation 135–6
chronic fatigue 26–7
Chun, Wendy 80
citizenship 61
Citton, Yves 102, 110
class struggle 109
cognitive labor 102, 107, 111
co-isolation 92
collective self 52
commodification 149
  and loss of ritual 146
commodity-space 92
community 91
  and digital gaplessness 78–9, 81
comparative political theory 59
*conatus* (Hobbesian) 25, 29, 30
consubstantiality 107–8
consumption 6, 18, 39, 56, 119, 128, 146, 149
contemplation 49, 57, 61, 123–8, 131, 133–6, 151, 169
  and action 127–8, 135
  and Arendt 135–6
  and beauty 164
  and Christianity 135–6
  and deep boredom and tiredness 133
  and encountering of the Other 123–4, 148–72
  as a form of resistance 134
  of God 135
  lingering attentively in the moment 124–47
contemplative duration 123–8
contemplative freedom 56–7
contemplative lingering 6, 61, 128–9, 130, 131–2, 133, 137, 142, 148, 164
  and beauty 164, 165
  and friendliness 166–7
  and works of art 165
control society, towards the total 94–122
cosmopolitanism, deep 5, 57–61, 62, 63, 148, 170
COVID-19 pandemic 146
Cowen, Tyler, *Average is Over* 126
Crawford, Matthew 12, 141
critical media theory
  Berardi's 106
  Han's 5, 90, 93, 94, 96
critical-cultural approach
  and media 96–7
critical-theoretical approach
  and media studies 67
cult value
  distinction between exhibition value and 143, 144
cultural studies research 67
cultural techniques 69
cyberbullying 20

Dallmayr, Fred 59
data collection 116–17
dataism 97, 116–17, 118
death 32, 51–2

# Index

anxiety about 5, 37, 41, 56
  of the ego 167
  and Heidegger 37, 41, 47–8, 49, 52
  and Levinas 49
  of the subject 117–22
  and Zen Buddhism 37, 48, 49, 50
"debt trap" 19
deep boredom, *see* boredom
deep cosmopolitanism 5, 57–61, 62, 63, 148, 170
deep ecology 58
deep tiredness, *see* profound boredom
Deleuze, Gilles 36, 96, 99
democratic theory
  and friendliness 61–3
Deneen, Patrick 29
depoliticization 18, 33
depression 14, 24, 26, 27, 87, 88, 110
Desmond, William 153
determinism, technological 94
dialectic 149, 153–4
digital bias 3, 5–6, 64–93, 94–5, 97, 122
  and analog technologies 92
  and control society 96
  and neoliberal hypercapitalism 72–3, 95
  and positivity 5–6, 28–9, 66, 72, 73, 79, 81, 90, 91, 95, 97, 98, 113–14
  and transparency 5–6, 66, 72, 81, 90, 95, 97, 113
digital communication 2, 4, 78
  without community 78
digital gaplessness 73–81
digital immortality 125–6
digital media 3
  becoming-invisible 80–1
  and control society 6, 100–2, 103
  dismantling of respect 82, 86
  and entrepreneurs of the self 109–10
  refashioning freedom into coercion and compulsion 105–6
  and transition from subject to project 108–10, 118
digital organicism 89–93, 91
digital panopticon 6, 112–15, 116, 118, 123
digital psychopolitics 94–122
digital surveillance 104, 111, 112, 116
digital swarms 83, 84–6, 87, 88, 95, 150
digital Taylorism 21
*Digitale Rationalität und das Ende des kommunikativen Handelns* 65
*The Disappearance of Rituals* 66, 142–7
disciplinary society 4–5, 11, 14–16, 17, 97, 103
Dōgen 50, 55, 60–1
Dufourmantelle, Anne 156, 157, 165
*Power of Gentleness* 148
Duration 123–8, 151–2, 165
dwelling 129–32, 137

East Asian philosophy 37
ecology, deep 58
education system 27
ego 5, 7, 30, 31, 44, 148–53, 167–8
Ehrenberg, Alain 26
Ellul, Jacques 106, 126
emphatic thinking 121, 122
employee monitoring 21
empowerment
  and freedom 14, 29, 33, 34
emptiness 38, 50, 59, 60, 61, 167, 168; *see also* śūnyatā
enframing 41, 42, 43, 71
Enlightenment 69, 125
entrepreneurs of the self 108–11, 112, 118
eros 7, 57, 60, 77–8, 91, 148–70, 172
  and beauty 158–64
  and the Other 156–8
  and positivity 97

Esposito, Roberto 99
*Euphoria* (TV drama) 85
Euripides, *Medea* 156
exhibition value 143, 144
exploitation
  allo- 13, 17–18, 106
  auto- 17–18, 106, 108, 110, 112
*The Expulsion of the Other* 7, 28, 148, 151, 154, 164, 165, 166–7, 169
extremism 127

factories 100–1
Fanjul, Sergio C. 127
festival, religious 135–6, 142, 145–6, 163
*Fight Club* 24
fingertip revolution 102, 103
Flusser, Vilém 70, 79, 102
  *Into the Universe of Technical Images* 73–4
Foucault, Michel 10, 14, 34, 96, 97–100, 103, 116
  and biopower 97–100
  *Discipline and Punish* 112
  Han's critique of 99–100
  *The History of Sexuality* 97
  and power 97
  and soul 15–16
Franklin, Samuel W., *The Cult of Creativity* 9
free will 119, 120
freedom 14, 35–7, 54, 104
  and achievement society 3, 6, 11–12, 14, 16, 17, 18–19, 20, 29, 30, 31, 33, 35, 97
  and boredom 37
  contemplative 56–7
  crisis of 4, 18–19, 36–7, 61, 110, 119
  and digital panopticon 113
  and friendliness 5, 53, 54–5, 63, 122
  Han's philosophy of 29–30, 35–45, 36, 38, 43
  Hegelian 54
  and Heidegger 41–2, 43–4, 54, 55
  and Hobbes 29
  and Merleau-Ponty 40, 44–5
  political 34, 40, 42, 59
  and Romantics 39–40
  and Rousseau 56–7
  subjective 37, 43, 59, 172
  and technology 33, 36, 37, 43–4
Freiburg Minster 144
Freud, Sigmund 15, 16
  *Civilization and its Discontents* 23
Freudenberger, Herbert 26–7
friendliness 31, 38–9, 71–2, 113, 122, 148, 154, 166–70, 172
  and artists 51, 54, 55, 166
  and death 51
  and deep cosmopolitanism 58–9, 148, 168, 170
  and democratic theory 61–3
  dialogical 48–9
  and digital panopticons 113–14
  eco-spirituality of 56
  and freedom 5, 53, 54–5, 63, 122
  and Hegel 53
  and Heidegger 48–9, 169–70
  and openness 5, 60, 166, 168
  and receptivity towards otherness 154–5
  and religion 48, 144–5
  and Romanticism 149, 168–9
  and Zen Buddhism 48, 60, 148, 166, 167–8, 170
friendly boredom 5, 45–50, 52, 56, 57, 63, 132–3
friendly tiredness 5, 37, 57
friendship 151, 152–3
  and Agamben 154
  and Aristotle 153, 154

gaplessness, digital 73–81, 86, 101, 108
gaplessness of the same 74–5, 86, 101, 108
gaze 113, 154, 155, 165
gentleness 157
German media theory 69, 70, 71, 90

German Romantics 37, 39–40
Gertz, Nolen 81
*Gewalt* 17
gift exchange 153, 163
gig economy 21
Gill, Rosalind, *Confidence Culture* 9
Girard, René 84
globalization 59, 149
God 38
   contemplation of 135
   existence of 39
Google 76, 120–1
goosebumps 47, 48
Greenfield, Adam 116
Gregory the Great 135
Guattari, Félix 96
Gumbrecht, Hans Ulrich 155

Habermas, Jürgen 62, 65, 70
haiku 50, 53
Handke, Peter 5, 12, 44, 51, 133, 166, 167
   and boredom 46
   "Essay on Tiredness" 12, 35, 45, 46, 52, 57
Harari, Yuval Noah 125
Haraway, Donna 91
Hardt, Michael 101
Hayek, F. A. 19–20, 34
Hayles, N. Katherine 91
health 22
Hegel, G. W. F. 4, 17, 32, 34, 37, 51, 167, 171
   and art 53
   dialectic 153–4
   *Elements of the Philosophy of Right* 117
   and freedom 54
   and friendliness 53
   *Introductory Lectures on Aesthetics* 53
   master/slave dialectic 52
   ontology of spirit 30
   and the Other 153
   and power 38, 53

*Hegel und die Macht* 32, 38, 53, 71, 153
Heidegger, Martin 4, 5, 29, 31, 32, 33–4, 41–3, 55, 59, 61, 71, 72, 129–30, 137–8, 141, 163, 166, 167
   *Being and Time* 37, 41, 52
   and boredom 5, 44, 46, 47–8, 52, 55, 132
   "Building Dwelling Thinking" 18, 131
   and death 37, 41, 47–8, 49, 52
   and dwelling 129–31, 137
   and freedom 41–2, 43–4, 54, 55
   and friendliness 48–9, 169–70
   *The Fundamental Concepts of Metaphysics* lectures 46
   interview in *Der Spiegel* 43
   lectures on Heraclitus 48
   and mood 40, 41, 42, 53
   *Parmenides* 90
   "The Question Concerning Technology" 41–2, 55, 138
   and releasement 42, 43, 48, 49, 130, 132, 169
   and technology 36, 37, 41–3
   and things 137, 138
   "turning" 41, 42, 43
   and Zen Buddhism 59, 132
*Heideggers Herz* 3, 37, 44, 46–7
hell of the same 148–51, 152, 153, 158, 160, 161
*Her* (film) 77–8
Heschel, Rabbi Abraham Joshua 146
historical time 124, 125, 130
Hobbes, Thomas 25, 29, 55
   *Leviathan* 29
Hölderlin, Friedrich 42, 48, 169
   *Hyperion* 169
   "Patmos" 55
Holzer, Jenny 12
Hong, Renyi, *Passionate Work* 9
Horn, Eva 70
hyperactivity 10, 117, 123, 133, 145

hyperculture 58–9, 171
*Hyperculture: Culture and Globalisation* 58–9, 149

*I Ching* 55
*Iliad* 124–5
immortality 25, 100
  digital 125–6
  illusion of 46
*In the Swarm: Digital Prospects* 4, 5, 20, 65, 66, 71
inactivity, politics of 5, 38, 57–8, 169
incense clock 128–9
"indebted man" 118
industrial era 100–1
inequality, wealth 16, 19
*Infocracy: Digitization and the Crisis of Democracy* 64, 66
Information Age 120
Innis, Harold 5, 72
  Presidential Address to the Royal Society of Canada (1947) 117
internalization thesis 15–16, 24–5, 26, 28, 46
Internet of Things (IoT) 115–16, 119
Ionesco, Eugène, *Exit the King* 51–2
Irigaray, Luce 150, 153
Italian autonomists 95

Japan
  bowing culture 48–9
Jones, Luke *Square Eyes* 64, 78
Jonze, Spike 77
Judge, Mike 21
jukebox 141
Jünger, Ernst 86, 91

Kant, Immanuel 51
  and beauty 158, 159, 160, 161, 162
Kateb, George 61
  *The Inner Ocean* 61
Katz, Elihu 67
Kierkegaard, Søren 57

Kittler, Friedrich 69, 70, 94
Klee, Paul 116
Koons, Jeff
  polished balloon sculptures 161
Kuniavsky, Mike 115

labor 100–2
  cognitive 102, 107, 111
  digitization of 107
  free 109–10
  and play 110
Lacan, Jacques
  and symbolic order 15, 74, 77
Lang, Fritz, *Metropolis* 120
Lazzarato, Maurizio 96, 106, 117–19
Lee, Stan 11
Levertov, Denise
  "The Métier of Blossoming" 132
Levinas, Emmanuel 5, 49, 52–3, 63, 153, 154
  *Otherwise than Being* 49
liberalism 29–30, 31–2
life hacks 8–14
"life logged in full" 112–17
lifelogging 112
lingering *see* contemplative lingering
LinkedIn 109
liquid love 157
listening 62, 151
*Lob der Erde* 59–60, 131–2, 156, 162–4, 166, 170, 172
Lomasky, Loren 30, 31, 34
love 4, 151, 154, 156
  eros and romantic 148
  liquid 157
Lovink, Geert 120
Luther, Martin 39
Lyon, David 104
Lyotard, Jean-François 96, 128, 129, 164

Machiavelli, Niccolò 18
Macho, Thomas 70
MacIntyre, Alasdair 31, 32

# Index

Mahieu, Eduardo 26
Marazzi, Christian 106
Marcuse, Herbert 24
market(s) 16, 19–20, 99, 149
*Martin Heidegger* 35, 47, 59
Marx, Karl 15, 19, 107
mass-produced goods 40, 139, 141
master/slave dialectic 52, 58, 153
Matrix 102–3, 107
Mau, Steffen, *The Metric Society* 20
McLuhan, Marshall 70–1, 80–1, 117
  *Understanding Media* 68
media
  as active mediators 68, 70–1
  critical-cultural approach 96–7
  as environments 68
  onto-mutational view of 71
  relationship with empire 72
  and subjective economy 96–7
media bias 72
media ecology 72–3, 120
media effects research paradigm 67
media marathoning 77
media studies 64–73
  critical-theoretical approach to 67
  technological tradition 67–9, 70–1
"medium is the message" 70–1, 117
Melville, Herman 15
meritocracy 2, 14, 19, 27, 28
Merkel, Angela 17
Merleau-Ponty, Maurice
  and freedom 40, 44–5
  *The Phenomenology of Perception* 40
metallurgy 2, 89
metanarratives, collapse of 128
*Mickey Mouse Clubhouse* 141
Mill, Anna, *Square Eyes* 64, 78
Mill, John Stuart 11, 30, 34
mimetic theory 84–5
mindfulness 33, 123, 124
Minerva's owl 117, 118
mirror stage 74
modernity 65
  digital bias and neoliberal 72–3
  and historical time 124, 125
  privileging of action over contemplation 127–8
  and the religious festival 145
  restlessness as a defining mark of 134
  temporal dimension of neoliberal 65–6
Montesquieu 18–19
Moses 132
*Müdigkeitsgesellschaft: Byung-Chul Han in Seoul and Berlin* (documentary) 2, 138
multitasking 18
Mumford, Lewis 89, 91
  *The Myth of the Machine* 89, 91
music 51, 156
mythic time 124–5, 130
mysticism 163–4

narcissism 32, 74, 153
  and the digital 77, 168
  Romanticism and modern 169
narrative(s) 31–2, 65, 142, 147
natality 133
*The Nation* 11
nature 29, 44, 53, 55, 89, 169
  as an exploitable resource 25, 168
  and Zen Buddhism 60
negative violence 4, 13, 20
negativity 54
  abolishing of in achievement society 10, 11, 14–23, 53
  and internalization thesis 15
  of the Other 15, 73, 80, 83, 86, 87, 93
Negri, Antonio 101
Nehamas, Alexander 165
  *Only a Promise of Happiness* 159
neoliberalism 2, 3, 4, 6, 17, 67, 92, 99, 104, 106, 108, 110, 117–19
  and meritocracy 3, 19, 27, 28
  and subjectivation 100, 118
Neruda, Pablo 138
networked perception 75, 115

Neumann, Adam 94, 102
*New York Times* 27
Nietzsche, Friedrich 31, 34, 38, 46–7, 61, 62–3, 171
   and beauty 159
   *Thus Spoke Zarathustra* 22
   *What Is Power?* 47
Nolan, Christopher, *Inception* 120
non-things 2, 119, 140–1
*Non-Things: Upheaval in the Lifeworld* 54–5, 66, 89, 115–16, 137–8, 141, 164
Notre-Dame Cathedral 144
Novalis 38, 60, 61, 169

Obama, Barack 9
O'Brien, Tim, *The Things They Carried* 139
Odell, Jenny 12
   *Saving Time* 123, 132
Odysseus 132
Oedipus complex 15
*Office Space* (film) 21
ontological passivity 43, 56, 58, 133
ontology 63
   weak 62
opioid crisis (US) 22
"ordered liberty" 34
Orgad, Shani, *Confidence Culture* 9
Orwell, George 113
Other 52, 57, 86, 91
   art and saving of the 161, 165
   *atopic* 157–8, 162, 163
   contemplation and the encountering of the 123–4, 148–72
   and ego 150, 151
   and eros 156–8
   ethics of the 149
   expulsion of the 6, 28, 87, 148, 151, 154, 164, 165, 166–7, 169
   finding the 148–70
   gift of the 152–3
   and Levinas 49, 51, 52–3, 153, 154, 157
   negativity of the 15, 73, 80, 83, 86, 87, 93
   positivity of the 96
   relationship with the 73, 148, 150, 151–6
   romantic relationship with the 156–7
   self-erosion and expulsion of the 88, 110
   and Selfsame 86
outrage 22, 83–4
   digital 83, 85, 88
owl of Minerva 117, 118

Padusniak, Chase 124
pain 22, 33, 86
*The Palliative Society* 22, 66, 126
panopticon 112
   digital 6, 112–15, 116, 118, 123
passivity 30–1, 57, 151, 157
   Heideggerian 44
   and Levinas 53
   ontological 43, 56, 58, 62, 133
peace
   and freedom 54
Peters, John Durham 68
*The Philosophy of Zen Buddhism* 167
Pinker, Steven 125
Plato 37, 42
   *Apology* 136
   and beauty 158, 159, 162, 163
   *Phaedo* 51
   *Phaedrus* 158, 162
   *Symposium* 158, 162, 163
playbor 110
poetry 55
   and incense clock 129
point-time 124
*polis* 135, 136
political economy 20
   and subjective economy 96
political theory/theorists 42, 61, 62
politics of inactivity 5, 38, 57–8, 169
pornographic 16, 82, 157–8

positive bias
  and the digital 5–6, 28–9, 66, 72, 73, 79, 81, 90, 91, 95, 97, 98, 113–14
positive violence 14, 17, 28, 35, 83, 121
  absoluteness of 13
  and negative violence 20
  operation of on a systemic basis 18
  paradigm shift to 4, 13
  of self-exploitation 3, 4
  as self-inflicted harm 10
positivity 91, 95–6, 105, 109, 160
  and achievement society 1–2, 9–10
  burnout and excess 9–10, 22–33, 29–34
  and eros 77
  and neoliberal psychopower 105
  of the Other 96
  social control and digital 6
  toxic 9, 171
  of the transparency society 64–93, 113, 114
Poster, Mark 96
power
  and Foucault 97
  and freedom 29
  Han's flexible concept of 16–17
  and Hegel 38, 53
  and politics 17
  "smart, friendly" 113, 115
private
  loss of distinction between public and 82
profound boredom *see* boredom
profound tiredness 7, 52, 55, 132–3
progress 65, 125–6, 128, 131, 144
Pronger, Brian 98
Protestant work ethic 127–8
Proust, Marcel 134
psychoanalysis 15
  Lacanian 74
psychopolitics 6, 14, 67
  and digital media 94–122
  neoliberal 97, 102
  resistance to 123
  surveillance 112
*Psychopolitics: Neoliberalism and New Technologies of Power* 4, 66
psychopower 100–1, 105, 112
public
  loss of distinction between private and 82
public sphere 70
"Purge" 24

quantified self 111–12

radio 90
Rawls, John 61
receptivity 38, 46, 57, 124, 133
  to freedom 33, 37, 42
  to nature 29
  to others/otherness 3, 6, 31, 34, 41, 154
  to relationships 139
  to a world beyond power 44, 65
relationship(s)
  with the Other 73, 148, 150, 151–6
  romantic 154, 156
  and self-esteem 152–3
releasement 41, 42, 43, 49, 50, 59, 130
religion
  capitalism as not a 144–5
  and friendliness 48, 144–5
  and ritual 145
repetition 107, 130, 142, 143
repression 4, 13–14, 23–4
resonance
  and the internet 73–4
restlessness 152
  as a defining mark of modernity 134
  and historical time 125
resurrection 60, 63
rights 30, 31

Rilke, Rainer Maria
  "Archaic Torso of Apollo" 136, 162
ritual(s) 89, 142–7, 163
ritual sites
  distinction between tourist sites and 143–4
rivalry, disappearance of 14, 22–3
Romantics/Romanticism 33–4, 45
  and art 53
  and freedom 38–40
  and friendliness 149, 168–9
  sacralization of the earth 60, 61
Ronell, Avital 69
Rorty, Richard 59, 62
Rosa, Hartmut 28
Rose, Julie 90–1
Rothstein, Jed 102
Rousseau, Jean-Jacques 24–5, 29, 33, 56–7
  *The Reveries of a Solitary Walker* 56

Sandel, Michael 27
Sartre, Jean-Paul 152, 155, 156
*Saving Beauty* 4, 7, 66, 148, 160–1, 163, 164, 169
scapegoating 84–5
Scarry, Elaine 162, 166
*The Scent of Time: A Philosophical Essay on the Art of Lingering* 6, 31, 65, 123, 124, 125, 127, 129, 130, 137, 142, 163, 166
Schelling, F. W. J. 34, 37, 39, 40, 42
Schmitt, Carl 17, 84
Schopenhauer, Arthur 167
Schweblin, Samanta, *Little Eyes* 114–15
self 47, 50, 51, 66–7, 172
  collective 52
  entrepreneurs of the 108–11, 112, 118
  paroxysms of an alienated 81–8
  quantified 111–12
  relation to the Other 73
  selfless 167
  Zen Buddhism and the 167
self-alienation 87, 88, 92
self-entrepreneurship 104, 111–12, 118
self-esteem
  and relationships 152–3
self-exploitation 3–6, 10, 13–14, 18–19, 108–9, 110–11, 113, 171
self-expression 6, 13, 14, 21, 53
self-harm 4, 9, 15, 25, 153
"self-made man" 8–9
self-optimization 6, 97, 108, 110
  of achievement subject 9, 12, 151–2
self-surveillance 171
self-tracking devices 111–12
selfie 88, 160
Selfsame 86
semantic web 75–6
semiocapitalism 106–7, 109
*Shanzhai: Deconstruction in Chinese* 144, 167
sharing economy 21, 92
Shewmon, Paul G., *Transformations in Metals* 140
Shinto Ise Shrine (Japan) 144
shitstorms, social media 84–5, 91
Shklar, Judith 62
Siegert, Bernhard 69, 70
Silicon Valley 125–6
sleep 134–5
Sloterdijk, Peter 56, 92, 136–7
  *Rage and Time* 83
  *You Must Change Your Life* 136
slow beauty 164–6
smart home 115, 116, 140–1
smartphones 43, 74, 103–4, 116, 134, 149
  and selfie 160
  and smoothness 160
smooth/smoothness 16, 24, 74, 80–1, 88, 95, 96, 113, 159–61
Snyder, Gary 61
social capital 82

social media 22, 75, 80, 81, 121, 134
  algorithms 5–6
  shitstorms 84–5, 91
Socrates 32, 39, 51, 57, 150
sovereignty 33, 84
  post-digital 84
spirit 46, 53
  Hegel's ontology of 30
*Squid Game* 127
Srnicek, Nick
  *Platform Capitalism* 106
stabilizing things 137–41, 155
Strauss, Leo 55
students
  and burnout 27–8
subject
  death of the 117–22
  transition to project from 108–10
subjectivity 29, 71, 86–7, 91, 96, 111, 117–18, 138, 153
sublime 128–9, 158–61
suicide 2, 88, 110
*śūnyatā* 38, 59, 61, 50, 167, 168; *see also* emptiness
*Super-Cannes* 26
super-ego 16, 30
surveillance
  auto- 104, 113
  culture 104–5
  digital 104, 111, 112, 116
  and digital panopticon 112–13
  psychopolitical 112
  self- 171
swarms, digital 83, 84–6, 87, 88, 95, 150
symbolic order
  and Lacan 15, 74, 77
symbolic perception 142–3

Taoism 37, 129, 168
Taylor, Charles 30, 32
Taylor, Francesca Teltscher 162
Taylor, Frederick 116
Taylorism, digital 21

technics
  Mumford on 89
technological determinism 55, 93, 94
technological tradition
  and media studies 67–9, 70–1
technology 33, 70–1, 89, 126–7
  Borgmann's paradigm of 117
  and consciousness 65
  and freedom 33, 36, 37, 43–4
television 90
Tellenbach, Hubertus 26–7
temporal architectures, erosion of 65–6
Terranova, Tiziana 109–10
theory/theorizing 120–2, 122
Theweleit, Klaus 69
Things 119, 137–41, 155,
thinking 50
  emphatic 121, 122
Thoreau, Henry David 61
time 6, 123–47
  historical 124, 125, 130
  mythic 124–5, 130
  scent of 31; *see also The Scent of Time*
  stabilizing of by ritual 142
  whizzing 65, 123–8, 124, 164, 165
tiredness 5, 7, 30, 35, 49, 52, 55, 133
  deep 56, 133
  friendly 5, 37, 57
  Handke's essay on 12, 35, 45, 46, 52, 57
  profound 7, 52, 55, 132–3
  *see also* we-tiredness
"The Tiredness Virus" 11
Tocqueville, Alexis de 11
*Tod und Alterität* 5, 32, 37, 51, 53, 154
*Todesarten* 47, 51
*The Topology of Violence* 13, 16
toxic positivity 9, 171
transparency 81–2, 82, 91, 95–6, 105
  imperative of 83
  and positivity 83

transparency bias
  and digital 5–6, 66, 72, 81, 90, 91, 95, 97, 113
transparency society 64–93
  completion of 115
  positivity of the 95, 113, 114
trucking industry 21
Trump, Donald 26
Trump, Melania 8
Tsutsui, Yasutaka, *Paprika* 120
Twitter swarm 84
typewriter 90
tyranny 25

uncanny 155
universities
  American elite 27–8
  burnout and students at 27–8
  impact of achievement society on 27
Urueña, Sergio 86

violence
  and *Gewalt* 17
  negative 4, 13, 20
  positive *see* positive violence
Virilio, Paul 65, 90–1, 116
Virno, Paolo 106
virtual reality 43
Vismann, Cornelia 70
*vita activa* 135, 136, 143
*vita contemplativa* 132–7, 143
*Vita Contemplativa: In Praise of Inactivity* 3, 23, 43, 57–8, 134–6, 149, 164, 168, 169, 170, 172

Wallace, David Foster, *The Pale King* 45
wandering 49, 60, 87, 132
  Bashō's 132
Wark, McKenzie 73, 78
we-tiredness 46, 167, 168
weak ontology 62
Weber, Max 11, 127

*The Protestant Ethic and the Spirt of Capitalism* 26
Wenders, Wim 2
West, Adrian Nathan 4, 84
Western philosophy 15, 29, 32–3, 37, 51, 53, 56, 59, 129, 167, 168
*What is Power?* 65
White, Stephen 61, 62, 63
Whitman, Walt 61
whizzing time 65, 123–8, 124, 164, 165
"Who Is a Refugee?" 34
*Wings of Desire* (film) 2–3
Winthrop-Young, Geoffrey 69
wonder 41, 49, 138, 155, 163
work/workers 106–7
  as entrepreneurs of the self 108–11
  positive identification with one's 107–8
  and social affectivity 106
world-friendliness 37, 38

Yeager, B. R., *Amygdalatropolis* 87–8
Yü-Chien, *Eight Views of the Xiao-Xiang* 168

*Die Zeit*
  Han's interview (2014) 89
Zen Buddhism 4, 5, 37, 41, 50, 59, 63, 166, 166–8, 172
  and death 37, 48, 49, 50
  and death of the ego 167
  and dwelling 132
  and emptiness 60, 61, 167, 168
  and friendliness 48, 60, 148, 166, 167–8, 170
  and Heidegger 59, 132
  and nature 60
  and "not-to" 133–4
  as a religion of "absencing" 48–9
Zuboff, Shoshana
  *The Age of Surveillance Capitalism* 104
Zuckerberg, Mark 8, 10
Zuckert, Catherine 42